Pro-active in plant care with pest control and fertilisers since 1974, Efekto has introduced hundreds of products to local gardeners, nurseries and plantgrowers. Many of these, such as Rosecare and Wonder fertilisers, have become part of the gardening lingo. As leaders in the garden care market and a member of the international Dow Agrosciences Group, an important part of the company's credo is its commitment to the protection of the environment. All products meet stringent statutory requirements and the responsible use of pesticides is always emphasised. The range of products containing natural ingredients is constantly being expanded as organic alternatives are identified and developed.

AUTHOR'S ACKNOWLEDGEMENTS

Putting a new book together always takes an enormous amount of effort by a number of people and I would firstly like to express my sincere appreciation and thanks to not only a good friend, but also a great horticulturalist – Lizelle Meyer-Faedda – who has assisted admirably in making this book possible. The assistance on many fronts from those who have supplied photographs, answered queries, proofread manuscripts and searched for that one specific photograph is much appreciated. My thanks go to the publishing and editing team from Struik Publishers, in particular to Annlerie van Rooyen for her patience and relentless nagging to keep things on track. A special thank you to Carmen Swanepoel of Struik Image Library, to Illana Fridkin who has so painstakingly designed the page-by-page content of the book, and to Sylvia Grobbelaar for editing the text. Special thanks go to my able secretary Margie Foggitt, to Paul Vonk of Hadeco Bulbs for some of the bulb photographs, and to Leale Wright of Flora Print (Alex White Printers) for supplying his photographs from the Flora Print library at a reasonable price. Thanks also to Bruno Bossi at Hurricanes Photographic Agency for photographs of myself on a great February afternoon in Cape Town. Last but by no means least, thank you to Dirk Visser and Efekto who generously co-sponsored the photographs, making it possible to produce this book at a reasonable price. I trust that everyone will enjoy this book – I hope that it will go a long way to assist both the novice and seasoned gardener when making a choice of plants for their own gardens, whether old or new, and that readers will get as much fun and enjoyment out of the book as we had putting it together!

KEITH KIRSTEN

CONTENTS

SYMBOLS

 Grows best in full sun

 Grows best in partial shade

 Grows best in shade

 Deciduous tree/shrub

 Semi-deciduous tree/shrub

 Evergreen tree/shrub

 Semi-evergreen tree/shrub

 Flowers are an attractive feature

 Fruit is an attractive feature

 Attracts butterflies

 Attracts birds

 Attracts bats

 Grows well in clay

 Survives severe drought

 Survives moderate drought

 Grows well in coastal sand and withstands coastal wind

 Grows in waterlogged soil

 Scrambler

 Needs a lot of water

 Needs a moderate amount of water

 Wind-tolerant

 Indigenous

 Survives harsh frost

 Survives moderate frost

 Survives light frost

No frost symbol: Cannot survive frost

 Grows best in area with high rainfall

 Grows best in area with moderate rainfall

Grows best in area with low rainfall

6

HOW TO USE THIS BOOK

The feature below explains each aspect of the entries, and the symbols used in the book are explained in the key, to the left.

PERENNIALS & GROUND COVERS

❶Hemerocallis x hybrids
❷ Day lily, Daglelie

❸

❹Size: 40 x 40 cm
❺Growth habit: The day lily is very easy to grow and is an evergreen or deciduous, clump-forming perennial with tuberous, fleshy roots. Lily-like flowers in branched clusters appear from spring to autumn in shades of rust, red, orange and yellow. Flowers open progressively as each flower only lasts for one day. Flowers are also edible. Divide clumps every three to four years in autumn, and cut back the foliage to 10 cm when replanting. Watch out for slugs and snails, aphids and red spider mite attack.
❻Planting: To prepare the bed, dig over the soil and work in a large quantity of compost and well-rotted manure, with some general fertiliser and superphosphate or bone meal.
❼Watering and feeding: Water regularly and feed with a general fertiliser for flowering plants in spring.
❽Uses: Ideal for mass planting or for the herbaceous border.
❾Varieties: 'Crystal Cupid' with ruffled yellow flowers on short stems is a low-growing miniature that flowers early in the season. 'Fleeta' has dark burgundy flowers. 'Frank Gladney' has coral-pink flowers with golden throats late in the season and is of medium height. 'Lemoine' bears single, salmon-pink flowers. 'Joan Senior' has whitish flowers in mid-season.

Impatiens x 'New Guinea' hybrids
'New Guinea' impatiens

Size: 50 x 40 cm
Growth habit: This fast-growing perennial is popular as much for its attractive foliage as its bright flowers. New Guinea impatiens requires at least four hours' sun a day to retain the colour of its leaves and blooms. The plant provides a great variety of different leaf variegations in greens, yellows, bronzes and pinks, together with many different flower colours from white and pale pink, through mauve, cerise and orange to bright red.
Planting: It prefers moist but well-drained soil. To prepare the bed, dig over the soil and work in a large quantity of compost and well-rotted manure, together with some general fertiliser and superphosphate or bone meal.
Watering and feeding: Water regularly to keep the plant moist and feed with a general fertiliser for flowering plants during spring.
Uses: This is an excellent container plant for colour on the cool to sunny patio. Lovely in the mixed perennial border with afternoon shade.
Varieties: 'Tango' has bright orange flowers and dark green flowers and compact growth. 'Spectra Mixed' features many colours and a variety of decorative foliage.

❿ Hide dying spring foliage Grow spring-flowering bulbs between summer-flowering day lilies to disguise the dying foliage of the bulbs with the fresh new growth from the day lilies in early summer. By the time the bulbs have died down the day lilies will have grown out fully and started to flower beautifully, effectively hiding the dead bulb foliage.

100

❶ The plant's newest scientific name (old scientific names have been given in the index).

❷ The best-known common name(s). If preceded by a number, this refers to the National List of Indigenous Trees and Shrubs.

❸ Symbols showing the plant's characteristics, and the conditions in which it grows best, at a glance (see the key to the left).

❹ Size the plant reaches. Sizes are approximate, as they vary depending on growth conditions. No sizes are given for climbers, as there are too many variables to determine the plant's spread.

❺ The way the plant typically develops – its main characteristics, such as shape, foliage, fruit and flowers.

❻ How you can go about growing the plant.

❼ How to take care of the plant in the garden.

❽ The best uses for the plant in the garden, and the climate and conditions in which it will grow best.

❾ Descriptions of the different varieties and species of the plant that are available.

❿ Practical and user-friendly gardening hints.

Trees are an essential part of our environment and form a natural, harmonious link between our homes and nature around us, softening harsh lines and blending textures.
They should always be the first plants to be chosen for a garden as, being the biggest and most conspicuous plants, they form the basic skeleton.

The value of a tree in a garden depends on the character of that specific variety – its shape, size, texture, colour and foliage. Besides providing shade in a parking area or in the children's playing corner, it could become a feature on an open lawn, form a screen or supply height to create architectural balance.

Trees are of great value to humans. They help to reduce air pollution, form a barrier against noise and wind, are wonderful oxygen producers, and provide shade and shelter for people, as well as birds and other wildlife. Choose your trees carefully as an inappropriate choice could be costly as regards time, effort and money. For instance, you would not plant an evergreen tree against the house where it would block the heat and light in winter. A deciduous tree, likewise, cannot form a screen. Another important consideration is the root system, as not all trees can be planted near a wall or swimming pool without causing damage. So choose a tree which meets as many of your requirements as possible, always making sure that it is a variety that will flourish in your area.

trees

Acacia galpinii
(166) Monkey thorn, Apiesdoring

Size: 18–25 x 12 m

Growth habit: Fast growing, up to 1 m per year with luxuriant growth, this large acacia has a dense, spreading crown. The stem is pale cream with rough, papery bark. Typical acacia-like foliage is light green. Slender flower-spikes appear in spring. They are creamy-yellow with a pink tinge. Reddish to purple-brown pods are long and flat, ripening in autumn. Hooked thorns occur in pairs along branches.

Planting: Dig a hole 75 cm square and deep. Mix two thirds of the topsoil with one third compost in the bottom of the hole, add one cup of bone meal or superphosphate and mix well. Stake young trees.

Watering and feeding: Water regularly until established. Feed in spring with a general fertiliser.

Pruning: Not necessary. Occasional shaping can be done throughout the year.

Uses: Attractively shaped and fine for avenue plantings. Excellent shade tree for large gardens and parking areas. Does not drop its thorns. Has a taproot and should not be planted closer than 3 m from a wall. Drought tolerant and termite resistant.

Acacia karroo
(172) Sweet thorn, Soetdoring

Size: 6–20 x 4 m

Growth habit: The most common thorn tree of the veld occurring throughout Southern Africa, it has a spreading, rounded crown with dense to sparse foliage. Leaves are dark green and it bears quantities of sweetly scented, mimosa-like flowers up to four times during summer, depending on rain. The stem is dark red-brown to dark brown. Grows up to 60 cm per year. It is drought resistant but will also tolerate damp growing conditions.

Planting: Dig a hole 75 cm square and deep. Mix two thirds of the topsoil with one third compost in the bottom of the hole, add one cup of bone meal or superphosphate and mix well. Stake young trees.

Watering and feeding: Avoid overwatering and too much feeding as this will result in roots developing too shallowly, causing the tree to blow over in strong wind.

Pruning: Not necessary. Cut off lower branches until the desired crown height is reached.

Uses: Excellent hardy tree for medium gardens. Tolerates salt-laden coastal winds and will grow in brackish soils. Termite resistant. Can be grown up to 3 m from a wall without causing damage. Attracts insects and birds. Used medicinally by indigenous people for wounds and treating sore throats.

Planting trees To ensure quick root development and strong growth, always make large holes of at least 75 cm square when planting trees. Add a few spades of compost and a mixed general fertiliser like 2:3:2 at a rate of 1 cup per hole as well as 1 cup of bone meal or superphosphate, well mixed with the soil and compost in the hole.

Acacia sieberiana var. woodii
(187) Paperbark thorn, Papierbasdoring

Size: 8–13 x 10 m
Growth habit: Attractively shaped with a flat crown covered in bright green foliage, this is a moderately fast-growing acacia, up to 60 cm per year. It has a straight stem with conspicuous, peeling, yellow-grey bark. It provides a light shade beneath which plants may be grown. Semi-deciduous with creamy-white, ball-shaped flowers in spring followed by woody, grey pods in autumn. Straight white thorns are borne in pairs.
Planting: Dig a hole 75 cm square and deep. Mix two thirds of the topsoil with one third compost in the bottom of the hole, add one cup of bone meal or superphosphate and mix well. Stake young trees.
Watering and feeding: Avoid overwatering and too much feeding as this will result in roots developing too shallowly, causing the tree to blow over in strong wind.
Pruning: Not necessary. Remove lower branches until the desired crown height is reached.
Uses: Extremely useful shade tree for the garden. Avoid planting this acacia on the lawn where children play, as it tends to drop twigs with thorns. Drought tolerant. Tolerates salt-laden winds near the coast and is termite resistant. It is a favourite nesting tree for barbets in the bushveld.

Acacia xanthophloea
(189) Fever tree, Koorsboom

Size: 10–19 x 7 m
Growth habit: This tree with its very distinctive lime-green stem is commonly seen in the Kruger National Park and northern KwaZulu-Natal. Its common name was derived from early travellers who associated it with fever contracted in malaria-rife areas. Upright in habit with a sparse crown, it is ideal for large gardens in warm areas and will tolerate both poor soil and swampy conditions. Bears yellow, ball-shaped flowers in spring, followed by brown, papery seed pods in midsummer.
Planting: Dig a hole 75 cm square and deep. Mix two thirds of the topsoil with one third compost in the bottom of the hole, add one cup of bone meal or superphosphate and mix well. Stake young trees.
Watering and feeding: Water regularly during dry periods. It is not as drought tolerant as other acacia species. Feed during spring with a general fertiliser.
Pruning: Not necessary. Remove lower branches until the desired height of the crown is reached.
Uses: Ideal shade tree on the lawn in large gardens. Avoid planting this tree where children play as it occasionally drops branches with thorns. This tree is irresistible to weaverbirds for nesting purposes. Traditional healers use the bark medicinally for treating fevers and eye complaints.

Leaves on lawns Plant trees with fine leaves – like acacias or the leopard tree (see p. 14) – on lawns, as the fallen leaves will disappear into the lawn without having to be swept up. They also provide a light enough shade to let the lawn grow successfully.

9

Acer buergerianum
Chinese maple, Chinese esdoring

Size: 6 x 3,5 m
Growth habit: This small tree with dark green, three-lobed foliage turns red in autumn in regions with cold winters and it has a rounded dense crown. Slow growing, up to 30 cm per year. Beautiful, fresh green foliage in early spring. Does not tolerate salt-laden winds.
Planting: Prefers acid soil. Dig a hole 75 cm square and deep. Mix two thirds of the topsoil with one third peatmoss or acid compost in the bottom of the hole, add one cup of bone meal or superphosphate and mix well. Stake young trees.
Watering and feeding: Maples prefer cool, well-drained soil with lots of water in spring. Does not need much attention once established. Must not suffer from drought in summer. Water regularly throughout the year. Feed with a general balanced fertiliser like 2:3:2 at a rate of 60 g per square metre once a month during the active growing season.
Pruning: Stake trees and prune to obtain specimens with higher branches.
Uses: Most suitable for a small garden on the lawn or patio area in colder areas. Can be planted up to 2 m from a wall without causing damage. They also make popular bonsai subjects and are excellent in large containers.

Alberta magna
(701) Natal flame bush, Breekhout

Size: 7 x 3 m
Growth habit: This medium-sized, dark green, glossy-foliaged tree has a narrow to rounded crown. Its clusters of scarlet flowers in summer are followed by bunches of scarlet bracts, making this tree a striking choice for coastal gardens. It is slow growing, up to 20 cm per year.
Planting: It needs fertile soil. Dig a hole 75 cm square and deep. Mix two thirds of the topsoil with one third compost in the bottom of the hole, add one cup of bone meal or super-phosphate and mix well. Stake young trees.
Watering and feeding: This plant cannot tolerate drought and needs to be watered and fed regularly throughout the year.
Pruning: Not necessary.
Uses: Very colourful tree for coastal and subtropical warm gardens. It can be grown in shade, but is difficult to maintain under adverse conditions. The bark has medicinal properties.

Winter warmth, summer shade Plant deciduous trees like acacias, maples or birches relatively close to the house on its north side to let in light and to help warm the house during winter. During the hot summer months, they will provide cool, dappled shade.

Albizia julibrissin
Silk tree, Pienk Siris/Syboom

Size: 5 x 8 m

Growth habit: A very elegant umbrella-shaped tree, it has dark green, fern-like foliage. Highly ornamental when in bloom, it produces heads of pink flowers which shimmer above the foliage in late spring and early summer. It throws a light shade under which other plants can successfully be grown. Rather slow growing, at 40 cm per year. It tends to sucker if the roots and lower main stem get damaged.

Planting: Prefers well-drained, sandy soil. Dig a hole 75 cm square and deep. Mix two thirds of the topsoil with one third compost in the bottom of the hole, add one cup of bone meal or superphosphate and mix well. Stake young trees.

Watering and feeding: Water and feed regularly until established whereafter it needs little attention.

Pruning: Not necessary, only to shape until the required crown height is reached.

Uses: Very ornamental medium-sized tree for lawns and near patios or for parking areas in town gardens. Once established it is quite drought tolerant. It will also tolerate salt-laden coastal air. Can be planted within 3 m from walls.

Apodytes dimidiata
(422) White pear, Witpeer

Size: 10 x 3 m

Growth habit: This medium-sized tree has a compact crown. It has glossy foliage and hanging bunches of white flowers in summer, followed by decorative bunches of black and red berries. Straight stem with grey bark and white patches. Slow growing, up to 30 cm per year, and tolerant to salt-laden air. It can also be grown in the shade of other trees.

Planting: Dig a hole 75 cm square and deep. Mix two thirds of the topsoil with one third compost in the bottom of the hole, add one cup of bone meal or superphosphate and mix well. Stake young trees.

Watering and feeding: Water and feed regularly to obtain a faster growth tempo.

Pruning: Not necessary.

Uses: This is a decorative tree that lures birds to the garden. Excellent for screening unsightly views. It will also grow in large containers on the patio.

Removing branches To remove a large branch from a tree, always make the first cut at the bottom of the branch flush with the main stem and then only make the final cut from the top, again flush with the main stem. This will prevent tearing the bark from the stem and avoid leaving unsightly torn bark and a protruding stump.

Betula pendula
Silver birch, Silwerberk

Size: 10 x 4 m

Growth habit: This is an upright-growing tree with a sparse crown and delicate hanging branches. It is neat in appearance and after a few years of growth, its striking silvery-white bark becomes evident. Has lovely yellow autumn foliage. A fine specimen tree, especially in a group, but it is also showy in winter when it loses its leaves. Expected growth tempo is approximately 60 cm per year under ideal conditions.

Planting: Dig a hole 75 cm square and deep. Mix two thirds of the topsoil with one third compost in the bottom of the hole, add one cup of bone meal or superphosphate and mix well. Stake young trees.

Watering and feeding: Water well in dry areas. In hot, dry climates it is best grown on the south or east side of the house. Feed with a general balanced fertiliser like 2:3:2 at a rate of 60 g per square metre once a month during the active growing season.

Pruning: Not necessary, except to remove side branches to obtain a single stem.

Uses: Very hardy in cold areas. An excellent choice for small or townhouse gardens on the Highveld. Very effective in creating a woodland effect. Can be grown as close as 3 m from a wall without causing damage.

Bolusanthus speciosus
(222) Tree wisteria, Vanwykshout

Size: 6–12 x 3 m

Growth habit: One of our most beautiful small to medium-sized indigenous trees, it has a weeping shape with a narrow crown. This tree produces long sprays of violet-blue flowers (a rare white form exists) after it loses its feathery, light green leaves in spring. They are followed by papery, brown seedpods in hanging clusters. It grows with an upright, brown stem, which becomes deeply grooved. Expected growth rate is about 60 cm per year.

Planting: Dig a hole 75 cm square and deep. Mix two thirds of the topsoil with one third compost in the bottom of the hole, add one cup of bone meal or superphosphate and mix well. Stake young trees.

Watering and feeding: This tree does very well in sandy soils. Water and feed regularly until it is well established, after which it is drought resistant. Avoid watering during winter to promote flowering.

Pruning: Not necessary, except for occasional shaping.

Uses: Decorative tree on the lawn for small gardens. It is termite resistant. It can also be planted as close as 3 m from a wall. Bark is used medicinally by indigenous people.

Trees close to paving When growing trees in or close to paved areas you should always leave enough space in the paving for the stem to develop and for water to reach the root system freely. Too small a space will cause the tree to grow stunted and eventually die. Try to keep the paving at least 75 cm away from the trunk.

Bridelia micrantha
(324) Mitzeeri, Mitserie

Size: 10–21 x 7 m
Growth habit: A relatively fast-growing tree with a dense spreading crown, its glossy, dark green leaves are rather large and turn a golden-red in autumn. Beautiful spring foliage with a coppery tinge. Bears small, edible, black fruits in late summer. Upright stem is grey and quite smooth.
Planting: Dig a hole 75 cm square and deep. Mix two thirds of the topsoil with one third compost in the bottom of the hole, add one cup of bone meal or superphosphate and mix well. Stake young trees.
Watering and feeding: Water and feed this tree regularly until mature.
Pruning: Only needs occasional shaping.
Uses: Lovely shade tree for medium gardens, with beautiful golden-orange autumn foliage. Birds love the berries. Do not plant closer than 5 m from walls. It is termite resistant. Traditional healers use the bark and roots for treating sterility as well as gastric, eye and respiratory complaints.

Buddleja saligna
(636) False olive, Witolienhout

Size: 4–15 x 3 m
Growth habit: This small, fast-growing tree has a weeping crown. It has dark green, shiny foliage with a silvery reverse. The main stem is usually twisted and light brown to dark brown. It bears creamy-white flowers in dense bunches towards the ends of the branches in summer. Flowers are sweetly scented.
Planting: Dig a hole 75 cm square and deep. Mix two thirds of the topsoil with one third compost in the bottom of the hole, add one cup of bone meal or superphosphate and mix well. Stake young trees.
Watering and feeding: Water and feed regularly until established. Drought resistant.
Pruning: Not necessary.
Uses: Ideal screening plant. It tolerates salt-laden winds at the coast. The false olive is an excellent plant for attracting butterflies and bees. Indigenous people use the plant medicinally for treating coughs and colds.

Watering trees When watering trees always water deeply to encourage a deep root system. Avoid regular shallow watering, as this will force the roots to the surface to get to the water, leading to a shallow root system which will cause large trees with big crowns to blow over in strong wind.

Butia capitata
Jelly palm, Jelliepalm

Size: 4 x 2 m
Growth habit: A large, single-stemmed palm with lovely, silver-grey, arching, feather-like fronds, it is slow growing but very hardy. Produces fleshy orange-yellow edible seeds.
Planting: Dig a hole 50 cm square and deep. Mix two thirds of the topsoil with one third compost in the bottom of the hole, add one cup of 5:1:5 fertiliser and one cup of bone meal or superphosphate and mix well.
Watering and feeding: Water and feed regularly until it is well established.
Pruning: Remove the old fronds from the tree as soon as they start to discolour.
Uses: An excellent focus plant in larger gardens and is also striking in a large container near the pool or patio. Birds enjoy the seeds. Do not plant closer than at least 3 m from a wall or swimming pool.

Caesalpinia ferrea
Leopard tree, Luiperdboom

Size: 12 x 8 m
Growth habit: One of the most splendid shade trees from Brazil, the leopard tree is so named because of its beautifully marked bark. It also has fine, attractive, acacia-like foliage, which is rosy-red when it emerges in spring. It throws such a light shade that it is possible to grow grass under it. Bears yellow flowers in summer. It is fairly fast growing. Tolerates salt-laden winds at the coast.
Planting: Dig a hole 75 cm square and deep. Mix two thirds of the topsoil with one third compost in the bottom of the hole, add one cup of bone meal or superphosphate and mix well. Transplants well in spring when cut back by a third. Stake transplanted trees.
Watering and feeding: Water and feed regularly until established. Does very well in warm dry soils. Does not require a lot of attention.
Pruning: Not necessary to prune, except when removing unwanted branches.
Uses: Not suitable for townhouse gardens. This is an excellent specimen shade tree on the lawn. It can be planted up to 3 m from walls.

Scale and balance Before planting any trees, consider the size of the house, the garden and the full-grown tree before making a decision. Too large a tree in a small garden will create an unbalanced effect. Do not plant too many large trees too close together as this will cause an unmanageable jungle, which may lead to too much shade in the garden.

Calodendrum capense
(256) Cape chestnut, Wildekastaiing

Size: 9–18 x 8 m

Growth habit: This handsome, medium-sized flowering tree grows into a well-shaped, spreading specimen with glossy, dark green foliage and masses of rosy-pink flowers in early summer. It develops a tall stem with smooth, pale grey bark. It has a faster growth rate at the coast, otherwise it is quite slow growing.

Planting: Needs fertile soil. Dig a hole 75 cm square and deep. Mix two thirds of the topsoil with one third compost in the bottom of the hole, add one cup of bone meal or superphosphate and mix well. Stake young trees.

Watering and feeding: Water and feed regularly during the active growing season.

Pruning: Not necessary, except for shaping when young.

Uses: A very showy shade tree and a fine tub subject. It tolerates salt-laden winds at the coast.

Celtis africana
(39) White stinkwood, Witstinkhout

Size: 12–38 x 9 m

Growth habit: One of our most glorious, spreading, indigenous trees, it is a fairly fast grower, up to 1 m per year, and one of the finest trees coming into leaf in spring, when it produces magnificent, pale green foliage. Casts dense shade. It has a smooth, pale grey stem. Many trees in the Pretoria area have a virus that gives leaves a yellow margin or yellow tips. Tolerates salt-laden winds.

Planting: Dig a hole 75 cm square and deep. Mix two thirds of the topsoil with one third compost in the bottom of the hole, add one cup of bone meal or superphosphate and mix well. Stake young trees.

Watering and feeding: Prefers fertile soil. Water and feed regularly until established. It is fairly drought hardy.

Pruning: Not necessary, except to shape.

Uses: Beautiful shade tree for the larger garden and works well as a street tree. Attracts birds and insects to the garden. Indigenous people use the wood for magical purposes.

Spacing trees Do not be afraid to plant upright-growing trees close together in a group. They are ideal to create a woodland effect. Some excellent species to grow close together are silver birch, *Heteropyxis natalensis*, white stinkwood, sneezewood and palms.

Ceratonia siliqua
Carob tree/Locust tree, Johannesbroodboom

Size: 10 x 7 m

Growth habit: Attractive and symmetrical in shape, this is one of the most useful medium-height evergreen trees. Dark green, leathery foliage forms a dense, spreading crown. Flowers appear in sprays 3–6 cm long on the old wood during summer. Flowers can be either predominantly male or female, with the male flowers emitting a disagreeable odour. From the female flowers develop large, thick, dark brown seedpods up to 30 cm long. Pods ripen in late summer and contain a sweetish, pulpy substance rich in proteins and sugars. Rather slow growing, up to 30 cm per year.

Planting: Dig a hole 75 cm square and deep. Mix two thirds of the topsoil with one third compost in the bottom of the hole, add one cup of bone meal or superphosphate and mix well. Stake young trees.

Watering and feeding: Water and feed this tree regularly until it is established.

Pruning: Not necessary, only needs occasional shaping.

Uses: An excellent hardy shade tree for the highveld and dry interior. Do not plant closer than 5 m from walls. Drought and termite resistant. Seeds can be used for fodder.

Cercis siliquastrum
Judas tree, Judasboom

Size: 6 x 4 m

Growth habit: This small to medium-sized tree has a sparse, spreading crown. It flowers just before coming into leaf in spring. When its branches are covered in purple-pink, butterfly-like blooms, it provides an amazing spectacle. Flowers are followed by long, flat seedpods. Expected growth rate is about 60 cm per year.

Planting: Prefers fertile soil. Dig a hole 75 cm square and deep. Mix two thirds of the topsoil with one third compost in the bottom of the hole, add one cup of bone meal or superphosphate and mix well. Stake young trees. Does not transplant well.

Watering and feeding: Water and feed this tree regularly until it is established.

Pruning: Only needs occasional shaping.

Uses: Lovely flowering tree for town gardens. Very popular with flower arrangers, as flower buds keep opening in the vase. Can be planted up to 3 m from walls. Drought tolerant. Tolerates salt-laden winds at the coast, but performs better in drier inland regions.

Planting depth When planting out trees or shrubs, always plant them at the same depth at which they were growing in the nursery bag or pot. Planting them too deep or too shallow will cause poor growth. Use the original mark on the stem, and plant at the same depth.

Combretum erythrophyllum
(536) River bushwillow, Riviervaderlandswilg

Size: 6–17 x 8 m

Growth habit: A medium-sized to large deciduous tree with a spreading crown. It has dense, pale green foliage that is attractively red and yellow in autumn. It develops a single or multi-branched stem with smooth, cream to pale brown bark that becomes flaky with age. Spikes of greenish-white flowers appear in early summer followed by four-winged seeds. Fast growing, up to 1 m per year.

Planting: Dig a hole 75 cm square and deep. Mix two thirds of the topsoil with one third compost in the bottom of the hole, add one cup of bone meal or superphosphate and mix well. Stake young trees and shelter from frost in their first two years.

Watering and feeding: Water regularly until well established. Feed during spring with a general fertiliser, then water in well.

Pruning: Not necessary, except to remove unwanted side branches until the required crown height is reached.

Uses: Excellent large shade tree for damp soil and in parking areas. Termite resistant. Drought tolerant once established. Do not plant closer than 5 m from walls.

Other species: *C. kraussii*, the forest bushwillow, is a fast-growing deciduous tree with glossy, dark green leaves and lovely red autumn colouring. Decorative medium-sized tree for town gardens.

Cunonia capensis
(140) Red alder, Rooiels

Size: 8–25 x 10 m

Growth habit: This decorative evergreen spreading tree rarely reaches more than 6 m in garden conditions. Its young leaves have a rosy tinge and stems are red. It bears spikes of sweetly scented white flowers in autumn and small sticky seeds are released from May to July. Fast growing, up to 1 m per year.

Planting: This tree prefers moist, fertile soil. Dig a hole 75 cm square and deep. Mix two thirds of the topsoil with one third compost in the bottom of the hole, add one cup of bone meal or superphosphate and mix well. Stake the young trees. Mulch with compost.

Watering and feeding: Water and feed this tree regularly until it is established.

Pruning: Not necessary, except for occasional shaping.

Uses: An excellent tub subject for patios in either sun or shade. The red alder tolerates salt-laden wind. The flowers and seeds attract insects and birds.

Maintaining trees Remember to regularly remove old, damaged, dry and sick branches from trees, especially evergreen ones, to help keep them in shape. This will let light into the crown and encourage new shoots to develop, giving the trees a healthy appearance.

Cussonia spicata
(564) Common cabbage tree, Gewone kiepersol

Size: 5–26 x 3 m

Growth habit: This tree grows up to 1 m per year, particularly in the warmer parts of the country. It has a slender stem, which develops into a thickset form with a rounded crown. Bark is corky, rough and grey. It has large, dark green leaves clustered at the tips of the branches. Flowers resembling candelabra are borne in summer, followed by small, round fruits with a purple colour. Will not survive severe frost.

Planting: Dig a hole 75 cm square and deep. Mix two thirds of the topsoil with one third compost in the bottom of the hole, add one cup of bone meal or superphosphate and mix well. Stake young trees.

Watering and feeding: Water and feed this tree regularly until it is established.

Pruning: Not necessary.

Uses: Very decorative tree. Can be planted in seaside gardens as it tolerates salt-laden winds. Do not plant too close to any permanent structure – keep it at least 4 m away. Flowers and fruit attract birds and butterflies. Medicinally used against malaria and stomach complaints by traditional healers.

Dais cotinifolia
(521) Pompon tree, Kannabas

Size: 5–8 x 2 m

Growth habit: This neat, upright-growing, small tree has a rounded crown. It is evergreen in warm areas but loses half its leaves in colder regions. Round clusters of pale mauve-pink flowers are borne from spring to the end of summer. It can be single or multi-stemmed, and its bark is smooth and grey. It is fast growing, up to 1 m per year.

Planting: Prefers well-drained, fertile soil. Dig a hole 75 cm square and deep. Mix two thirds of the topsoil with one third compost in the bottom of the hole, add one cup of bone meal or superphosphate and mix well. Stake young trees.

Watering and feeding: Water and feed this tree regularly until well established.

Pruning: Not necessary, except for occasional shaping.

Uses: Decorative tree ideal for small gardens in retirement villages and townhouse complexes. Excellent in coastal gardens, tolerates salt-laden wind. Bark is traditionally used for plaiting into ropes, for binding and whips.

Common cabbage tree Do not be tempted to grow this tree in small gardens in the open ground, especially close to the pool, a wall or paved areas. It has a large root system that will eventually cause a lot of damage. Rather grow it in a large container or at least 4 m away from any permanent structure.

Dombeya rotundifolia
[471] Common wild pear, Gewone drolpeer

Size: 5–7 x 2 m
Growth habit: A small, gracefully shaped tree with a rounded crown, its leaves are large and rounded, dark green above and pale green on the reverse. The crooked trunk is a dark grey-brown. Clusters of scented, creamy-white flowers cover the bare tree in late winter. Fast growing under cultivation, up to 60 cm per year.
Planting: Dig a hole 75 cm square and deep. Mix two thirds of the topsoil with one third compost in the bottom of the hole, add one cup of bone meal or superphosphate and mix well. Stake young trees.
Watering and feeding: Only needs to be watered until established. Feed during spring with a general fertiliser, then water in well.
Pruning: Not necessary, except for occasional shaping.
Uses: Excellent flowering tree for indigenous gardens. The flowers can be used in dried arrangements. It is drought tolerant. Medicinally used for heart problems and stomach complaints by traditional healers.

Ekebergia capensis
[298] Cape ash, Essenhout

Size: 10–30 x 8 m
Growth habit: This showy tree has shiny leaves and its stem is usually tall and straight with smooth to rough grey-brown bark. It produces panicles of tiny, ivory-coloured flowers followed by red berries. Male and female flowers occur on separate trees. It is reasonably fast growing, up to around 60 cm per year. It has a very attractive shape with a tall, spreading crown. It is evergreen in frost-free areas and semi-evergreen in cooler regions.
Planting: Dig a hole 75 cm square and deep. Mix two thirds of the topsoil with one third compost in the bottom of the hole, add one cup of bone meal or superphosphate and mix well. Stake young trees.
Watering and feeding: Water and feed this tree regularly until well established.
Pruning: Not necessary.
Uses: Beautiful shade tree suitable for large gardens and street avenues. Do not plant closer than 5 m from walls. The fruit is very popular with birds. It is also a host tree for *Bunaea alcinoe* moth larvae. It has magical and medicinal uses. The bark is used for coughs and the roots to treat dysentery.

Watering new trees and shrubs Always water trees well in their container before planting out. After planting, make a shallow basin around the stem to keep water from running off in all directions. Water deeply and provide a mulch of compost within the basin to help with moisture retention and to keep the soil cool.

Erythrina lysistemon
(245) Common coral tree, Gewone koraalboom

Size: 8–16 x 6 m

Growth habit: A medium-sized tree with a spreading crown, it develops a broad stem with smooth, pale grey bark. Leaves are trifoliate and light green. It is grown for its showy flowers, which are orange-red and appear in late winter. Branching low down, this is one of our most sublime coral trees. Does well in dry winters.

Planting: Dig a hole 75 cm square and deep. Mix two thirds of the topsoil with one third compost in the bottom of the hole, add one cup of bone meal or superphosphate and mix well.

Watering and feeding: Don't water in winter as it prefers dry winters to flower well. Feed during spring with a general fertiliser, then water in well.

Pruning: Not necessary except for occasionally removing dead branches.

Uses: Beautiful flowering tree for medium to large gardens. Flowers attract many birds and insects. Hole-nesting birds also like this soft-wooded species. Has medicinal properties.

Ginkgo biloba
Maidenhair tree, Vrouehaarboom

Size: 15–23 x 6 m

Growth habit: This prehistoric tree is the oldest flowering tree known. It is a tall, narrow tree which develops a spreading crown when mature. It has lovely, light green, fern-like leaves, with beautiful yellow autumn colouring on the highveld. Slow growing, only about 30 cm per year.

Planting: Prefers fertile, acid soil. Dig a hole 75 cm square and deep. Mix two thirds of the topsoil with one third compost in the bottom of the hole, add one cup of bone meal or superphosphate and mix well. Stake young trees.

Watering and feeding: Needs regular, deep watering until well established. Feed during spring with a general fertiliser, then water in well.

Pruning: Not necessary, only needs shaping while young.

Uses: This elegant specimen tree is particularly suitable for cold gardens. Effective for narrow, enclosed spaces. Can be grown up to 3 m from walls. It tolerates salt-laden wind and has medicinal properties.

Feeding newly planted trees After planting out a tree into the garden, it will only be necessary to fertilise it the following spring at the start of the new active growing season. Spread a handful of fertiliser evenly around the tree, at a distance from the stem to prevent burning, and water well.

Harpephyllum caffrum
(361) Wild plum, Wildepruim

Size: 14–26 x 7 m
Growth habit: This medium-sized to large, reasonably fast-growing, evergreen tree has a dense, spreading crown and an expected growth rate of up to 60 cm per year. It has dark green, glossy leaves, which are sickle-shaped. The odd red-coloured dead leaf on the tree is a feature. The stem is usually tall, with smooth bark when young, becoming rough with age. The branches on young trees develop a distinctly candelabra-like shape. Sprays of small, cream-coloured flowers appear during summer followed by sour, edible, red fruit ripening during winter.
Planting: Dig a hole 75 cm square and deep. Mix two thirds of the topsoil with one third compost in the bottom of the hole, add one cup of bone meal or superphosphate and mix well.
Watering and feeding: Water and feed regularly to obtain a faster growth rate.
Pruning: Not necessary.
Uses: A beautiful evergreen shade tree for medium to large gardens. Also makes an excellent street tree. Light frost will not damage established trees. Tolerates salt-laden wind at the coast. Fruit attracts birds, fruit bats, bushbabies and monkeys. Fruit can also be used to make a tasty jelly. The bark is utilised for medicinal purposes by traditional healers.

Heteropyxis natalensis
(455) Lavender tree, Laventelboom

Size: 5 x 4 m
Growth habit: This small to medium-sized tree has strongly aromatic, light green foliage, turning into attractive red autumn colours. Its flowers are small, yellowish-green and fragrant, and appear from December to March. The stems usually develop a crooked shape in dry, rocky areas but can be quite elegant under garden conditions. Bark is an ornamental white with pale orange blotches. Slow growing, with an expected rate of approximately 30 cm per year.
Planting: Prefers well-drained soil. Dig a hole 75 cm square and deep. Mix two thirds of the topsoil with one third compost in the bottom of the hole, add one cup of bone meal or superphosphate and mix well. Stake young trees.
Watering and feeding: Water regularly until well established. Quite drought tolerant when mature. Feed during spring with a general fertiliser, then water in well.
Pruning: Not necessary, only needs occasional shaping.
Uses: A very attractive small tree with glossy foliage for townhouse gardens. Excellent indigenous option to the silver birch (*Betula pendula*). Can be grown up to 3 m from walls. Termite resistant. Flowers attract bees, butterflies and wasps. Traditional healers use roots and leaves to treat worms in cattle and stock.

Autumn leaves Sweep fallen leaves from lawns to prevent them from looking untidy, but leave them where they fall in beds to act as a mulch which will help to keep the soil damp. They will eventually decompose to form compost.

Hymenosporum flavum
Scented blossom tree, Gevlerktesaadboom

Size: 10–21 x 3 m

Growth habit: This tall, columnar, evergreen tree is suitable for both large and small gardens. Its foliage is dark green and shiny, forming a small crown. It is fast growing, 60 cm per year or more. From spring to summer trees are festooned with sprays of cream to golden-yellow flowers, followed by winged pods in autumn.

Planting: Prefers fertile, well-drained soil. Dig a hole 75 cm square and deep. Mix two thirds of the topsoil with one third compost in the bottom of the hole, add one cup of bone meal or superphosphate and mix well. Stake young trees.

Watering and feeding: Water and feed this tree regularly until well established.

Pruning: Not necessary.

Uses: Excellent slender tree for town and coastal gardens. Can be used for screening tall water tanks or as a windbreak.

Ilex mitis
[397] Cape holly, Without

Size: 10–25 x 5 m

Growth habit: A medium-sized to large evergreen tree with glossy, dark green foliage forming a dense, spreading crown, it develops a tall stem with rough, light brown bark. Bears small, white, scented flowers during summer followed by red berries in autumn. Male and female flowers occur on separate trees. Relatively fast growing, approximately 60 cm per year.

Planting: Dig a hole 75 cm square and deep. Mix two thirds of the topsoil with one third compost in the bottom of the hole, add one cup of bone meal or superphosphate and mix well. Stake young trees.

Watering and feeding: Water regularly until well established, and during dry spells; fertilise during spring.

Pruning: Not necessary to prune, but it can be pruned into a standard shape.

Uses: Excellent choice for damp areas or near water. It can also be grown in a large container on the patio. Birds like the fruit. Foliage and bark have medicinal uses.

Planting time Most trees and shrubs can be planted out into the garden throughout the year. However, bare-rooted deciduous plants like fruit trees and roses must be planted out in winter and early spring for best results. The best time to plant is autumn, as this will give them enough time to develop a good root system before winter.

Kiggelaria africana
(494) Wild peach, Wildeperske

Size: 8 x 6 m
Growth habit: This medium-sized tree has dense foliage developing into a spreading crown. The main stem can be single or multi-stemmed with pale brown bark on young trees becoming dark and rough on older specimens. Small, yellow flowers appear during spring to summer, with male and female flowers on separate trees. Round fruit about 2 cm in diameter ripen late summer into winter by splitting into four sections to expose black seeds in a bright orange-red coating. Fast growing, up to 60 cm per year, and hardy.
Planting: Prefers fertile soil. Dig a hole 75 cm square and deep. Mix two thirds of the topsoil with one third compost in the bottom of the hole, add one cup of bone meal or superphosphate and mix well. Stake young trees.
Watering and feeding: Water and feed regularly to accelerate the growth tempo and to obtain a well-shaped tree.
Pruning: Not necessary, except for occasional shaping.
Uses: Excellent decorative tree for all gardens. Fruit attracts insects and many bird species to the garden. It is also a butterfly host plant. Tolerates salt-laden wind. It can be planted up to 3 m from walls. Traditionally used for magical purposes.

Lagerstroemia indica
Pride of India/Crepe myrtle, Trots van Indië

Size: 5 x 3 m
Growth habit: A small, colourful tree suitable for all seasons, it develops a spreading crown. Usually multi-stemmed but can be pruned into single-stemmed specimens. Bark is light brown to grey-mottled and smooth, becoming flaky on mature plants. Masses of flowers on terminal panicles appear in early summer. Available in a range of colours, including lilac, mauve, pale pink, rose pink, red and white. It is also very colourful in autumn when foliage turns to orange, red and golden shades. Susceptible to mildew in humid areas. Tends to form suckers on damaged roots. Slow growing, up to 30 cm per year.
Planting: Dig a hole 75 cm square and deep. Mix two thirds of the topsoil with one third compost in the bottom of the hole, add one cup of bone meal or superphosphate and mix well. Stake young trees.
Watering and feeding: Water until established. Annual feeding will improve flowering and growth tempo. Drought tolerant once mature.
Pruning: Winter pruning produces lots of flowers in summer.
Uses: Very colourful small tree for any garden. Tolerates salt-laden winds, grows well in brackish soils. Termite resistant. Very few other plants will still perform as well under general conditions of neglect as the Pride of India.

Pruning young specimen trees Remove low-growing shoots and branches from the main stems of young trees which are to become shade trees. This will help to channel the energy from this growth, which will have to be removed at a later stage anyway, into stronger and taller growth.

Liquidambar styraciflua
Liquidambar/American sweet gum, Amberboom

Size: 10–30 x 3 m
Growth habit: Upright growing with a pyramidal form, the liquidamber is an ornamental shade tree with brilliantly coloured foliage of yellow, orange, red and plum during autumn. New foliage in spring is an attractive light green turning darker green towards summer. Insignificant yellow-green flowers are followed by prickly, brown seeds in late summer. It is slow growing, up to 40 cm per year.
Planting: Dig a hole 75 cm square and deep. Mix two thirds of the topsoil with one third compost in the bottom of the hole, add one cup of bone meal or superphosphate and mix well.
Watering and feeding: Water regularly and keep trees well mulched. Feed during spring with a general fertiliser.
Pruning: Not necessary.
Uses: Excellent for specimen and background planting. It also makes a good avenue tree. The liquidambar tolerates salt-laden wind and waterlogged soil conditions.

Loxostylis alata
(365) Tarwood, Teerhout

Size: 3–8 x 2,5 m
Growth habit: A small tree with either a single or multi-stemmed main stem, it has attractive, light green, compound foliage with a drooping habit. The flowers are small and white, and borne in dense sprays with prominent sepals, which turn reddish-pink on the female trees during summer. Male and female flowers feature on separate trees. Rather slow growing, with an expected growth rate of about 40 cm per year under ideal conditions.
Planting: Dig a hole 75 cm square and deep. Mix two thirds of the topsoil with one third compost in the bottom of the hole, add one cup of bone meal or superphosphate and mix well. Stake young plants.
Watering and feeding: Water regularly to accelerate growth tempo. Mature trees are drought tolerant. Feed during spring with a general fertiliser, then water in well.
Pruning: Not necessary, except for occasional shaping.
Uses: Lovely tree for small gardens. Bark and leaves are used medicinally by traditional healers at childbirth.

Pyramid-shaped trees These trees – for instance the yellowwoods, the pinoak and the liquidambar – have a growth habit with naturally low-growing branches. Do not remove these low-growing branches if you want to keep the natural growing shape of these plants.

Magnolia grandiflora
Tree magnolia, Magnolia

Size: 10–19 x 5 m
Growth habit: One of the most glorious evergreen trees, it is pyramidal in shape, has large, leathery, dark green leaves and bears showy, saucer-shaped, creamy-white flowers during summer and autumn. This magnificent but slow-growing tree has an expected growth rate of 30 cm per year.
Planting: Dig a hole 75 cm square and deep. Mix two thirds of the topsoil with one third compost in the bottom of the hole, add one cup of bone meal or superphosphate and mix well. Stake young trees.
Watering and feeding: Must be watered during dry weather but does not need regular feeding.
Pruning: Not necessary except for shaping.
Uses: This is an ideal shade tree for the large garden and also excellent in large tubs. Flowers are lovely for picking. Tolerates salt-laden winds and shady growth conditions. It can be propagated with cuttings.

Malus floribunda
Japanese flowering crab apple, Japanse blomappel

Size: 4 x 3 m
Growth habit: Remarkably beautiful, and probably the most sought-after crab apple for the garden, it has long, arching branches. In spring it is covered with crimson buds that open to white and pale pink flowers. Yellow and red fruits follow. Slow growing, about 30 cm per year.
Planting: Dig a hole 75 cm square and deep. Mix two thirds of the topsoil with one third compost in the bottom of the hole, add one cup of bone meal or superphosphate and mix well. Stake young trees.
Watering and feeding: Regular watering will ensure good flowering. Keep well mulched. Mature plants are drought tolerant but need water to flower well. Feed during spring.
Pruning: Not necessary, only needs occasional shaping.
Uses: Very ornamental and ideal for cold gardens. Provides cut flowers. Fruit can be used to make an excellent jelly.
Varieties: *M.* 'Oekonomierat Echtermeyer' (weeping crab apple) grows to approximately 5 m tall. Its long, pendulous branches bear masses of bright red blossoms in spring and red fruit in autumn. Best of the weeping cultivars.

Noise buffer Evergreen trees and large shrubs in particular are ideal to form a screen next to busy roads, as they effectively absorb the noise of the traffic and provide a measure of privacy in these busy areas.

Milettia grandis
(227) Umzimbeet, Omsambeet

Size: 10–18 x 5 m

Growth habit: This medium-sized flowering tree has a spreading, rounded crown with a tall main stem featuring light brown-grey, flaking bark. It bears shiny, compound leaves which may be shed during summer. Erect panicles of mauve to lilac, pea-shaped flowers appear from November to March. Woody seedpods are decorative and split open on the tree during winter. It has a moderate growth tempo, with an expected growth rate of 40 cm per year.

Planting: Dig a hole 75 cm square and deep. Mix two thirds of the topsoil with one third compost in the bottom of the hole, add one cup of bone meal or superphosphate and mix well. Stake young trees.

Watering and feeding: Water regularly until well established. Regular feeding will hasten the growth rate.

Pruning: Not necessary, only needs occasional shaping.

Uses: The umzimbeet is a decorative and elegant garden tree for medium gardens. It will start flowering while still young. It is wildlife-friendly and is a butterfly host plant. It tolerates salt-laden winds. The seeds can be poisonous, and roots are used medicinally. Wood is heavy and hard and used for walking sticks, furniture and knobsticks.

Olea europaea subsp. africana
(617) Wild olive, Olienhout

Size: 6–18 x 3 m

Growth habit: A beautiful, medium-sized tree with a spreading, rounded crown, it has a slender stem with grey bark, which is fairly smooth on young trees. The foliage is leathery and grey-green with a paler reverse. Small, creamy-white flowers appear in tight bunches during early summer followed by round to oval purple fruits. It is rather slow growing, with an expected growth rate of 30 cm per year.

Planting: Dig a hole 75 cm square and deep. Mix two thirds of the topsoil with one third compost in the bottom of the hole, add one cup of bone meal or superphosphate and mix well. Stake young trees.

Watering and feeding: Do not overwater. Feed during spring with a general fertiliser, then water in well.

Pruning: Not necessary, only needs occasional shaping.

Uses: Useful as a windbreak or screener and excellent as a contrast tree. Tolerates alkaline soil conditions. It is hardy and drought resistant. Ideal for the small to medium garden. Fruit attracts birds, monkeys and bats. Foliage and bark medicinally used by traditional healers for headaches, respiratory and renal ailments.

Windbreaks Trees planted as windbreaks are usually effective for approximately 20 times their height in distance behind the tree. Ideal windbreak trees are the wild olive, carob, conifers and yellowwoods.

TREES

Peltophorum africanum
(215) Weeping wattle, Huilboom

Size: 5–15 x 4 m
Growth habit: This lovely, medium-sized, spreading tree has a rounded crown. Its main stem is low branching with grey-brown bark, smooth when young, becoming rough with age. Acacia-like foliage is a dull olive-green with a paler reverse. Terminal sprays of yellow flowers appear for many months during summer, followed by yellow-brown, flat leathery fruit pods. It is moderately fast growing, up to 60 cm per year. It can be parasitised by spit-bugs which gives the tree its common name of weeping wattle.
Planting: Dig a hole 75 cm square and deep. Mix two thirds of the topsoil with one third compost in the bottom of the hole, add one cup of bone meal or superphosphate and mix well. Stake young trees.
Watering and feeding: Water and feed regularly during the active growth season to obtain a faster growth tempo.
Pruning: Not necessary, only needs a little shaping.
Uses: A lovely shade tree for the medium garden. Traditional healers use the roots and the bark medicinally for treating sterility and backache.

Platanus x acerifolia
London plane, Gewone plataan

Size: 12–30 x 25 m
Growth habit: A large tree with a spreading crown, it develops a substantial upright main stem with attractive, smooth, grey-mottled bark. The leaves are large and during autumn they change into lovely yellow colours. The flowers are insignificant. It is a fairly fast-growing tree, with an expected growth rate of about 60 cm per year.
Planting: Dig a hole 75 cm square and deep. Mix two thirds of the topsoil with one third compost in the bottom of the hole, add one cup of bone meal or superphosphate and mix well. Stake young trees.
Watering and feeding: Water and feed regularly during the active growth season.
Pruning: Not necessary.
Uses: An outstanding shade tree for large gardens in cold climates. It tolerates salt-laden winds.

Staking trees Newly planted trees must always be tied to a sturdy stake to prevent damage caused by wind. Thread some wire through a piece of hosepipe for tying the tree to the stake. Leave enough space between the tying material and the trunk for it to develop. Strips cut from a rubber inner tube or old pantyhose make good tying material.

Podocarpus henkelii
(17) Henkel's yellowwood, Henkel-se-geelhout

Size: 10–36 x 5 m

Growth habit: A tall, upright-growing tree with a pyramidal shape, its main stem is straight, with brown bark flaking off in long strips. The most attractive of the yellowwoods, it has dense foliage with dark green leaves on closely arranged horizontal branches. New foliage is light green turning dark green and leathery with age. Relatively slow growing, with an expected growth rate of about 30 cm per year.

Planting: Dig a hole 75 cm square and deep. Mix two thirds of the topsoil with one third compost in the bottom of the hole, add one cup of bone meal or superphosphate and mix well. Stake young trees.

Watering and feeding: Water and feed regularly during the active growth season.

Pruning: Not necessary.

Uses: Ornamental tree suitable for tub planting. It can be grown in the shade. It tolerates salt-laden winds and some drought once established. Makes an excellent indigenous Christmas tree.

Prunus serrulata
Japanese flowering cherry, Japanse blomkersie

Size: 3–6 x 3 m

Growth habit: This is one of the most beautiful trees in early spring with its clusters of hanging double, semi-double and single flowers in shades of pink to white. Its new bronze-coloured foliage appears after flowering. During autumn, foliage changes to attractive yellow and red shades. These trees enjoy cold, frosty winters and bear their flowers when most of the other flowering fruits have stopped blooming.

Planting: Dig a hole 75 cm square and deep. Mix two thirds of the topsoil with one third compost in the bottom of the hole, add one cup of bone meal or superphosphate and mix well. Stake young trees.

Watering and feeding: Water regularly throughout the active growing season. Feed with a general fertiliser during spring. Keep trees mulched with compost.

Pruning: Prune after flowering to stimulate new growth.

Uses: Lovely small tree for planting on the lawn or in the mixed border in cold areas.

Varieties: *P. serrulata* 'Kanzan' bears dark pink double flowers and has an upright growth habit. *P. serrulata* 'Mammoth Rose' bears large, rose-pink double flowers with frilly edges. *P. serrulata* 'Shirofugen', a strong grower, bears flesh-coloured buds which open to double pale pink to white flowers.

Central growing tip If the central growing tip of a tree with a pyramid shape (such as a yellowwood) breaks or gets damaged, you can successfully train a side branch lower down to become the central leader, by cutting off the damaged piece above this new leading branch and tying the new branch onto a stake.

Ptaeroxylon obliquum
(292) Sneezewood, Nieshout

Size: 10–20 x 5 m
Growth habit: This tall, upright-growing tree has a narrow, rounded crown. It is usually single stemmed, with pale grey bark becoming rough with age. Glossy, dark green leaves are compound and are borne in clusters at the ends of branches. Leaves turn yellow in autumn before they drop. Sweetly scented yellow to white flowers are borne in bunches from August to November, followed by reddish-brown capsules. Male and female flowers occur on separate trees. Expected growth tempo is about 60 cm per year under ideal conditions.
Planting: Dig a hole 75 cm square and deep. Mix two thirds of the topsoil with one third compost in the bottom of the hole, add one cup of bone meal or superphosphate and mix well. Stake young trees.
Watering and feeding: Water and feed this tree regularly until it is established.
Pruning: Not necessary.
Uses: Ideal tree for medium gardens. A butterfly host plant and relatively fast growing at the coast. Tolerates salt-laden winds and can be grown in shade. Traditionally used for magical and medicinal purposes to treat headaches, sinusitis and rheumatism.

Quercus palustris
Pin oak, Moeraseik

Size: 15–30 x 9 m
Growth habit: This upright-growing tree has a pyramidal shape and branches that sweep the ground. Its foliage makes a lovely show in spring when light green new leaves appear and in autumn when leaves turn all shades of red. A moderately fast grower, with a growth rate of 60 cm per year.
Planting: Dig a hole 75 cm square and deep. Mix two thirds of the topsoil with one third compost in the bottom of the hole, add one cup of bone meal or superphosphate and mix well. Stake young trees.
Watering and feeding: Water regularly. These trees do not tolerate drought. Feed young trees during spring in order to hasten growth.
Pruning: Not necessary, except for occasional shaping.
Uses: Excellent shade and street tree. Also beautiful avenue tree in cold areas.

Too dense shade on lawn A problem area under a large shade tree where the lawn doesn't want to grow can be converted into a focal point by mulching with large bark chips or gravel, enclosed by a low edging. Place a bench or a group of containers with colourful shade-loving plants on the mulched area as a focal point.

29

Quercus robur
English oak, Akkerboom

Size: 18 x 18 m

Growth habit: Many places in the Cape owe their charm to this stately tree. A large, spreading tree with a straight stem and wide, rounded crown. The stem becomes gnarled and covered with irregularly furrowed, dark brown bark. Foliage is an attractive dark green and lobed. Autumn foliage is yellow and rust brown. Acorns are borne singly or in short sprays. It initially grows slowly, but grows faster once well established. The expected growth rate is about 30 cm per year in deep, fertile and moist soil conditions. It is susceptible to heart rot and powdery mildew fungi, especially in the Western Cape.

Planting: Dig a hole 75 cm square and deep. Mix two thirds of the topsoil with one third compost in the bottom of the hole, add one cup of bone meal or superphosphate and mix well. Stake young trees.

Watering and feeding: Water and feed the young trees until well established.

Pruning: Not necessary, except for occasional shaping.

Uses: A fine, well-shaped tree, it is ideal for cold areas. It is a lovely, big shade tree for street plantings or large estates.

Rhamnus prinoides
(452) Dogwood, Blinkblaar

Size: 2–6 x 3 m

Growth habit: This small tree is usually multi-stemmed, has glossy, dark green leaves and is reasonably frost resistant. It bears tiny green flowers followed by shiny, red-purple berries in late summer. Has a moderately fast growth tempo of about 60 cm per year.

Planting: Dig a hole 75 cm square and deep. Mix two thirds of the topsoil with one third compost in the bottom of the hole, add one cup of bone meal or superphosphate and mix well. Stake young plants.

Watering and feeding: Water and feed regularly during the active growth season.

Pruning: Only to shape. Can be pruned into a hedge.

Uses: Excellent for town gardens. Makes a lovely hedge. Tolerates salt-laden winds and shade. Looks good in a large container on the patio. Birds and insects like the fruit. Traditionally used for magical purposes against evil spirits and for protection against lightning. Medicinally used for the treatment of skin complaints and respiratory infections.

Trees close to pools Avoid planting deciduous trees, flowering trees and berry-bearing plants close to the swimming pool as they make a mess in the pool. Plant taller shade trees or palms on the southeast side of the swimming pool to eliminate shade on the pool as shade will prevent the water temperature from heating up early in summer.

Rhus lancea
(386) Karee, Kareeboom

Size: 6–16 x 6 m

Growth habit: A medium-sized, dark green shade tree with a spreading crown, its bark is dark brown and rough. It has small, brown-yellow, edible berries in summer and autumn. It is drought tolerant and moderately fast growing, with an expected growth rate of about 60 cm per year.

Planting: Dig a hole 75 cm square and deep. Mix two thirds of the topsoil with one third compost in the bottom of the hole, add one cup of bone meal or superphosphate and mix well. Stake young trees.

Watering and feeding: Water and feed these trees regularly while they are young.

Pruning: Not necessary, except for occasional shaping.

Uses: An excellent, hardy, evergreen tree for dry and cold regions. It can also be used effectively as a windbreak on the Highveld. It tolerates alkaline soils and it is termite resistant. Fruits are traditionally used to ferment in water to make beer.

Rothmannia globosa
(695) September bells, Septemberklokkies

Size: 4–10 x 3 m

Growth habit: A small, bushy tree with a narrow crown, its main stem can be single or multi-stemmed, with brown bark becoming rougher with age. Foliage is dark green. Beautiful bell-shaped, ivory-coloured, scented flowers are borne in spring, followed by round fruits which are woody and brown. Prefers a semi-shaded position. It has a slow to moderate growth tempo of about 40 cm per year.

Planting: Dig a hole 75 cm square and deep. Mix two thirds of the topsoil with one third compost in the bottom of the hole, add one cup of bone meal or superphosphate and mix well. Stake young trees.

Watering and feeding: Water and feed regularly throughout the active growth season.

Pruning: Not necessary.

Uses: Very decorative garden plant especially for small gardens. Traditional healers use powdered roots medicinally.

Feeding established plants Start feeding trees and shrubs in spring with 3:1:5 for flowering plants and 2:3:2 for non-flowering plants, at a rate of 60 g per square metre, and do this every two months until autumn. Spread the plant food evenly over the drip area of the plant and water well after each application.

Schotia brachypetala
(202) Tree fuchsia, Huilboerboon

Size: 10–15 x 6 m

Growth habit: A medium-sized to large tree with a rounded crown, its main stem is grey-brown in colour and rough in texture. Leaves are compound and dark green in colour. New foliage is bronze turning to pale green and later to dark green. Mature trees usually flower at their best after a very dry winter. Green foliage is dropped just before flowering. During early spring, it gets covered in crimson flowers with copious nectar. It is rather slow growing, with an expected growth rate of 30 cm per year.

Planting: Dig a hole 75 cm square and deep. Mix two thirds of the topsoil with one third compost in the bottom of the hole, add one cup of bone meal or superphosphate and mix well. Stake young trees.

Watering and feeding: Water regularly until well established. Keep mature trees dry during winter to promote flowering. Feed during spring with a general fertiliser, then water in well.

Pruning: Not necessary except for occasional shaping.

Uses: This well-shaped shade tree is suitable for the medium to large garden. A butterfly host plant. Sunbirds, monkeys and insects love its nectar. Traditional healers use the bark medicinally for the treatment of heartburn and hangovers. Seeds can be roasted and eaten.

Stenocarpus sinuatus
Queensland fire wheel tree, Vuurwielboom

Size: 12–23 x 10 m

Growth habit: A large tree with a rounded crown, its large-lobed leaves are glossy and dark green. This tree is particularly handsome in late summer and autumn when it bears large, round umbels of scarlet flowers. It is a moderately fast grower, with an expected growth rate of 60 cm per year under ideal conditions.

Planting: Dig a hole 75 cm square and deep. Mix two thirds of the topsoil with one third compost in the bottom of the hole, add one cup of bone meal or superphosphate and mix well. Stake young trees.

Watering and feeding: Water and feed regularly. Do not let it dry out during winter.

Pruning: Not necessary.

Uses: A fine specimen or avenue liner. This evergreen tree is a must for large gardens in regions with mild winters. It tolerates salt-laden winds near the coast.

Buying plants, especially trees Never buy a plant if you do not need it. If you do not have a place for it, you will probably plant it in the wrong place and then wonder why it does not flourish, or it could overcrowd other smaller plants.

Tabebuia chrysotricha
Yellow tabebuia, Geeltrompetboom

Size: 5–8 x 3 m

Growth habit: This small tree with a spreading crown develops an upright stem with brown, fissured bark. Compound leaves are velvety and mid-green in colour. It produces a spectacular display of bright golden, trumpet-like flowers in early spring before its foliage appears. Long, narrow seedpods are light brown and are produced in summer; they split open to set hundreds of papery seeds free. Flowers during its first season as a small plant.

Planting: Dig a hole 75 cm square and deep. Mix two thirds of the topsoil with one third compost in the bottom of the hole, add one cup of bone meal or superphosphate and mix well. Stake young trees.

Watering and feeding: Water and feed regularly throughout the active growth season.

Pruning: Not necessary.

Uses: A colourful tree in early spring for small to medium gardens. Plant it in a bed as seeds tend to be messy.

Other species: *T. pentaphylla* (*T. rosea*), the pink trumpet tree, is deciduous and bears lovely lilac-pink, trumpet-shaped flowers in early spring. Very decorative.

Trachycarpus fortunei
Chinese windmill palm, Houtpalm

Size: 4 x 1,5 m

Growth habit: One of the toughest of the palms, this tree is even seen in parks in Scotland. It thrives in temperate climates, as it is inclined to scorch in full, hot sun. Developing a single trunk covered with coarse, brown-grey fibres, it is crowned with dense, fan-shaped foliage. Although rarely seen much higher than 2 m it may, when mature, reach 10 m or more. It is a slow-growing tree.

Planting: Dig a hole 75 cm square and deep. Mix two thirds of the topsoil with one third compost in the bottom of the hole, add one cup of bone meal or superphosphate and mix well.

Watering and feeding: Water and feed regularly throughout the active growth season.

Pruning: Not necessary to prune, except for the removal of dead leaves.

Uses: Ideal focus plant in the garden, the windmill palm is seen to advantage in groups, but it also makes a fine tub subject for patios and terraces. It will even grow indoors with good light.

Forked trunks Trees prone to form forks in the main trunk must be cut back hard close to the fork to encourage new denser growth. This will help prevent the trunk from splitting during stormy weather. Stinkwood, tabebuia and leopard trees are prone to form forked trunks.

33

Trichilia emetica
(301) Natal mahogany, Rooiessenhout

Size: 15 x 10 m
Growth habit: A medium-sized to large tree with a wide-spreading crown, its main stem is sturdy and develops branches fairly low down. Bark is grey-brown. Compound leaves are dark green and glossy. Silvery-green flowers in dense bunches are sweetly scented and appear during early summer among the leaves. Round fruits develop to split into three segments to expose large, black seeds covered with an orange-red skin during late summer. Relatively fast growing, with an expected growth rate of 60 cm per year. Plant at least 10 m away from walls, as roots tend to sucker.
Planting: Dig a hole 75 cm square and deep. Mix two thirds of the topsoil with one third compost in the bottom of the hole, add one cup of bone meal or superphosphate and mix well. Stake young trees.
Watering and feeding: Water and feed plants regularly during the active growing season.
Pruning: Not necessary.
Uses: A fine shade tree for tropical and subtropical gardens. Nectar and seeds attract birds and monkeys. A butterfly host plant. Tolerates salt-laden winds, can be grown in shade and is termite resistant. Seeds used as a vegetable by indigenous people. Traditional healers use powdered bark medicinally.

Vepris undulata
(261) White ironwood, Witysterhout

Size: 10 x 5 m
Growth habit: A small to medium-sized tree with a spreading, rounded crown, it develops a tall stem with smooth, grey bark. Glossy foliage has an apple-green colour. The aromatic leaves are trifoliate with wavy margins and have a lemon scent when crushed. Small green flowers appear in the middle of summer in terminal bunches and are followed by small, fleshy fruits, which are black when ripe in autumn. It is slow growing, with a growth tempo of about 30 cm per year. It can be planted up to 3 m from walls.
Planting: Dig a hole 75 cm square and deep. Mix two thirds of the topsoil with one third compost in the bottom of the hole, add one cup of bone meal or superphosphate and mix well. Stake young trees.
Watering and feeding: Water and feed regularly during the active growth season. Not drought hardy.
Pruning: Not necessary, except for occasional shaping.
Uses: Ideal tree for smaller gardens. Fruits attract birds and it is also a butterfly host plant. Tolerates salt-laden wind and is termite resistant. Traditional healers use powdered roots medicinally against influenza.

Placing birdbaths Always place a birdbath in a sheltered spot surrounded by or close to trees and shrubs to give the birds a place to perch and to provide some protection for them. This will also help to attract more birds to your garden.

Warburgia salutaris
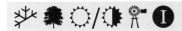
(488) Pepper-bark tree, Peperbasboom

Size: 8 x 4 m
Growth habit: A medium-sized tree with a rounded crown, its main stem is dark brown with branches developing low down. Dark green leaves are glossy with a paler reverse. Flowers are small and green and appear in autumn, followed by round, green fruits which ripen in early summer. Leaves and bark have a sharp peppery taste. It is slow growing, with an expected growth rate of about 30 cm per year. It can be planted up to 3 m from walls.
Planting: Dig a hole 75 cm square and deep. Mix two thirds of the topsoil with one third compost in the bottom of the hole, add one cup of bone meal or superphosphate and mix well. Stake young trees.
Watering and feeding: Water and feed regularly until well established. Established trees are drought tolerant.
Pruning: Not necessary, except for shaping.
Uses: Excellent for screening purposes. It is drought tolerant and the bark is used for medicinal purposes, especially for the treatment of common colds and chest ailments. Very rare in the wild due to overexploitation.

Wodyetia bifurcata

Foxtail palm

Size: 10–15 x 4 m
Growth habit: A graceful palm with a smooth, ringed, single stem. Its fronds are dark green with leaflets densely arranged in a circular plume, giving the appearance of a 'foxtail'. The arching fronds make this a truly elegant palm. The old leaves are shed cleanly to give a smooth, ringed appearance to the stem, giving it a very neat appearance. It grows rather slowly when young but grows faster after a few years.
Planting: Dig a hole 75 cm square and deep. Mix two thirds of the topsoil with one third compost in the bottom of the hole, add one cup of bone meal or superphosphate and mix well.
Watering and feeding: Water and feed regularly during the active growth season until well established. It is quite drought tolerant once established.
Pruning: Not necessary.
Uses: The foxtail palm is excellent for avenue planting. It is also beautiful as a specimen on the lawn, or anywhere else requiring a tropical appearance.

Evergreen trees When growing evergreen trees on the lawn, regularly remove lower branches as this will encourage the tree to develop a high crown. This will let enough sunlight reach the lawn for it to grow successfully.

Shrubs have the most important function of providing the garden with body and interest. They are by far the most significant feature in helping to create a maintenance-free garden. Because shrubs are such long-lived plants, most achieving their full potential in under five years, very few will have to be replaced in an average lifetime. Once they are planted, they need little care and attention except for periodic pruning or occasional trimming.

Shrubs with interesting foliage are very useful in supplying all-year-round colour, and those that produce flowers and berries give excellent offerings for the vase. Flowers and berries also have the added bonus of attracting birds and butterflies. Shrubs are also useful for screening off different areas in the garden and as windbreaks, to help deaden intrusive traffic noises, to give definition to boundaries and to help blend walls and houses with their surroundings by softening outlines and hiding foundations.

Shrubs are very versatile and you should not plant them too closely together, or put too many different varieties in the same bed, else the effect will be spoiled. Stick to the general design and theme of the garden as a whole to achieve a harmonious and pleasing overall picture.

It is important to remember when planting new shrubs to make decent holes and to provide them with enough compost and fertiliser to give them a good start in life. A little extra time invested in the preparation of the planting area will reap rich rewards in the long run. The wonderful thing is that there is a shrub suitable for every aspect, be it north, south, east or west, and for every situation be it sunny, shady, boggy or rocky, and for every climate, no matter how harsh.

shrubs

Abelia x grandiflora 'Francis Mason'
Glossy abelia, Blink-abelia

Size: 1,5 x 1,5 m

Growth habit: 'Francis Mason' is a medium-sized shrub with arching canes, and is excellent for colour contrast in the garden. It has shiny, variegated golden-green foliage, with white, trumpet-shaped flowers from spring to autumn. Fast growing.

Planting: Abelias prefer well-drained soil. Dig a hole 60 cm square and deep. Mix two thirds of the topsoil with one third compost in the bottom of the hole, add one cup of bone meal or superphosphate and mix well. Large plants can be transplanted successfully during late winter if cut back to one third.

Watering and feeding: Water regularly in summer. Fertilise during spring with a general fertiliser.

Pruning: Can withstand heavy pruning. To keep variegated foliage, remove the branches that revert to green.

Uses: It is good for hedging and its graceful branches are ideal for flower arranging.

Varieties: 'Confetti' has creamy-white and green foliage in summer; may become pink-tinged in colder weather. Bears small, white flowers in summer. Excellent for foreground shrub border and tub culture. 'Dwarf Queen' makes an effective small hedge. 'Prostrata' (0,7 x 1 m) is fine for banks and as a ground cover. It has spreading branches, shiny green foliage and white flowers. New growth is tinged with red.

Acalypha wilkesiana
Copper-leaf/Fijian fire bush, Koperblaar

Size: 1,5 x 1,5 m

Growth habit: Fast growing, suitable for tropical climates. There are over 200 species of copper-leaf, also referred to as Jacob's coat. Attractive foliage in shades of red, copper, pink, yellow and maroon. Flowers are inconspicuous. Neglected plants can be susceptible to mealy bug and red spider mite.

Planting: Does better in well-drained, loamy soil. Dig a hole 60 cm square and deep. Mix two thirds of the topsoil with one third compost in the bottom of the hole, add one cup of bone meal or superphosphate and mix well.

Watering and feeding: Water regularly throughout the year. Feed during spring and in midsummer after pruning, with a balanced general fertiliser.

Pruning: Needs pruning twice a year, in midsummer and early spring, to keep plant bushy.

Uses: Excellent for colour contrast in a mixed border. Makes an ideal hedge at the coast.

Varieties: 'Blushing Thai' has smaller, bronze-red leaves with a pink edge, which turn to a soft luminous pink. 'Java Yellow' is large with green, yellow, cream, and white variegated foliage. 'Pink Sport' is outstanding, with variegated foliage in shades of pink and maroon. 'Tropica' has curly, brick-red leaves with shades of carmine and pale green, splashed with olive-green.

Shaping a flowerbed An easy way to obtain the shape of a bed is to leave a hosepipe in the sun to soften, and to then lay it in the desired shape, marking the outline with a spade.

Agathosma ovata
False buchu, Basterboegoe

Size: 0,3–1 m

Growth habit: Agathosma is a small, low-growing shrub with compact growth. Its aromatic, heath-like foliage is dense and mid-green in colour. Small, white, star-shaped flowers appear from late winter to spring.

Planting: Buchu does better in well-drained soil. Dig a hole 60 cm square and deep. Mix two thirds of the topsoil with one third acid compost or peat, add one cup of bone meal or superphosphate and mix well.

Watering and feeding: Water during dry weather. Feed with a general fertiliser for flowering plants during the active growth season. Mulch with compost.

Pruning: Not necessary, but responds well to pruning.

Uses: Good next to pathways, where its aromatic foliage can be touched and smelled. Very good tub subject. Tolerates salt-laden wind near the coast. Foliage has medicinal properties.

Varieties: *A. ovata* 'Kluitjieskraal' is a low-growing shrub, 70 cm high, with small, dark green aromatic leaves and a profusion of pink flowers in winter. Good container plant.

Aloe arborescens
Krantz aloe, Kransaalwyn

Size: 3 x 3 m

Growth habit: This species usually forms a dense, shrubby bush with rosettes of fleshy leaves. Leaves are edged with recurving prickles. Flower-spikes with hanging tubular flowers appear freely from May to June and are usually red. The colour of the flowers may also be yellow or orange, depending on the locality. Slow growing and drought tolerant. The krantz aloe is prone to scale insect infestations which can be treated with mineral oil-based insecticide.

Planting: The krantz aloe needs well-drained soil and will flourish in a well-prepared hole containing compost and bone phosphate when planted.

Watering and feeding: It does not need a lot of attention but will respond well to occasional watering and feeding during dry weather.

Pruning: Not necessary.

Uses: Makes an excellent impenetrable hedge or screen. Flowers attract honeybirds. Outstanding for harsh conditions, and a good container subject in hot dry areas. Extract from leaves has medicinal uses for skin ailments or burns.

Aloes It is illegal to remove aloes out of the veld without a permit in order to transplant them into the garden. Make sure you buy these plants from legal growers like nurseries or botanical gardens.

Aucuba japonica 'Crotonifolia'
Japanese laurel, Japanse lourier

Size: 1,5 x 1 m
Growth habit: This medium-sized, slow-growing shrub is ideal for cool, shady places and has large, dark green leaves speckled with yellow. The plants are of different sexes. A female plant will produce red berries if a male plant with pollen is available.
Planting: It prefers fertile soil with lots of organic material. Dig a hole 60 cm square and deep. Mix two thirds of the topsoil with one third acid compost or peat in the bottom of the hole, add one cup of bone meal or superphosphate and mix well.
Watering and feeding: Water and feed regularly by mulching plants with compost and kraal manure.
Pruning: Not necessary.
Uses: Very good hardy shrub for shady areas. Also makes a good container plant for the shady patio.
Varieties: 'Goldeyana' has dark green leaves with big yellow spots. 'Variegata' has leaves with creamy-white spots.

Azalea indica
Azalea, Asalea

Size: 1,5 x 1,5m
Growth habit: Azalea is the common name given to those hybrids developed mainly from Japanese rhododendron species. Three of the most popular azaleas are the large-growing red 'Flambeau', the white 'Grandiflora Alba' and the cerise-pink 'Magenta'. These are free flowering, fast growing, and make excellent standard specimens. Avoid too much shade which will cause poor growth and few flowers.
Planting: The ideal soil pH for the azalea is 4,5–5,5, and it is important to plant it with peat moss. Dig a hole 60 cm square and deep. Mix two thirds of the topsoil with one third acid compost or peat in the bottom of the hole, add one cup of bone meal or superphosphate and mix well. Large plants transplant well during winter.
Watering and feeding: Too much water causes browning of leaves. Too little water causes leaf drop and droopy leaves. Feed regularly in active growing season with blue hydrangea food, to keep the soil acid. Mulch plants with acid compost.
Pruning: Not necessary except for occasional shaping. Can be pruned into standard forms.
Uses: Ideal tub subject on the patio. It also thrives under deciduous trees, for it needs the sun in winter.

Growing acid-loving plants To grow acid-loving plants – such as azaleas, gardenias, hydrangeas, fuchsias and camellias – in alkaline soil, use large plastic pots filled with acid potting soil and then plant these containers in the ground. Mulch each plant with acid compost to hide the rim and to keep the soil moist and cool.

Barleria obtusa
Bush violet, Bosviooltjie

Bauhinia galpinii
(208.1) Pride-of-de-Kaap, Vlam-van-die-vlakte

Size: 1 x 1,5 m

Growth habit: This medium-sized to large indigenous shrub is ideal for warmer parts of the country and has a scrambling growth habit. Foliage is dark green and covered in fine hairs. It bears a mass of mauve-blue flowers during April, May and June. It is relatively fast growing and spreads by suckering and seeding.

Planting: Dig a hole 60 cm square and deep. Mix two thirds of the topsoil with one third compost, add one cup of bone meal or superphosphate and mix well.

Watering and feeding: Does not need a lot of attention but will benefit by watering during dry weather and occasional feeding with a general fertiliser for flowering plants.

Pruning: It needs severe winter pruning after flowering.

Uses: This plant is excellent for banks and dry areas. The flowers attract butterflies. Drought tolerant.

Other species: *B. repens* 'Tickled Pink' bears lovely clear pink flowers. It has shiny foliage and does not grow as high as the bush violet.

Size: 3 x 2 m

Growth habit: This spreading, long-flowering shrub is worth its place in any garden, featuring leaves that are two-lobed and dark green when mature. Masses of brick-red flowers appear from spring into summer. It has a rampant, sprawling habit. It will not suffer any lasting damage from light frost. Relatively fast growing.

Planting: Prefers well-drained soil. Dig a hole 60 cm square and deep. Mix two thirds of the topsoil with one third compost, add one cup of bone meal or superphosphate and mix well.

Watering and feeding: Does not need a lot of attention, but responds well to extra water during dry weather and occasional feeding.

Pruning: Needs severe winter pruning to keep it in shape.

Uses: Ideal for embankments and rock gardens. It is drought tolerant. Will do well against a north-facing wall in full sun.

Other species: *B. natalensis*, the Natal bauhinia, is a lovely fast-growing, evergreen shrub and bears white flowers for a long period. Drought resistant.

Pruning evergreen shrubs Evergreen shrubs are not pruned like deciduous ones as they usually only need occasional shaping. All dead, diseased or damaged wood should be removed as soon as it is noticed, irrespective of the time of the year.

Berberis thunbergii 'Rose Glow'
Barberry, Berberis

Size: 0,5 x 0,5 m

Growth habit: This small, purple-leaved shrub is one of the most spectacular of the barberries, with pink-flushed, bronzy-purple foliage. Stems are spiny; small, yellow, bell-shaped flowers are borne in clusters during early summer.

Planting: It is easy to grow and thrives in most garden soils. Dig a hole 60 cm square and deep. Mix two thirds of the topsoil with one third compost in the bottom of the hole, add one cup of bone meal or superphosphate and mix well.

Watering and feeding: Once established, it only needs water during dry weather. Feed with a general fertiliser for flowering plants in spring and midsummer, then water in well.

Pruning: Can be pruned into a low hedge.

Uses: Excellent for colour contrast in front of larger shrubs or as a low hedge.

Varieties: 'Atropurpurea' is bigger, growing up to 1,5 m, and is useful for its brilliant purple foliage. 'Atropurpurea Nana' is similar to the above, but is low growing, reaching a height of up to 0,5 m. 'Red Chief' grows to 1,2 m and is a compact shrub with purplish-red, round leaves and red stems and is very effective in landscaping.

Brunfelsia pauciflora 'Floribunda'
Yesterday, Today and Tomorrow, Verbleikblom

Size: 3 x 1,5 m

Growth habit: Undoubtedly one of the most popular larger shrubs, bearing masses of fragrant flowers varying from purple through lilac to white from spring to summer. Semi-deciduous in colder climates, but only for a short time. New foliage has a bronze tinge and develops into pale green leaves.

Planting: Prefers light, well-drained soil. Dig a hole 60 cm square and deep. Mix two thirds of the topsoil with one third compost, add one cup of bone meal or superphosphate and mix well. Keep well mulched with compost and kraal manure.

Watering and feeding: Water it regularly and feed during spring with a general fertiliser for flowering plants.

Pruning: Not necessary, but it can be shaped and pruned into a hedge.

Uses: Plant near a window or the patio for its lovely scent. Excellent for screening. Makes a good container plant.

Varieties: 'Sweet Petite' is a compact form of yesterday, today and tomorrow. It is an evergreen shrub and becomes semi-deciduous in cooler areas. Makes an excellent feature plant in the garden or as a tub specimen to brighten up patios, verandahs, courtyards and balconies. It reaches a height of 1 m and a spread of up to 75 cm.

Pruning hedges When pruning hedges make sure that the base of the hedge is thicker than the top. This will ensure even light distribution, promoting denser growth from the bottom right up to the top of the hedge.

Buddleja salviifolia
(637) Sagewood, Saliehout

Size: 5 x 3 m

Growth habit: This large, multi-stemmed shrub or small tree has slightly drooping branches and its blue-green foliage has a grey reverse. It bears strongly scented mauve flowers in winter and spring. Fast growing.

Planting: Dig a hole 60 cm square and deep. Mix two thirds of the topsoil and one third compost in the bottom of the hole, add one cup of bone meal or superphosphate and mix well.

Watering and feeding: Does not need a lot of attention but will benefit from water during dry weather and occasional feeding with a general fertiliser for flowering plants.

Pruning: Cut back after flowering to keep the plant neat.

Uses: Makes a good windbreak or screening plant in a dry position. Attracts butterflies and birds to the garden. It is drought tolerant

Other species: *B. auriculata* (636.5), the weeping sage, is a beautiful, large, arching shrub featuring dark green, leathery foliage with a white reverse and sprays of sweetly scented, cream-coloured flowers in spring.

Burchellia bubalina
(688) Wild pomegranate, Wildegranaat

Size: 3 x 1,5 m

Growth habit: It is an outstanding large shrub with neat, glossy, dark green leaves and has showy scarlet to orange flowers appearing in clusters, from late spring into summer. Flowers contain nectar, and fruit is urn-shaped. It is slow growing. Plants start to flower while still small.

Planting: This shrub does better in well-drained soil. Dig a hole 60 cm square and deep. Mix two thirds of the topsoil with one third compost in the bottom of the hole, add a cup of bone meal or superphosphate and mix well.

Watering and feeding: Water and feed regularly, and keep plants well mulched with compost.

Pruning: Not necessary, can be shaped occasionally.

Uses: The flowers and fruit of this plant attract many varieties of birds. Ornamental evergreen shrub for the shrub border and excellent as a container plant on the patio.

Gardening for birds To attract birds to the garden, provide a variety of plants and habitats. Include a tall canopy area for safe nesting sites, a low-traffic area where birds can go about undisturbed, an open lawn for species feeding on pests, water for bathing and drinking, and a variety of fruit, berry and seed-bearing plants as food supply.

Calliandra brevipes
Shuttlecock/Powder puff tree, Poeierkwasboom

Size: 2 x 2 m
Growth habit: The shuttlecock is the most beautiful of all the *Calliandra* species and is a medium-sized to large shrub with a graceful growth habit. Silky, pink-white, powder-puff-like flowers appear during the summer months. Fine foliage is an attractive mid-green colour. It thrives in subtropical climates but will also do well on the Highveld given a sheltered corner on the north side.
Planting: Dig a hole 60 cm square and deep. Mix two thirds of the topsoil with one third compost and kraal manure, add one cup of bone meal or superphosphate and mix well.
Watering and feeding: Water regularly especially during hot, dry weather, and feed during spring with a general fertiliser for flowering plants.
Pruning: Prune lightly during late winter to promote denser growth and more prolific flowering.
Uses: Ideal for townhouse gardens in the background of the shrub border.
Other species: *C. tweedii*, the Mexican flame bush, has coarser foliage and bears brilliant red, powder-puff-like flowers during summer. *C. haematocephala* is a spreading shrub with similar large, reddish-pink flowers from autumn to spring. This shuttlecock is also available with pure white flowers.

Callistemon citrinus 'Hot Pink'
Pink bottlebrush, Pienk bottelborsel

Size: 2,5 x 1,5 m
Growth habit: Sturdy large shrub with leathery, dark green foliage. Bears large, shocking pink bottlebrush flowers on the tips of its branches in summer. Tips of flower-spikes continue to grow as leafy shoots with long-lasting woody seed capsules.
Planting: It prefers well-drained soil. Dig a hole 60 cm square and deep. Mix two thirds of the topsoil with one third compost in the bottom of the hole, add one cup of bone meal or superphosphate and mix well.
Watering and feeding: Water and feed regularly until well established. Does not need a lot of attention once settled except for water during dry weather.
Pruning: Not necessary but can be cut back if it becomes woody with age, to promote bushy new growth. It is also a good idea to cut back spent flowers to prevent woody seed capsules from developing, as they can be messy.
Uses: Excellent background shrub in every garden. Nectar-rich flowers attract honeybirds to the garden.
Varieties: *C. citrinus* 'Endeavour' (red bottlebrush) is free flowering with large, rich, crimson brushes in spring, early summer and again in autumn. New growth is silky-red. 'Perth Pink' (3 x 2 m) bears soft pink, bottlebrush-like flowers in summer. New growth is brownish-pink.

Gardening for wildlife Most birds and butterflies prefer indigenous plants for nesting and feeding activities. Plant a selection that will provide fruit, berries and nectar throughout the year and not only during one season. Bird feeders are a good idea for smaller gardens.

43

Camellia japonica
Camellia, Japonika

Size: 4 x 3 m
Growth habit: Large, evergreen shrub with lovely, glossy, dark green foliage. Spectacular when flowering in autumn through winter to early spring. Flower forms are classified as single, semi-double, anemone form, peony form, rose form or formal double. If flowers turn brown or buds drop, it can be due to a lack of humidity, particularly in summer rainfall areas, but is usually caused by a mite. Plant in a south- or east-facing position where it will be protected from the hot afternoon sun.
Planting: Prefers acid, well-drained, humus-enriched soil. Dig a hole 60 cm square and deep. Mix two thirds of the topsoil with one third acid compost or peat, add one cup of bone meal or superphosphate and mix well. It transplants well, especially in autumn and early spring.
Watering and feeding: Mulch the camellia regularly with acid compost to conserve water. Feed regularly with blue hydrangea food to keep the soil acid.
Pruning: Not necessary except for occasional shaping.
Uses: It is excellent in tubs on patios where it has filtered sun. Very good as a background screener in shady areas.
Varieties: 'Kramers Supreme' bears large, peony-shaped, dark red flowers. 'Francie L' bears semi-double, large rose-pink flowers.

Chamaerops humilis
European fan palm, Europese waaierpalm

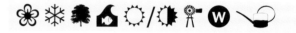

Size: 3 x 2 m
Growth habit: This is a small, multi-stemmed palm. The leaf colour may vary from blue-green to grey-green, and the leaf is fan-shaped. Slow growing. This is one of very few palms that can be grown throughout the country.
Planting: Dig a hole 60 cm square and deep. Mix two thirds of the topsoil with one third compost in the bottom of the hole, add one cup of bone meal or superphosphate and mix well.
Watering and feeding: Water when dry and feed regularly until it is well established. It does not need a lot of attention once settled.
Pruning: Not necessary except for removal of spent leaves.
Uses: This palm is ideal for small gardens. It makes a good container subject for the pool or patio area. It is hardy to cold and drought.

Acid-loving plants To encourage healthy growth in acid-loving plants such as hydrangeas, azaleas, fuchsias and camellias, fertilise them regularly with special 'Blue Hydrangea food'. Use a mulch of acid compost or peat moss to maintain the acidity of the soil.

Choisya ternata
Mexican orange

Size: 1,5 x 1,5 m

Growth habit: This lovely, rounded, compact shrub is medium in size and its leaves consist of 3 glossy deep green leaflets. Clusters of fragrant, star-shaped, white flowers appear during spring and sometimes in late summer and show up well against the dark green foliage. This shrub belongs to the citrus family and has aromatic leaves. It prefers a cooler climate and does not do well in subtropical areas.

Planting: Prefers slightly acid soil, which is well drained and rich in compost. Dig a hole 60 cm square and deep. Mix two thirds of the topsoil with one third acid compost or peat in the bottom of the hole, add one cup of bone meal or superphosphate and mix well. Keep plants mulched with compost.

Watering and feeding: Water during dry weather and feed during spring with a general fertiliser for flowering plants.

Pruning: Prune lightly after flowering if you wish to promote bushy growth.

Uses: A wonderful screening shrub for courtyards or for the patio and the mixed border. Also good for large pots.

Cistus x hybrids and species
Rock rose/Sun rose, Kliproos

Size: 1 x 1 m

Growth habit: This evergreen shrub is very well adapted to the winter rainfall regions. Medium in size, it forms a dense, mound-shaped shrub. It bears attractive, saucer-shaped flowers with 5 crinkly petals and comes in shades of white, pink and purple with a yellow centre. It flowers throughout the warmer seasons. It does not grow well in warm subtropical areas.

Planting: It prefers sandy, well-drained soil. Dig a hole 60 cm square and deep. Mix two thirds of the topsoil and one third compost in the bottom of the hole, add one cup of bone meal or superphosphate and mix well.

Watering and feeding: It does not need a lot of attention, but water during dry spells. Feed with a general fertiliser for flowering plants during spring and midsummer, then water in well.

Pruning: Not necessary, but some shaping can be done during late winter to promote a bushy shape.

Uses: This plant is excellent in shrub borders, and also in pots on the sunny patio. It is drought tolerant during summer.

Varieties: C. x *aguilari* is bushy, with sticky, wavy leaves and large white flowers in summer. It grows slightly bigger, reaching 1,5 x 1,5 m. C. x *purpureus* 'Brilliancy' features crimson-pink flowers with maroon spots in the centre.

Weed removal Never let weeds go to seed. The best method to get rid of weeds without using chemicals is still by hand-weeding, hoeing and digging. Small weeds can be smothered by placing black plastic sheeting over the weeds where this is possible to do without covering your precious plants as well.

X Citrofortunella mitis
Calamondin, Kalamondin

Size: 1,5 x 1 m

Growth habit: This dwarf citrus plant which originated from crossbreeding a kumquat with a tangerine is a beautiful little tree. It bears small, orange fruits like mini-oranges that ripen during July. It is always either in flower or fruit which shows up strikingly against the dark green foliage. It does very well in subtropical areas.

Planting: Dig a hole 60 cm square and deep. Mix two thirds of the topsoil with one third compost in the bottom of the hole, add one cup of bone meal or superphosphate and mix well.

Watering and feeding: Water and feed regularly.

Pruning: Can be pruned into a standard shape. Cut back in July, after fruit has ripened, to promote bushy growth.

Uses: Fine container subject for poolside pots, patios or decks. Very good focal point in the herb garden. Fruit can be used to make marmalade.

Varieties: *X C. mitis* 'Variegata', the variegated calamondin, is similar to the above but has cream and green variegated foliage, with green-, yellow- and orange-striped fruit in July.

Codiaeum variegatum
Croton, Kroton

Size: 2 x 2 m

Growth habit: This tropical plant with brilliant colour combinations is the ideal foliage plant for warm climates. Colours range from bright oranges and reds to mahogany and green, yellow and cream. It is at its most beautiful during autumn. This is a tender plant and is not suitable for cold climates. Sap stains clothing permanently.

Planting: It prefers well-drained soil rich in organic material. Dig a hole 60 cm square and deep. Mix two thirds of the topsoil with one third compost in the bottom of the hole, add one cup of bone meal or superphosphate and mix well.

Watering and feeding: Water and feed regularly. Keep plants well mulched.

Pruning: Tolerates heavy pruning. Cut back during late winter to promote low, bushy growth.

Uses: An excellent plant for colour contrast planting in the shrub border or as container plant on the patio. Popular for flower arranging.

Varieties: Many hybrids are available and they are usually sold just as croton hybrids – when names do appear they are usually wrong or confused.

Pruning flowering shrubs Make it a rule always to prune flowering shrubs once they have finished flowering, even if it is in summer. This will ensure a longer growth season and encourage new shoots to develop for the next flowering period.

Coleonema album
Confetti bush, Aasbossie/Wit konfettiebos

Size: 1 x 0,5 m

Growth habit: It is a small shrub. This bushy buchu has aromatic, heath-like foliage dark green in colour, with masses of tiny, white flowers from late winter to summer.

Planting: Prefers well-drained soil. Dig a hole 60 cm square and deep. Mix two thirds of the topsoil with one third compost in the bottom of the hole, add one cup of bone meal or superphosphate and mix well.

Watering and feeding: Does not need a lot of attention once established. It is drought tolerant in the winter rainfall regions. Water during winter in summer rainfall areas. Keeping plants mulched will help to preserve moisture. Feed with a general fertiliser for flowering plants during spring and midsummer, then water in well.

Pruning: Cut back lightly after flowering, but avoid cutting into the hard wood.

Uses: Ideal for rock gardens and in the front of the shrub border. Tolerates salt-laden winds at the coast.

Varieties: *C. pulchrum* bears masses of purplish-pink flowers from spring to summer. *C.* x 'Sunset Gold' has pale pink flowers and yellow-green fine foliage.

Coprosma repens 'Marble Chips'
Mirror bush, Spieëlplant

Size: 1,5 x 1,5 m

Growth habit: This shrub is medium in size. Glossy foliage is variegated with combinations of green and white. Its speckled and margined leaves are very striking. A more upright-growing coprosma, it is excellent in semi-shade.

Planting: Dig a hole 60 cm square and deep. Mix two thirds of the topsoil with one third compost in the bottom of the hole, add one cup of bone meal or superphosphate and mix well.

Watering and feeding: Does not need a lot of attention once established. Feed with a general fertiliser during spring and midsummer, then water in well.

Pruning: Only for shaping.

Uses: A background and foreground screening shrub with a dense habit and glossy foliage.

Varieties: Many cultivars available. *C. repens* 'Coffee Cream' is similar to the above but with creamy-yellow edges on foliage. 'Picturata' is similar to 'Marble Chips', but its golden centre is surrounded by glossy, bright green edges. 'Pink Splendour' has dark green, glossy leaves with maroon and pink-shaded edges, best in winter. 'Rainbow Surprise' is low growing with small, yellow-green and pink glossy leaves. Ideal rock garden plant. 'Taupata Gold' grows taller to about 2 m and is decorative with glossy, cream-coloured leaves with green centres.

Spent flowers Many shrubs retain spent flowers for a long period for seed production. Most seeds produce a hormone which inhibits new growth and more flowers. By removing spent flowers regularly, the plant will be encouraged to produce more flowers and it will stimulate fresh growth.

Cordyline australis 'Red Sensation'
Cabbage palm/Cabbage tree, Palmlelie

Size: 3 x 1 m

Growth habit: With its palm-like stem and wine-red, strap-like foliage trailing from the terminal point, it is an extremely useful form plant for giving a palm-like effect in cold areas. It is reasonably fast growing.

Planting: Prefers well-drained soil. Dig a hole 60 cm square and deep. Mix two thirds of the topsoil with one third compost, add one cup of bone meal or superphosphate and mix well.

Watering and feeding: Does not need a lot of water once established. Feed with a general fertiliser during spring and midsummer, then water in well.

Pruning: If damaged or too tall, cut off at ground level during spring, and it will develop new shoots again.

Uses: Very good accent and structural plant, excellent near the patio or the pool area. Not good in containers as it can get top heavy.

Varieties: *C. australis* 'Albertii' is similar, but with beautiful cream and green striped foliage. New leaves have a salmon tinge in the middle. *C. australis* 'Atropurpurea' (purple cabbage tree) has brownish-purple, evergreen foliage and prefers full sun.

Cuphea hyssopifolia
Stardust bush/False heather, Valsheide

Size: 0,3 x 0,3 m

Growth habit: This small shrub has fine, twiggy growth covered in heath-like foliage and grows into a rounded shape. The plant is covered with small, purple-coloured, star-shaped flowers for most of the year. Fast growing. Tends to self-seed.

Planting: Dig a hole 60 cm square and deep. Mix two thirds of the topsoil with one third compost, add one cup of bone meal or superphosphate and mix well.

Watering and feeding: Water and feed regularly.

Pruning: Can be cut back lightly after a flower flush, to promote a bushy shape.

Uses: Excellent for the front border, in small flower beds or in containers on the sunny patio.

Varieties: 'Cocktail' has yellow-green foliage and purple-pink flowers. 'Midget' has fine, bright green foliage with masses of dark purple flowers. 'White Star' has dark green foliage with white flowers in summer and autumn. 'Lemon Squash' has a compact growth habit, with golden foliage and tiny amethyst flowers. It grows to 20–30 cm, and is 35 cm wide. An ideal border or pot plant, it can easily be shaped to form an excellent low hedge. Light pruning will encourage flushes of new growth.

Eye-catching form plants Choose a selection of plants with dramatic structure to add year-round interest to the garden. Some good examples are sago palm, cabbage palm, philodendron or aloes.

Cyathea australis
Australian tree fern, Australiese boomvaring

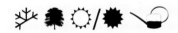

Size: 5 x 3 m

Growth habit: The Australian tree fern is single stemmed with a tall trunk and an umbrella-like crown of large fronds. Fronds are covered in prickly hairs. As beautiful as our indigenous *C. dregei*, this species grows both faster and taller. It grows best in dappled shade, but can tolerate a fair amount of sun or shade. It grows best in a humid atmosphere.

Planting: This plant prefers moist soil, rich in organic material. Dig a hole 60 cm square and deep. Mix two thirds of the topsoil with one third compost in the bottom of the hole, add one cup of bone meal or superphosphate and mix well. It transplants well during early spring.

Watering and feeding: It needs to be watered regularly as it will die if the soil dries out. Fertilise regularly with a nitrogen-rich fertiliser to obtain lush dark green fronds.

Pruning: Not necessary, except for the removal of dead or untidy fronds.

Uses: It makes a dramatic form plant and is also ideal for large shady areas.

Other species: *C. brownii* is a similar Australian tree fern, but more heat tolerant, with bigger and darker green fronds.

Cycas revoluta
Sago palm, Japanse sagopalm

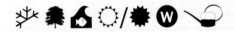

Size: 2 x 1 m

Growth habit: The sago palm is undoubtedly one of the finest form plants available for the garden. It has shiny green leaves, neatly and symmetrically arranged around its short trunk, and is a relatively quick grower compared to indigenous cycads, producing leaves up to three times a year. As it is not indigenous, no permit is needed for this cycad.

Planting: It prefers well-drained soil. Dig a hole 60 cm square and deep. Mix two thirds of the topsoil with one third compost in the bottom of the hole, add one cup of bone meal or superphosphate and mix well. Transplants well during late winter. The removal of side-shoots or suckers should also be done during late winter and wounds treated with flowers of sulphur to prevent stem rot.

Watering and feeding: Water when dry and feed during spring with a general fertiliser.

Pruning: Not necessary except for the removal of old or damaged fronds.

Uses: Popular ornamental plant for accent or as a tub subject on the patio.

Tea leaves Cold black tea and discarded tea leaves are excellent for increasing the acidity of soil. Use to mulch acid-loving plants like ferns, blue hydrangeas, azaleas, camellias and gardenias.

Diospiros whyteana
(611) Bladder-nut, Swartbas

Size: 5 x 3 m

Growth habit: This large, evergreen shrub has glossy, dark green foliage and develops a dense crown. White flowers appear from spring to summer, followed by red fruits enclosed by bladder-like structures. Rather slow growing, with an expected growth rate of about 30 cm per year.

Planting: Dig a hole 60 cm square and deep. Mix two thirds of the topsoil with one third compost in the bottom of the hole, add one cup of bone meal or superphosphate and mix well.

Watering and feeding: Does not need a lot of attention once established. Water when dry. Feed with a general fertiliser during spring and water in well.

Pruning: Cut back in order to promote a bushy form or to shape the plant.

Uses: Beautiful screening shrub also suitable as a hedge plant. It attracts birds to the garden and will tolerate shady growth conditions. It tolerates drought and salt-laden wind at the coast. It is also termite resistant.

Duranta erecta 'Sheena's Gold'
Forget-me-not tree, Vergeet-my-nie-boom

Size: 2 x 2 m

Growth habit: It is a small to medium-sized evergreen shrub with bright yellow foliage in full sun. Its foliage turns lime-green in dappled shade. Loose sprays of powder-blue flowers appear sporadically during spring and summer on the tips of branches. Beautiful for contrast planting in the mixed shrub border or as a clipped specimen in formal settings.

Planting: Dig a hole 60 cm square and deep. Mix two thirds of the topsoil with one third compost in the bottom of the hole, add one cup of bone meal or superphosphate and mix well.

Watering and feeding: Water when dry and feed during spring with a general fertiliser.

Pruning: Prune to shape; excellent topiary subject.

Uses: Ideal compact plant for patios and containers. Makes a lovely clipped hedge.

Topiary This is the art of clipping and pruning trees or shrubs into familiar shapes. Choose plants with small foliage and many dormant buds, so that new growth can start anywhere a cut is made. *Duranta erecta* 'Sheena's Gold', *Syzygium*, some conifer varieties and *Buxus* are good examples to use for this purpose.

Duvernoia adhatodoides
(681) Pistol bush, Pistoolbos

Size: 2,5 x 1 m
Growth habit: It is a medium-sized to large bushy shrub with large, dark green leaves. It bears showy, fragrant, white flowers in dense, compact sprays during summer. Flowers have purple markings in the throat. Seeds burst open with an explosive crack, hence the name 'pistol bush'.
Planting: It prefers deep soil rich in organic material and damp conditions. Dig a hole 60 cm square and deep. Mix two thirds of the topsoil with one third compost in the bottom of the hole, add one cup of bone meal or superphosphate and mix well.
Watering and feeding: Water regularly and feed in spring with a general fertiliser. Keep well mulched with compost.
Pruning: Not necessary except for occasional shaping.
Uses: Very good for the background of the shrub border in semi-shaded positions.

Erica species
Heath, Heide

Size: 1 x 2 m
Growth habit: Ericas are small, woody shrubs with small, narrow leaves. Flowers come in a great variety of colours, shapes and sizes. This plant loves acid soil. Do not disturb the roots by digging.
Planting: It needs a sandy, well-drained soil with a pH of 4–5,5. Dig a hole 60 cm square and deep. Mix two thirds of the topsoil with one third acid compost or peat, add one cup of bone meal or superphosphate and mix well.
Watering and feeding: Water well in the dry winter months of the interior. Mulching with acid compost, peat moss or pine needles is important to keep the soil moist, to protect the roots and feed the plant.
Pruning: Not necessary, but flower stems can be cut to promote bushier growth.
Uses: It makes an ideal rock garden plant. Also excellent as cut flower material.
Varieties: *E. baccans*, the berry heath, is vigorous, growing up to 2 m tall during winter and spring, with urn-shaped pink blooms. *E. bauera*, the bridal heath, has grey-green foliage and grows up to 1 m tall. During summer it bears masses of tubular flowers which are white, pale yellow or pale pink on long stems.

Labour saving You can save a lot of labour by placing a piece of plastic on the lawn when planting new shrubs or trees. Place dug-out soil on the plastic to prevent soil falling on the lawn, which leaves an untidy patch and requires a lot of time to clean up.

Escallonia x hybrid 'Apple Blossom'
Escallonia

Size: 2 x 1,5 m

Growth habit: This is a medium-sized to large shrub with attractive, glossy, dark green foliage. Its pale pink clusters of flowers in summer make this a lovely addition to any shrub border. It is fast growing and has a spreading growth habit.

Planting: Prefers well-drained, fertile soil. Dig a hole 60 cm square and deep. Mix two thirds of the topsoil with one third compost in the bottom of the hole, add one cup of bone meal or superphosphate and mix well.

Watering and feeding: Water and feed regularly, throughout the active growth season until well established.

Pruning: Cut back in winter to promote bushy growth. It can also be clipped into a hedge.

Uses: An excellent screening shrub or an informal hedge. It makes an attractive background shrub or can be used alone in a bed of annuals. It tolerates drought and salt-laden wind at the coast.

Varieties: *E. bifida* 'Donard Star' is an upright-growing, compact shrub with clusters of reddish-pink flowers in summer and autumn. *E. exoniensis fradesii* 'Gold Brian' grows up to 1 m tall and is a beautiful, medium-sized shrub with golden-coloured foliage, and bears pink flowers in midsummer.

Euonymus japonicus 'Microphyllus'
Spindle tree, Speekbeenboom/Kardinaalsmus

Size: 0,3 x 0,3 m

Growth habit: *Euonymus* is slow growing with small, dark green leaves and forms a dense little shrub. Flowers are inconspicuous.

Planting: Prefers fertile, well-drained soil. Dig a hole 60 cm square and deep. Mix two thirds of the topsoil with one third compost in the bottom of the hole, add one cup of bone meal or superphosphate and mix well.

Watering and feeding: Water and feed this shrub regularly until well established.

Pruning: Not necessary, except to shape.

Uses: It makes an excellent colour contrast shrub in the mixed border or can act as a ground cover. Tolerates adverse conditions such as wind at the coast, heat, cold and poor soil.

Varieties: *E. japonicus* 'Microphyllus Variegatus' has green leaves with a white edge and is ideal for a small as well as a rock garden. 'Microphyllus Gold Dust' grows up to 60 cm tall and has lime-yellow foliage which turns to golden-yellow in full sun. It is a slow, compact grower. 'Albomarginatus' (spindle tree) is much larger, growing to about 2 x 1,5 m. It has green leaves with a thin, white margin. It is good for screening and is wind resistant. 'Aureus' is compactly shaped. It has beautiful, gold-yellow leaves with a thin, green margin.

When to repot Roots growing out of the drainage holes of pots, leaves becoming smaller and stunted growth all are signs that plants are potbound and need to be planted into a container one size larger. You can replant in the same size pot by pruning the plant and the roots back by a third.

Fuchsia x hybrids
Fuchsia, Foksia

Size: 1,5 x 1,5 m

Growth habit: There are more than a hundred species, with many thousands of hybrids. Flowers are usually pendulous, but more and more erect and very floriferous varieties are becoming available. The fuchsia flowers from early summer into winter. Its foliage varies from lush green through to bronze, with some variegated varieties also available.

Planting: Prefers a south- or east-facing position, with morning sun and afternoon shade. It needs rich, moist but well-drained soil, sheltered from wind. Dig a hole 60 cm square and deep. Mix two thirds of the topsoil with one third compost, add one cup of bone meal or superphosphate and mix well.

Watering and feeding: Water regularly; keep mulched. This heavy feeder needs to be fed regularly during summer with a high nitrogen and potash fertiliser in order to flower well.

Pruning: Prune in early spring by cutting back two thirds of the plant.

Uses: Fuchsias make excellent tub subjects for a cool, light patio and cascading hybrids are excellent in hanging baskets.

Varieties: 'Lady Beth' has a weeping growth habit with double flowers, which have pale rose sepals with a violet-blue corolla. 'R.A.F.' has a bushy growth habit with double flowers with red sepals and a pale pink corolla.

Gardenia augusta
Gardenia, Katjiepiering

Size: 2 x 1,5 m

Growth habit: It is a medium-sized shrub with glossy, dark green foliage and fragrant, double white flowers during summer. It is rather slow growing.

Planting: This plant prefers well-drained, acid soil. Dig a hole 60 cm square and deep. Mix two thirds of the topsoil with one third acid compost or peat, add one cup of bone meal or superphosphate and mix well.

Watering and feeding: Water this plant regularly and keep it well mulched. The gardenia flourishes in acid soil and needs to be fertilised with blue hydrangea food, for instance, to keep the soil acid.

Pruning: It can be trained into a standard form. Cut back stray shoots.

Uses: Excellent near a window or as a tub subject on the patio where the lovely perfume can be appreciated.

Varieties: 'Golden Magic' (yellow gardenia) is similar to the above with lovely dark green, glossy foliage and pale yellow, fragrant flowers that appear in summer. 'Radicans' is low growing, up to 30 cm. This small shrub has a spreading habit. Bears small, fragrant, white flowers throughout the year. Ideal ground cover for warm areas. Also very good in containers and hanging baskets.

Red spider mite Fuchsias and azaleas are very susceptible to red spider mite and white fly during hot, dry weather and when plants are under stress from lack of moisture. Keep plants well watered during hot, dry spells and spray with appropriate insecticide to avoid attack from these pests.

Hibiscus rosa-sinensis
Hawaiian hibiscus, Chinese stokroos

Size: 2 x 2 m

Growth habit: A medium-sized to large evergreen shrub with dark green, shiny foliage. Flowers can be single, semi-double or fully double with colours from white through pinks, yellows and reds. It flourishes in warm areas, is adaptable and can be grown in most regions, except where there is severe frost in winter. Protect plants in areas where light frosts occur.

Planting: Dig a hole 60 cm square and deep. Mix two thirds of the topsoil with one third compost in the bottom of the hole, add one cup of bone meal or superphosphate and mix well.

Watering and feeding: Water regularly during dry weather. Feed with fertiliser for flowering plants in spring, midsummer and autumn.

Pruning: Prune lightly in spring, once danger of frost is over, for better flowering and to maintain bushy growth. The standard form should be cut back in the middle of summer as well, to maintain its standard shape.

Uses: It is ideal for large pots or tubs. It makes a lovely informal hedge or screening plant.

Varieties: 'Canary Island' (apple blossom), prolific and one of the most popular, has pale pink single flowers with a cerise-pink eye. 'Ross Estey' has large flowers that open orange, turning to salmon-pink.

Hydrangea macrophylla x hybrids
Hydrangea, Krismisroos

Size: 1 x 1,5 m

Growth habit: Among the showiest flowers in the summer garden. The first hydrangea flowers appear in early summer, carrying on well into autumn. Many of the old cultivars lose their colour, eventually turning green. Modern hybrids retain their colour far longer.

Planting: For blue hydrangeas, which need a soil pH of as low as 4,5, add a lot of peat moss when planting to make it more acid. For pink hydrangeas, the soil does not need to be as acid (pH 6,0) so plant with compost or peat moss.

Watering and feeding: Water deeply, particularly during hot, dry spells. Use Hydrangea food at regular intervals throughout the growing season. Keep plants mulched.

Pruning: Prune at the end of winter. Cut back the previous year's growth to three pairs of buds, to promote sturdy new stems with large blooms.

Uses: Lovely grown in tubs on a shady patio. Flowers are ideal for the vase. Cut the flowering stem in the hard wood, otherwise the flower will not last when picked.

Varieties: 'Bodensee' has sky-blue flowers, depending on the soil pH. 'Daphne' has pink flowers and retains its colour. 'M. E. Moulliere' has white flowers, aging to a pinkish hue.

Pruning hibiscus Prune hibiscus twice a year to encourage flowering, as flowers are only borne on new shoots. Cut back all branches by a third during winter and in mid-summer, and pinch out new growing tips to ensure lots of flowers.

Hydrangea quercifolia
Oak-leaf hydrangea, Eikeblaar-krismisroos

Size: 2 x 2 m

Growth habit: This plant has leathery, deeply lobed, dark green leaves that turn red in autumn. The white flower heads appear from midsummer until autumn. The flowers open as white but then fade to pink and violet.

Planting: It prefers well-drained soil in a dappled shade position. Dig a hole 60 cm square and deep. Mix two thirds of the topsoil with one third acid compost or peat in the bottom of the hole, add one cup of bone meal or superphosphate and mix well.

Watering and feeding: Water and feed regularly during the active growth season. Keep the plant mulched.

Pruning: Cut back lightly during winter in order to promote new growth.

Uses: This is a very good provider of colour in the mixed border for cold gardens.

Hypoestes aristata
Ribbon bush, Seeroogblommetjie

Size: 1,5 x 1 m

Growth habit: This small to medium-sized shrub with downy, dark green leaves gets covered in masses of purple-pink flowers from autumn to the end of winter. It grows very easily and multiplies rapidly by seeding itself.

Planting: Dig a hole 60 cm square and deep. Mix two thirds of the topsoil with one third compost in the bottom of the hole, add one cup of bone meal or superphosphate and mix well.

Watering and feeding: Water during dry weather. Does not need a lot of attention. Feed with a general fertiliser for flowering plants during spring and midsummer, then water in well.

Pruning: Keep trimmed or it becomes untidy.

Uses: Very good shrub for colour during winter, in dry semi-shaded positions. The flowers attract insects which in turn are preyed on by birds. It is traditionally used as a vegetable in some areas.

Varieties: *Hypoestes* 'Purple Haze' is a compact, smaller shrub with light to dark purple flowers.

Blue hydrangeas The colour of most hydrangeas depends on the soil acidity – the more acid the soil, the more intense the blue colour; the more alkaline, the pinker the colour. Add one of the following to increase the blue colour: iron chelate, flowers of sulphur or diluted aluminium sulphate. Mulch with peat moss.

55

Ixora coccinea
Flame-of-the-woods, Vlam-van-die-woud

Size: 1,5 x 1,5 m

Growth habit: This small to medium-sized tropical shrub has shiny, dark green leaves and showy, vivid crimson, tubular-shaped flowers borne in flat heads.

Planting: It prefers well-drained, acid soil in a semi-shaded position. Dig a hole 60 cm square and deep. Mix two thirds of the topsoil with one third acid compost or peat moss in the bottom of the hole, add one cup of bone meal or superphosphate and mix well.

Watering and feeding: Water regularly and keep well mulched to conserve moisture and feed during spring with a general fertiliser for flowering plants.

Pruning: It can be pruned to shape, and flowers will appear on new shoots.

Uses: Lovely colourful shrub for any tropical garden.

Other species: *I. javanica* from Java is a large 3-m shrub with shiny green leaves and wide, flat clusters of coral flowers. *I. macrothyrsa* 'Super King' is a tropical hybrid with 3-m tall erect branches and large, glossy green leaves. Bright crimson clusters of flowers are borne in flat heads. *I. chinensis* is a medium-sized, tropical shrub with clusters of flowers borne in flat heads. Varieties in shades of pink, apricot, salmon, red and yellow are available.

Laurus nobilis
Bay laurel, Lourier

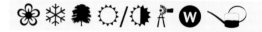

Size: 5 x 3 m

Growth habit: The bay laurel is a large shrub or small tree and is grown for its aromatic foliage and its lovely pyramidal shape. It has dark green, leathery leaves that form a dense shrub. The flowers are small and insignificant, and followed by black, rounded seeds. It is rather slow growing but worth the effort. New foliage might burn in areas with severe frost but it never causes lasting damage. It thrives in Western Cape coastal regions.

Planting: Dig a hole 60 cm square and deep. Mix two thirds of the topsoil with one third compost in the bottom of the hole, add one cup of bone meal or superphosphate and mix well.

Watering and feeding: Water and feed regularly until well established, whereafter it does not need a lot of attention.

Pruning: Can be pruned into a standard or a formal hedge.

Uses: The foliage is highly ornamental and useful in cooking. Excellent screening and hedge shrub. Makes a very good windbreak and tolerates dry spells.

Spray equipment Never leave leftover spraying chemicals in the spray container as they can be corrosive and also may not be effective after a time. Always rinse spray equipment thoroughly after every use as leftover poison or chemicals could damage plants and be dangerous for pets and humans if used incorrectly by uninformed persons.

Lavandula stoechas
French lavender, Laventel

Size: 0,6 x 0,4 m

Growth habit: All lavenders are aromatic shrubs. There are about 25 species, all with fragrant, greyish foliage. This particular one has grey-green, aromatic leaves with purple flowers in summer. Flowers of this species are the most striking of all the lavenders. Lavender will grow well in most areas except the humid subtropical areas.

Planting: It prefers fertile, well-drained soil. Dig a hole 60 cm square and deep. Mix two thirds of the topsoil with one third compost in the bottom of the hole, add one cup of bone meal or superphosphate and mix well.

Watering and feeding: Water when dry, especially during winter in the summer rainfall regions. It needs little attention once established. Feed during spring with a general fertiliser.

Pruning: Remove spent flower-spikes regularly. Prune back lightly during late winter to promote bushy growth.

Uses: Lavender oil is commercially obtained from this species. Ideal for a low hedge, in the herb garden and mixed border.

Varieties: *L. stoechas* 'Helmsdale' has grey-green foliage with dark purple flowers in spring and summer. *L. stoechas* subsp. *lusitanica* 'Marshwood' also has grey-green foliage but with purple-pink flowers. 'Papillon' bears pink-purple flowers in spring and autumn and is low growing.

Leonotis leonurus var. leonurus
Wild dagga/Lion's ear, Wildedagga

Size: 2 x 1 m

Growth habit: This lovely shrub is mostly evergreen but can lose its leaves in very cold areas. The plant quickly sprouts again after frost burn. It grows upright with tall stems covered in sparse, dull-green leaves. Flowers appear in whorls on the tips of the stems and are bright orange and tube-like. They appear during autumn and winter. Although fairly drought resistant, it thrives in good, moist soil.

Planting: Any well-drained soil is suitable. Dig a hole 60 cm square and deep. Mix two thirds of the topsoil with one third compost in the bottom of the hole, add one cup of bone meal or superphosphate and mix well.

Watering and feeding: It does not need a lot of attention. Water only during very dry weather, but be careful not to overwater. Feed with a general fertiliser for flowering plants during spring and midsummer, then water in well.

Pruning: Must be pruned to keep neat.

Uses: Very good accent plant in the back border. It is popular with flower arrangers, and attracts birds.

Varieties: *L. leonurus* var. *albiflora* similar to above, but with creamy-white instead of orange flowers.

Aromatic plants Grow plants with strongly aromatic foliage scent, for example buchu, lavender, herbs and geraniums, close to pathways where they can be brushed against to release their fragrance.

Leucospermum species
Pincushion protea, Speldekussingprotea

Size: 3 x 2 m
Growth habit: This protea is an evergreen, winter-flowering shrub and one of the most lovely indigenous plants. The pincushion flowers for 6 to 8 months. It is native to the southwestern Cape and is quite adaptable and will grow in most areas of the country. Plant in a sheltered spot in areas with severe frost. The shrub varies from upright growing to low spreading.
Planting: It needs well-drained, acid soil in a sunny position with good ventilation, and a good mulch of acid compost or wattle leaves. When planting, remember to prepare a hole just big enough to take the root ball; do not use manure and do not disturb the roots.
Watering and feeding: Water well during dry winter months in the summer-rainfall regions. Do not fertilise.
Pruning: Not necessary, except to remove spent flowers.
Uses: Wonderful cut flower and colourful in the shrub border. Attracts birds.
Varieties: Many pincushion species and varieties are available from nurseries. 'Ballerina', a spreading shrub, grows to about 1,5 m tall with pink flowers, July to October. 'Highgold' is a strong, upright-growing shrub with large, yellow flowers. 'Tango' is a rounded shrub also, 1,5 m tall, with peach flowers in early summer.

Mackaya bella
(681.1) River bells, Blouklokkiesbos

Size: 2 x 1 m
Growth habit: It is a multi-stemmed, medium-sized to large shrub with shiny, dark green foliage. Flowers appear on terminal sprays in late spring and are white, tinged pale pink with purple lines. Lavender-shaded flowers are also available. Does very well in humid subtropical regions.
Planting: Needs to be planted in semi-shade and preferably near water. Dig a hole 60 cm square and deep. Mix two thirds of the topsoil with one third compost in the bottom of the hole, add one cup of bone meal or superphosphate and mix well.
Watering and feeding: Water and feed regularly. Keep the plant well mulched with compost.
Pruning: Prune after flowering in early summer to promote bushy growth and to control the size. Can be pruned and trained into a standard shape.
Uses: Excellent shrub for warm and temperate gardens in semi-shade under big trees. Flowers last well in the vase.

Pesticides and fungicides If at all possible try to use alternative pesticides or fungicides for the same problem to prevent the insects or fungus from building up resistance to the chemical. For the same reason it is also not a good idea to use spray cocktails too often.

Mandevilla sanderi 'Rosea'
Brazilian jasmine, Brasiliaanse jasmyn

Size: 0,5 x 0,3 m

Growth habit: This is a lovely small, evergreen shrub with glossy, dark green, leathery foliage. It bears cerise-pink, trumpet-shaped flowers fading to lighter pink with a yellow throat, throughout the year. It has a twining growth habit.

Planting: It prefers fertile, well-drained soil. Dig a hole 60 cm square and deep. Mix two thirds of the topsoil with one third compost in the bottom of the hole, add one cup of bone meal or superphosphate and mix well. Use good quality potting soil when planting in containers for the patio.

Watering and feeding: Water regularly during hot weather and feed twice during the active growth season with a general fertiliser for flowering plants.

Pruning: Not necessary.

Uses: Ideal container and patio plant.

Varieties: *Mandevilla* x hybrid 'My Fair Lady' has pink buds opening into white flowers with a tinge of pink.

Melaleuca bracteata 'Johannesburg Gold'
Golden melaleuca

Size: 6 x 4 m

Growth habit: This popular, large-growing shrub can also become a small tree. It is widely used for its magnificent golden to yellow foliage. It is upright growing with a narrow crown and has a single stem with fissured brown bark. Flowers are insignificant. It is fast growing.

Planting: Prefers well-drained, fertile soil. Dig a hole 60 cm square and deep. Mix two thirds of the topsoil with one third compost in the bottom of the hole, add one cup of bone meal or superphosphate and mix well.

Watering and feeding: Water during dry weather in winter. Feed with a general fertiliser during spring and midsummer, then water in well.

Pruning: Not necessary, but can be cut and trained into a standard shape.

Uses: Excellent for contrast planting, it has fern-like foliage and may be cut for flower arranging. Established plants will tolerate drought and wind near the coast.

Varieties: *M. bracteata* 'Golden Gem' (1 x 1 m) is a low-growing shrub with fine, lemon-yellow leaves. It is a great rock garden plant and does not need pruning.

Automatic watering system Installing an automatic irrigation system can save a lot of water and effort. Many do-it-yourself kits are available from garden centres at very reasonable prices. You can also install a stopping device at the same time; this will keep the sprayers from spraying while it is raining.

Murraya exotica
Orange jasmine, Lemoenjasmyn

Size: 3 x 2 m

Growth habit: This attractive, medium-sized shrub with its glossy, dark green leaves has a shrubby, compact growth habit. Large heads of sweetly scented, small, white, jasmine-like flowers are borne during summer, followed by round, red fruits. It is relatively slow growing.

Planting: It prefers well-drained soil rich in organic material. Dig a hole 60 cm square and deep. Mix two thirds of the topsoil with one third compost in the bottom of the hole, add one cup of bone meal or superphosphate and mix well.

Watering and feeding: Water regularly and feed during spring with a general fertiliser for foliage plants. Keep plants well mulched.

Pruning: Prune this shrub during winter to promote bushy growth and flowers.

Uses: Very good dark green shrub in semi-shade or near the house for its perfumed flowers, or for screening in an informal hedge. Foliage is excellent for flower arranging.

Myrtus communis
Common myrtle, Gewone mirte

Size: 2 x 1,5 m

Growth habit: Myrtle is a bushy, medium-sized, evergreen shrub with shiny, dark green, pointed leaves. During summer, it produces star-shaped, pure white flowers with massed, brush-like stamens, followed by blue-black berries. It has aromatic foliage. Slow growing and drought tolerant.

Planting: Prefers fertile soil. Dig a hole 60 cm square and deep. Mix two thirds of the topsoil with one third compost in the bottom of the hole, add one cup of bone meal or superphosphate and mix well. Large plants transplant well during late winter if cut back by half.

Watering and feeding: Water during winter in summer rainfall regions and mulch both to conserve water and feed.

Pruning: Useful for clipping as a topiary subject. Trim during winter to keep plants compact and bushy.

Uses: Ideal for cold gardens in the shrub border or as an informal hedge. Excellent container subject. In Sardinia berries are used to produce a lovely digestive liqueur called 'Mirto'.

Varieties: 'Variegata' is a particularly attractive, variegated form of the common myrtle, with creamy-white foliage and violet fruits. It is slightly smaller than the green form. 'Compacta', a dwarf green variety, is also available and excellent for tub culture.

Wooden stepping stones Before using wooden sleepers and rounds as stepping stones in shady areas, treat the wood with diesel oil to prevent the wood from being destroyed by termites.

Nandina domestica
Sacred bamboo, Heilige bamboes

Size: 3 x 1 m

Growth habit: This is an upright-growing plant with cane-like stems and fern-like delicate foliage. In summer, it bears large sprays of creamy-white flowers in terminal panicles, followed by numerous bright red fruits. It has beautiful red autumn colouring and will grow in almost any position.

Planting: Prefers fertile soil. Dig a hole 60 cm square and deep. Mix two thirds of the topsoil with one third compost in the bottom of the hole, add one cup of bone meal or super-phosphate and mix well. Transplants easily during winter.

Watering and feeding: Water regularly for lush appearance and feed during spring with a general fertiliser for foliage plants. Keep well mulched but can tolerate drought.

Pruning: Prune untidy stems back to promote new growth.

Uses: Suitable for patios and containers. Popular with flower arrangers. Excellent in the background border and near the swimming pool.

Varieties: *N. domestica* 'Pygmaea' is a dwarf variety, grow-ing up to 50 cm tall. It is a rounded shrub with scarlet and red autumn shades in winter. Very attractive single or massed in the mixed shrub border or in containers.

Pentas lanceolata
Pentas

Size: 0,8 x 0,8 m

Growth habit: A fast-growing, small to medium-sized, herba-ceous shrub with light green foliage. Pentas flowers for a long period throughout the warmer months. Each branch tip bears a bunch of small flowers. Pentas comes in a variety of colours, including pink, red, mauve and white. It cannot with-stand severe frost but will tolerate a fair amount of drought once established.

Planting: Prefers rich, fertile soil. Dig a hole 60 cm square and deep. Mix one third of the topsoil with one third compost and one third kraal manure in the bottom of the hole, add a cup of bone phosphate and mix well.

Watering and feeding: Water regularly throughout the active growth season and feed during spring with a general fertilis-er for flowering plants. Keep the plant mulched with compost.

Pruning: Cut back in winter to promote new bushy growth. The regular removal of spent flowers will encourage more flowers.

Uses: Cut flowers last well in the vase. The shrub looks good in the mixed border in front of a dark green shrub or as a backdrop for annuals and perennials.

Varieties: *P. lanceolata* 'Candy Stripe' bears masses of pink, star-shaped flowers with a white centre. 'New Look Pink' has hairy green foliage with small, star-shaped flowers in summer.

Gutter runoff Place round pebbles in areas where gutter runoff causes the soil to be washed away in flowerbeds. Pebbles are available in a variety of colours and sizes and can look very attractive. Use a sturdy chain to conduct water from the gutter down into a bed of pebbles. This feature can be incorporated into the overall design.

61

Philodendron 'Xanadu'
Philodendron, Filodendron

Size: 1 x 1,5 m

Growth habit: A small to medium-sized, dense and compact-growing shrub. Striking, dark green foliage is serrated and red-veined when mature. It reaches 75 cm when fully grown. It needs afternoon shade in hot and dry interior regions.

Planting: Dig a hole 60 cm square and deep. Mix one third of the topsoil with one third compost and one third kraal manure in the bottom of the hole, add one cup of bone meal or superphosphate and mix well.

Watering and feeding: Water when dry and fertilise during spring with a general fertiliser for the lawn. Keep the plant well mulched.

Pruning: Not necessary.

Uses: Excellent for small and large gardens, containers on the patio, in beds and as a bold indoor plant. A wonderful all-rounder, it can be used as a solitary specimen, in a spacious container, in large lobbies or patios, and in the garden, either in sun or shade. It tolerates up to -3 °C of frost.

Varieties: *P. selloum* is bold and has lush foliage, so it is ideal where tropical effects are sought. Not unlike the delicious monster in looks, it has glossy, deeply divided, dark green leaves, segments of which are narrow and toothed. The broad, elegant leaves are on long, slender stems.

Phoenix roebelenii
Miniature date palm, Miniatuur-dadelpalm

Size: 1,5 x 1 m

Growth habit: One of the most popular small palms, it rarely tops 1,5 m. It has dark green, arching fronds, giving an elegant effect. The single stem is slender and rough. In summer, yellow flower bunches appear on the mature plants, and these are followed by elongated, black fruits. It has a more compact growth habit in full sun than in shade. Does very well in warm climates.

Planting: It prefers well-drained soil. Dig a hole 60 cm square and deep. Mix two thirds of the topsoil with one third compost, add a cup of bone meal or superphosphate and mix well.

Watering and feeding: Water regularly during dry weather and feed once a month during the active growing season with a general fertiliser for foliage plants. Do not overwater when grown indoors, as this will cause browning of leaftips.

Pruning: Not necessary except for the removal of untidy fronds and spent flower bunches.

Uses: This strikingly stunning palm is ideal for hot decks, patios and entrances, but also does well indoors, provided it has good light and sun for at least a few hours a day. An ideal container subject.

Cutting back frostbitten plants
Always wait until danger of late frost has passed before cutting back frostbitten plants, as dead plant material can help prevent further damage. New shoots growing out after pruning will be damaged again by late frost.

Phormium cookianum 'Yellow Wave'
Green mountain flax, Vlas

Size: 1,75 x 1,5 m

Growth habit: This is an invaluable foliage plant with gracefully arching blades of yellow, grass-like leaves with a green edge, 2 m in length and about 5 cm broad. Both hardy and evergreen, it adapts to practically any position, and makes an ideal focus plant in semi-shade areas.

Planting: It needs well-drained soil. Dig a hole 60 cm square and deep. Mix two thirds of the topsoil with one third compost in the bottom of the hole, add one cup of bone meal or superphosphate and mix well.

Watering and feeding: Water it regularly and feed during spring with a general fertiliser for foliage plants.

Pruning: Not necessary, though it is good to remove untidy-looking leaves regularly.

Uses: Excellent for foliage contrast planting in the shrub border. Foliage is popular with flower arrangers.

Varieties: 'Flamingo' grows only about 75 cm tall. It is a tuft-forming plant with pastel pink, yellow-orange and green leaves. Ideal patio plant for semi-shade or shade areas.

Photinia x fraseri 'Red Robin'
Chinese hawthorn, Chinese haagdoring

Size: 3,5 x 1,5 m

Growth habit: Foliage is the main feature of this photinia, with its glistening, coppery-red leaves on bright red stems. Delightful spring blossoms, with pink buds opening to dazzling white, are a bonus. It is a must for any garden, being drought resistant yet able to stand soggy growing conditions. It is a slow-growing plant.

Planting: Dig a hole 60 cm square and deep. Mix two thirds of the topsoil with one third compost in the bottom of the hole, add one cup of bone meal or superphosphate and mix well.

Watering and feeding: Water regularly and feed during spring with a general fertiliser for foliage plants. Keep plants well mulched.

Pruning: Prune during winter to promote bushy growth and new foliage.

Uses: Ideal for cold gardens in the background border or for an informal hedge.

Varieties: *P. glabra* 'Rubens' grows up to 2 m tall and is covered with coppery-red foliage for many months of the year.

Transplanting trees or shrubs To transplant a tree or shrub successfully, wait until the late winter to do this, just before the active growing season starts. Always mark the plant to be able to plant it facing in the same direction as its previous growing position; this will help prevent transplant shock and unnecessary stress.

Plectranthus fruticosus
Forest spur-flower/Fly bush, Spoorsalie

Size: 2 x 1,5 m

Growth habit: This upright and fast-growing herbaceous shrub has purplish stems covered in sparse hairs. It bears branched sprays of pink or mauve flowers in autumn. Leaves have a toothed margin and a pink reverse.

Planting: For the best results, plant this shrub in humus-rich soil and water well.

Watering and feeding: Water regularly. Feed with a general fertiliser for flowering plants during spring and midsummer, then water in well.

Pruning: Not necessary.

Uses: Excellent for deep shade in the garden. Fast growing and very good for mass plantings, especially at the coast. Stems and leaves make an effective fly-repellent when rubbed on window sills. Flowers are attractive to butterflies.

Varieties: 'Behr se Trots' has purple flowers. 'Ellaphie' bears pale pink flowers. 'James' bears pinky-mauve flowers. 'Ngoye' has pink to mauve flowers.

Plumbago auriculata 'Royal Cape'
Cape forget-me-not, Blousyselbos

Size: 3 x 3 m

Growth habit: It is a medium-sized to large scrambling shrub and grows quickly by means of suckers. Foliage is deep green with a paler reverse. Clusters of phlox-like, deep blue flowers appear on branch tips throughout the warmer months, followed by sticky hairy seeds. Drought tolerant.

Planting: Plumbago is not fussy and will grow in almost any garden soil. It will, however, benefit from additional organic material. Dig a hole 60 cm square and deep. Mix two thirds of the topsoil with one third compost in the bottom of the hole, add one cup of bone meal or superphosphate and mix well.

Watering and feeding: Water when dry and feed during spring with a general fertiliser for flowering plants.

Pruning: Prune back short to control the size and to promote new shoots.

Uses: Excellent as a hedge or background plant. Will clamber into a tree if grown near one. Flowers attract butterflies. Used by traditional healers for medicinal purposes.

Varieties: *P. auriculata* 'Alba', a less common white form, is also available.

Snail and slug traps Place some bran under fresh cabbage leaves after watering the garden. Snails will congregate under the leaves, where you can collect them the next morning. Otherwise leave a shallow dish of beer overnight among plants that are eaten by snails. They will come to drink the beer, fall into the dish and drown.

Polygala myrtifolia
(302.1) Wild violet, Bloukappie

Size: 2 x 1 m

Growth habit: Polygala is a medium-sized, rounded shrub with pale green foliage and it grows quickly. The main flowering time is spring, but the bright purple-red flowers can be found on the bushes for most months of the year.

Planting: It is not very fussy but will benefit from fertile soil. Dig a hole 60 cm square and deep. Mix two thirds of the topsoil with one third compost in the bottom of the hole, add one cup of bone phosphate and mix well.

Watering and feeding: Water when dry and feed during spring with a general fertiliser for flowering plants.

Pruning: Not necessary but can be pruned hard to promote bushy growth close to the ground. It can also be pruned and clipped into a standard shape.

Uses: Excellent at the coast as it tolerates salt-laden wind and of short periods of drought. Also good in areas with moderate frost, for the shrub border. Flowers attract butterflies.

Other species: *P. fruticosa* 'Sugar Baby' is a smaller plant, only 50 cm tall with darker purple-blue flowers in summer.

Prunus laurocerasus
English laurel, Engelse lourier

Size: 4 x 3 m

Growth habit: It is one of the finest background and specimen foliage plants available. This large shrub forms a dense, rounded crown and its leaves are magnolia-like, thick, shiny and bright green. Bunches of small, white flowers appear in spring and are followed by purple-black berries which ripen in autumn. It has a slow growth rate while young but grows much faster with age.

Planting: Dig a hole 60 cm square and deep. Mix two thirds of the topsoil with one third compost in the bottom of the hole, add one cup of bone meal or superphosphate and mix well.

Watering and feeding: Water regularly during dry weather and feed during spring to speed up the growth rate.

Pruning: This shrub can be pruned back hard in winter to control the size.

Uses: It makes an excellent tub subject. One of the best large shrubs for screening or in the background shrub border in cold gardens.

Low-maintenance gardening For those people with a busy lifestyle, consider a formal design with paving and a few large containers with permanent trees and shrubs as this does not require a lot of time and energy to maintain.

Rhaphiolepis x delacourii 'Kruschenia'
Kruschens pink, Indiese meidoring

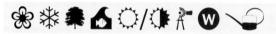

Size: 2 x 2 m

Growth habit: This beautiful, rounded shrub has dense, shiny, dark green, leathery foliage. New foliage in spring has a lovely red colour. The shrub becomes covered with clusters of rose-pink flowers in August and continues flowering for two months. Flowers are followed by blue-black berries. It is slow growing.

Planting: It prefers fertile soil. Dig a hole 60 cm square and deep. Mix two thirds of the topsoil with one third compost in the bottom of the hole, add one cup of bone meal or super-phosphate and mix well.

Watering and feeding: Needs little attention. Water during dry weather and keep the plant well mulched to obtain a faster growth rate. Feed during spring with general fertiliser.

Pruning: Not necessary, but the plant can be cut back in winter to shape.

Uses: One of the best shrubs for coastal gardens in the Cape. It makes a lovely informal hedge or screen. Branches with flowers are also good material for the vase. Drought tolerant, it can also withstand wind and heat.

Varieties: 'Alba' grows up to 80 cm tall and bears white, star-shaped flowers in spring. 'Enchantress' is also a smaller shrub with clusters of rose-pink flowers from late winter till early summer.

Rhus crenata
(380.1) Dune crowberry, Duinekraaibessie

Size: 4 x 3 m

Growth habit: It is a large, much-branched shrub with a rounded crown and has compound, trifoliate, glossy, dark green leaves. It bears small sprays of cream flowers in autumn that are followed by clusters of dark red-purple berries. Wind resistant.

Planting: It prefers well-drained soil. Dig a hole 60 cm square and deep. Mix two thirds of the topsoil with one third compost in the bottom of the hole, add one cup of bone meal or super-phosphate and mix well.

Watering and feeding: Water when dry and feed during spring with a general fertiliser.

Pruning: Not necessary.

Uses: A very useful shrub for a hedge, windbreak or accent plant in a coastal garden, or as a specimen plant. Very good for dune stabilisation. Berries attract birds.

Shaping while pruning To give a shrub an upright growth when pruning, cut back to an inward-facing bud, and to make a shrub spread out, cut back to an outward-facing bud.

Salvia africana-lutea
Beach salvia/Golden salvia, Bruinsalie/Strandsalie

Size: 2 x 2 m

Growth habit: This is a medium-sized shrub with aromatic, grey-green foliage. Its striking brown flowers are a feature of this very pretty shrub and appear during spring and summer. It is reasonably fast growing.

Planting: It has no particular soil requirements but must have good drainage. Dig a hole 60 cm square and deep. Mix two thirds of the topsoil with one third compost in the bottom of the hole, add one cup of bone meal or superphosphate and mix well.

Watering and feeding: Water during dry weather, but it does not need a lot of attention. Feed with a general fertiliser for flowering plants in spring and midsummer, then water in well.

Pruning: Prune back in winter to neaten the bush and to keep a compact shape.

Uses: A lovely shrub for coastal gardens and the rock garden, or in a mixed shrub border for colour contrast. Flowers attract honeybirds and butterflies. Fairly drought resistant.

Other species: *S. chamelaeagna* 'Bloublommetjiesalie' is a smallish, hardy shrub with clusters of blue flowers in summer.

Spiraea cantoniensis 'Flora Plena'
Cape may, Wit meidoring

Size: 2 x 2 m

Growth habit: This medium-sized shrub is one of the joys of spring when it gets covered with masses of fine, double white flowers borne along arching branches. Leaves are bright green and mature to a darker green with a paler reverse. Thrives in temperate climates, but will not do well in subtropical areas.

Planting: It prefers moist, well-drained soil. Dig a hole 60 cm square and deep. Mix two thirds of the topsoil with one third compost, add one cup of bone meal or superphosphate and mix well.

Watering and feeding: Water during dry weather, but it does not need a lot of attention otherwise. Keep the plant well mulched. Feed during spring with a general fertiliser.

Pruning: Can be clipped into a formal hedge. Cut back in spring after flowering.

Uses: This shrub is an ideal hedge plant. It is also lovely in the mixed shrub border.

Varieties: *S. cantoniensis* 'Ice' grows up to 1 m tall with mottled green-white foliage with white flowers in spring.

Dead flowers Use cut off dead flowers, fallen leaves and grass clippings to spread out under shrubs in beds to form a mulch. This will decompose and return valuable nutrients to the soil.

Strelitzia reginae
Bird of paradise/Crane flower, Kraanvoëlblom

Size: 1,5 x 1,5 m

Growth habit: This plant is indigenous to the Eastern Cape and southern KwaZulu-Natal coastal areas, where it grows in rocky grassland areas. It is a dark greyish-green, large-leafed shrub. Slow growing. Orange flowers are borne in winter. It is the floral emblem of KwaZulu-Natal.

Planting: It needs well-drained, fertile soil. Dig a hole 60 cm square and deep. Mix two thirds of the topsoil with one third compost in the bottom of the hole, add one cup of bone meal or superphosphate and mix well. Can be transplanted, which will result in several years of no flowering. Care should be taken not to damage the fleshy roots and not to give transplants too much water.

Watering and feeding: Water when dry and keep the plant well mulched. Feed during spring with a general fertiliser for flowering plants.

Pruning: Not necessary, except for the removal of spent flowers and untidy leaves.

Uses: The strelitzia is a very popular cut flower worldwide. Excellent in the mixed shrub border or rock garden. The thick nectar is enjoyed by honeybirds.

Varieties: *S. reginae* 'Mandela's Gold' is a lovely yellow-flowering form.

Streptosolen jamesonii
Marmalade bush, Marmeladebos

Size: 2 x 2 m

Growth habit: This medium-sized to large fast-growing shrub is popular because of its unusual orange colour. It produces rich orange and yellow flowers for many months from spring into summer. Grows in long, arching stems with flowerheads on the drooping ends. Brightly coloured flowers are long-tubed and funnel-shaped, covered in fine hairs.

Planting: It prefers a north-facing aspect in colder regions, protected from frost. Dig a hole 60 cm square and deep. Mix two thirds of the topsoil with one third compost in the bottom of the hole, add one cup of bone meal or superphosphate and mix well.

Watering and feeding: Water and feed regularly during spring and summer, otherwise it does not need a lot of attention.

Pruning: Cut back after flowering to promote bushy growth and prolific flowering.

Uses: Provides a lovely bright colour in the shrub border. Excellent on slopes and terraces as well.

Varieties: *S. jamesonii* 'Lutea' (yellow marmalade bush) is similar, but with yellow flowers instead of orange.

Lime sulphur When spraying lime sulphur after pruning, spray not only the plant but also the surrounding soil and clippings to kill all the fungus spores. Use fresh lime sulphur as it does not keep well from year to year. Do not place clippings on the compost heap; rather burn them to make sure of ridding the garden of unwanted pathogens.

Tecomaria capensis
(673.1) Cape honeysuckle, Kaapse kanferfoelie

Size: 3 x 3 m
Growth habit: This fast-growing, semi-creeper or scrambling shrub with dark green, shiny foliage bears bunches of orange honeysuckle flowers on the branch tips throughout the year. Plants with red, and all the shades of orange and yellow flowers, are also available. Frost usually does not damage the plant permanently.
Planting: It is not particular and will grow in almost any soil. Dig a hole 60 cm square and deep. Mix two thirds of the topsoil with one third compost in the bottom of the hole, add one cup of bone meal or superphosphate and mix well.
Watering and feeding: Water during dry weather for best results and feed during spring with a general fertiliser for flowering plants.
Pruning: Prune vigorous growth regularly. Cut back after flowering to control its size and to encourage bushy growth.
Uses: An ideal hedging plant to attract nectar-feeding birds and butterflies to the garden. Traditional healers use it medicinally to treat pain, sleeplessness and dysentry, to name but a few complaints.
Varieties: *T. capensis* 'Apricot' has pale orange-yellow flowers in summer; 'Coccinea' has dark orange, almost red flowers. 'Lutea' has yellow flowers in summer and is smaller.

Viburnum tinus 'Lucidum'
Laurustinus, Wildelourusboom

Size: 4 x 2 m
Growth habit: This is a vigorous, large shrub with fairly big, glossy, dark green leaves. It bears big clusters of flat, white flower heads in spring, followed by blue-black berries. Fairly fast growing. Will tolerate some shade.
Planting: It will grow in any well-drained soil. Dig a hole 60 cm square and deep. Mix two thirds of the topsoil with one third compost in the bottom of the hole, add one cup of bone meal or superphosphate and mix well.
Watering and feeding: Water and feed regularly until the shrub is well established. Once it is mature, the plant will only need to be watered from late winter until early summer. Keep it well mulched.
Pruning: Not necessary except to shape and control its size.
Uses: Excellent screening shrub and attractive in the background shrub border.
Varieties: *V. tinus* 'Variegatum' is similar to above but grows only 2 m tall. Foliage has conspicuous creamy-yellow variegations. Fine plant for large tubs in semi-shade.

Autumn leaves To keep the colour of autumn leaves in a vase, pick them when they are mature but not at the dropping stage. Crush the stems and place in a mixture of one part glycerine to two parts of warm water.

Climbers are ideal space-saving plants, as they grow in almost any position. They also provide a perfect foliage backdrop against a vertical wall for garden features like statues or furniture. They can be used to cover a pergola or an arch, to provide a screen, for cut flowers or container plants and they can even be used as ground covers. There is a climber for practically any position in the garden.

To get the best out of your climbers, you should prune, feed and water them regularly. Choose the correct climber for each position carefully. Do not let them grow unchecked as they can smother shrubs and trees if they are not cut back regularly. Self-clinging climbers are ideal for covering unattractive walls but must also be cut back regularly to prevent them from clogging gutters or lifting roof tiles.

A good way to cultivate twining climbers that are not self-clinging is to grow them on a hinged trellis. Mount the hinged trellis on to wooden blocks about 5 cm thick at the base of the wall, and fasten it to a wooden block at the top. In this way the trellis can be folded back when the wall behind the climber needs painting or cleaning.

climbers

Antigonon leptopus
Coral/Honolulu creeper, Koraalklimop

Size: 5 m

Growth habit: A fast-growing climber covered in large sprays of dainty, bright pink flowers from summer through to late autumn. This climber uses tendrils to attach itself to a support system and looks very pretty with its heart-shaped, mid-green foliage. Although it will be cut back by frost in cold areas, it usually recovers well. Prefers a warm sunny spot and thrives in subtropical climates.

Planting: Dig a hole, 60 square and deep, and mix two thirds of the topsoil with one third compost in the bottom of the hole. Add some general fertiliser plus a cup of superphosphate or bone meal and mix well.

Watering and feeding: Water regularly during the active growth season and feed with general fertiliser for flowering plants during spring.

Pruning: Cut back during spring, to promote new growth.

Uses: Fine cut flower. Ideal climber for the patio, or for covering a pergola, pillar or tree stump quickly, and excellent for hanging down a terrace. A white variety is also available. It is relatively drought tolerant once established.

Bougainvillea cultivars
Bougainvillea

Size: 0,3–10 m

Growth habit: Possibly the most spectacular climber – certainly there is none more colourful. Dozens of cultivars are available in shades of white, pink, red, orange, lilac, purple, cerise and copper; one even has pink and white flowers on the same plant. Double varieties, plus some with variegated leaves, also exist. It is evergreen in moist tropical climates and deciduous in cooler climates.

Planting: Flowers best if grown in poorish soil and given little water. Dig a hole, 60 cm square and deep, and mix two thirds of the topsoil with one third compost in the bottom of the hole. Add a cup of superphosphate or bone meal and mix well.

Watering and feeding: Water when needed and do not over-fertilise. Too much nitrogen fertiliser will cause luxuriant leaf growth but few colourful bracts.

Pruning: Prune after flowering, especially if grown in containers. Flowers appear on new wood.

Uses: Use in warm dry gardens, to cover walls and pergolas, as ground cover, specimen plant and in containers. Vigorous, heavy and thorny, the stronger growers need stout support.

Varieties: 'Tropical Rainbow' is a spectacular variegated creeper, with cream and green leaves tinged with pink. It is always attractive, even without its brilliant cerise flowers.

Pruning overgrown bougainvilleas Cut back the long shoots to about the fifth bud from the base at the main stem. Trim out all twiggy growth. Train and trim new shoots as soon as they start to grow long again. Usually bougainvilleas are not pruned very hard, because this will induce the plant to grow too vigorously.

Campsis radicans
Trumpet creeper/Trumpet honeysuckle

Size: 2–3,5 m

Growth habit: This is a vigorous, woody, self-clinging climber with aerial roots. The foliage is downy underneath. It bears small clusters of deep orange and red trumpet flowers in late summer to autumn, and forms suckers.

Planting: Dig a hole, 60 cm square and deep and mix two thirds of the topsoil with one third compost in the bottom of the hole. Add some general fertiliser plus a cup of super-phosphate or bone meal and mix well.

Watering and feeding: Water well during hot dry weather. Feed during spring with a general fertiliser for flowering plants, and water in well.

Pruning: Established plants can be cut back hard in early spring. Pinch back new shoots to promote bushiness. Remove suckers regularly as soon as they appear, otherwise they can smother other plants.

Uses: Excellent for large gardens, garden walls, pergolas and steep slopes. It is drought tolerant once established.

Clematis montana
Anemone clematis, Bosrank

Size: 2–4 m

Growth habit: Though rarely seen in South Africa, it is ideal for cold to temperate regions if given the right conditions. Clematis will grow in many different positions, provided its roots are shaded and the plant itself grows in the sun. Will grow several metres in a season. During late spring, it bears snow-white to pale pink vanilla-scented blossoms, 5 cm in diameter, with yellow stamens.

Planting: Prefers well-drained, fertile soil. Ensure that it has a generous-sized hole filled with lots of compost and fertiliser. Into a hole at least 50 cm square and deep, mix good potting soil or topsoil, two bucketfuls of imported Irish peat moss, and either well-rotted kraal manure or compost, ensuring that these latter two additions are below the root ball. Two good handfuls of bone meal should be well mixed into the soil.

Watering and feeding: Water and feed regularly. Keep well mulched at all times and feed with a general fertiliser once a month throughout the active growing season.

Pruning: Prune back hard after flowering.

Uses: It grows well against walls, on poles or pergolas, on trelliswork and on to trees and shrubs.

Varieties: 'Elizabeth' bears pale pink flowers. 'Rubens' produces pink flowers with purple-tinted foliage.

Pruning Remember the following general rule with pruning most plants: the more severely a plant is pruned, the more vigorous the regrowth will be. A good example of this is the bougainvillea.

Clerodendrum splendens
Scarlet clerodendrum

Size: 1,5–2 m

Growth habit: This climber is originally from tropical Africa and one of the showiest creepers, with brilliant red posies of flowers showing up beautifully against large, dark green, wrinkled leaves. Flowers mainly in winter in warm areas.

Planting: Prefers fertile, well-drained soil. Dig a hole, 60 cm square and deep, and mix two thirds of the topsoil with one third compost and well-rotted manure in the bottom of the hole. Add some general fertiliser and a cup of superphosphate or bone meal and mix well.

Watering and feeding: Water regularly during dry weather and feed once a month with a general fertiliser for flowering plants during spring and summer.

Pruning: Prune the plant back lightly after flowering to promote new growth.

Uses: Excellent against a wall, round a pillar or over a wire fence. It can also be used as a ground cover on a slope. Useful in tubs.

Varieties: *C. thomsoniae* 'Bleeding Heart' is not as showy, having scarlet flowers with white outer petals.

Distictis buccinatoria
Mexican blood trumpet, Mexikaanse trompetblom

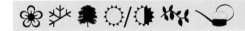

Size: 3–5 m

Growth habit: This beautiful, fast-growing creeper produces large clusters of unusual, long, deep yellow trumpet flowers with a scarlet mouth. They show up well against its large, green, oval leaves. Flowers during summer. It needs a strong support, as it can become very heavy with age.

Planting: Dig a hole, 60 cm square and deep. Mix two thirds of the topsoil with one third compost and kraal manure in the bottom of the hole. Add some general fertiliser plus a cup of superphosphate or bone meal and mix well.

Watering and feeding: Water regularly until well established, then only during very dry weather. Fertilise during spring with a general fertiliser for flowering plants.

Pruning: Cut back regularly to control the size as it is a vigorous climber and can become very overgrown.

Uses: Excellent for covering high walls and hedges, also for large pergolas.

Varieties: *D. laxiflora* (vanilla trumpet vine) is self-clinging on any rough surface, and is a magnificent creeper rather like *D. buccinatoria* in appearance, although its long trumpet flowers are mauve with pale throats. *Distictis x riversii* (*D. buccinatoria* x *D. laxiflora*) is similar to *D. buccinatoria*, but with much larger, paler mauve flowers in summer.

Water saving Use a watering can instead of the hosepipe to water containers. Water the garden and containers early in the morning or late afternoon when wind and evaporation are at their lowest. Install a rainwater tank to collect run-off water from gutters for watering container plants like pink dipladenia or clerodendrum.

Ficus pumila
Tickey creeper, Kruipvy

Size: 10 m and higher

Growth habit: Very neat and compact in growth habit, the tickey creeper is ideal for covering unsightly walls. Initially slow, it will cling to any support with suckers. It is fast growing once established. It has tiny round, rich dark green leaves in the juvenile stage, which become quite large with woody stems in the adult stage. Growth needs to be contained in the adult stage as hair roots can damage walls.

Planting: Dig a hole, 40 cm square and deep, and mix two thirds of the topsoil with one third compost in the bottom of the hole. Add some general fertiliser plus half a cup of superphosphate or bone meal and mix well.

Watering and feeding: This plant needs little attention once established. Feed it during spring with a general fertiliser, and water it in well.

Pruning: To prevent the plant from becoming too woody, cut back and remove old stems regularly, to promote the new growth with its small, heart-shaped foliage.

Uses: Excellent for clothing walls, but keep away from house foundations where it can cause problems. Can also be used as ground cover.

Varieties: *F. radicans* 'Variegata' is similar to the above but has narrower, white-flecked leaves.

Gelsemium sempervirens
Carolina jasmine, Valsjasmyn

Size: 3 m

Growth habit: Evergreen and hardy, it grows quickly and produces a mass of fragrant, yellow, trumpet-like flowers for nine months of the year, often more. Foliage is glossy and dark green. It needs a little help initially to support itself but, once established, it twines itself around the support very quickly. Prefers to have cool roots in the shade with shoots reaching for the sun.

Planting: Prefers fertile, well-drained soil. Dig a hole 50 cm square and deep, and mix two thirds of the topsoil with one third compost and kraal manure in the bottom of the hole. Add some general fertiliser plus a cup of superphosphate or bone meal and mix well.

Watering and feeding: Water regularly and fertilise during spring with a general fertiliser for flowering plants. Keep plants well mulched.

Pruning: Not necessary.

Uses: An ideal container plant for the patio, this light creeper is excellent for climbing on trelliswork and for twining around poles and pillars.

Garden tools Always clean garden tools after using them by brushing or rinsing off soil and stains, then wipe them down with an oily rag before putting them away in order to prevent them from rusting.

Jasminum multipartitum
Starry wild jasmine, Wildejasmyn

Size: 2–3,5 m

Growth habit: A lovely jasmine native to the Eastern Cape, KwaZulu-Natal and eastern Mpumalanga. Of the ten indigenous species the starry wild jasmine is the most decorative, with large star-shaped, fragrant, white flowers with a pink reverse. Flowering time is from August to January and flowers are followed by shiny black twin berries. Foliage is glossy and dark green in colour. It is quite fast growing.

Planting: Prepare a generous-sized hole, 50 cm square, and include an ample amount of compost and kraal manure with at least a third to two thirds of the soil from the hole. Mix in a cupful of general fertiliser plus a cup of superphosphate or bone meal.

Watering and feeding: Water regularly during dry weather and feed during spring and summer with general fertiliser for flowering plants.

Pruning: Not necessary but the plant will respond well to shaping after flowering.

Uses: Excellent container plant or to cover a hedge or pole. Fruit is eaten by birds and people. It is a traditional love charm and can be used to make a herbal tea.

Jasminum polyanthum
Chinese jasmine, Chinese jasmyn

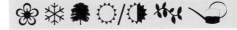

Size: 3–4m

Growth habit: This jasmine provides the garden with the first breath of spring, opening in warmer areas as early as the end of July. A fast-growing evergreen, it grows into a dense bush covered in clusters of pink buds opening to white flowers that are extremely fragrant. It can become invasive if not kept under control.

Planting: Dig a hole, 60 cm square and deep, and mix two thirds of the topsoil with one third compost and kraal manure in the bottom of the hole. Add some general fertiliser plus a cup of superphosphate or bone meal and mix well.

Watering and feeding: Water regularly until established. Feed it with a general fertiliser for flowering plants during spring, and water in well.

Pruning: Cut back after flowering to keep under control.

Uses: Ideal for covering pillars and lampposts or a trellis near the house, so that the scent can be enjoyed during spring. Can be grown in containers on the patio.

Ugly features Hide ugly features like tanks or compost heaps with trelliswork and a light creeper like star jasmine, pink dipladenia or Carolina jasmine, or use woven bamboo or bark panels. Manholes and drains can also be hidden by strategically placing containers with interesting plants over or in front of them.

Mandevilla amoena 'Alice du Pont'
Pink dipladenia, Pienk dipladenia

Size: 2,5 m
Growth habit: A lovely climber with spectacular, large, trumpet-like, bright pink flowers. This plant, which does not like growing against a hot wall, is ideal for training on a light trellis. Flowering while still small, once established it produces masses of flowers, starting in November and continuing through the summer right up to winter. Fast growing.
Planting: Needs a warm aspect and deep, rich, well-drained soil. Dig a hole, 60 cm square and deep, and mix two thirds of the topsoil with one third compost and kraal manure in the bottom of the hole. Add some general fertiliser plus a cup of superphosphate or bone meal and mix well.
Watering and feeding: Water regularly during the flowering season and feed once a month with liquid fertiliser in summer.
Pruning: Not necessary, but can be cut back lightly after flowering to stimulate new growth and to tidy plants up.
Uses: A light climber that is ideal for a trellis or for covering a pergola or pillar. Also excellent in containers on the patio or the pool area.

Mandevilla laxa
Chilean jasmine, Chileense jasmyn

Size: 6 m
Growth habit: With attractive, heart-shaped leaves, this half-hardy creeper bears masses of white, trumpet-shaped, heavily perfumed flowers in clusters throughout the summer. Remains evergreen in subtropical areas. Vigorous and fast growing, forming twining woody stems.
Planting: Prefers fertile, well-drained soil. Dig a hole, 60 cm square and deep, and mix two thirds of the topsoil with one third compost and kraal manure in the bottom of the hole. Add some general fertiliser plus a cup of superphosphate or bone meal and mix well.
Watering and feeding: Water during dry spells and fertilise during spring with a general fertiliser for flowering plants. Keep plants well mulched.
Pruning: Prune heavily in early spring to shape and encourage new growth.
Uses: Excellent for covering a fence or pergola. Lovely in large containers on a patio with a trellis. Useful for flower arrangements.

Watering Deep, thorough watering is much better than regular, shallow watering. Deep watering will encourage a deep root system, which will be better equipped to withstand heat and short periods of drought.

Pandorea jasminoides 'Rosea'
Australian bower plant, Australiese prieëlplant

Size: 3–4 m
Growth habit: This lovely Australian climber is fast growing. It is showy throughout summer when it is covered in masses of white, trumpet-shaped flowers with streaks of pinkish-red at the throat. The compound leaves are dark green and glossy. Twining stems attach themselves with tendrils. These plants prefer warmer climates but will not sustain lasting damage from light frost.
Planting: Dig a hole, 60 cm square and deep, and mix two thirds of the topsoil with one third compost and kraal manure in the bottom of the hole. Add some general fertiliser plus a cup of superphosphate or bone meal and mix well.
Watering and feeding: Water when dry and feed with a general fertiliser for flowering plants during spring. Keep plants well mulched.
Pruning: Cut back regularly after each flush of flowers to control the size and to promote new growth.
Uses: Excellent creeper for any position, especially on the patio, for covering walls, trellises and pergolas.
Varieties: 'Lady Di' is similar to the above but is pure white with a golden throat. 'Southern Belle' bears large clusters of pink, trumpet-shaped flowers throughout summer. It makes a very good container plant.

Parthenocissus quinquefolia
Virginia creeper, Virginiese klimop

Size: 7 m
Growth habit: There is no faster climber than the Virginia creeper. This self-clinging creeper attaches itself by tendrils with tiny, disc-shaped suckers. The vine-like leaves (having five leaflets) that change to bright autumn colours make a charming wall covering. Flowers are inconspicuous but are followed by small berries not unlike grapes.
Planting: Prefers fertile, well-drained soil. Dig a hole, 60 cm square and deep, and mix two thirds of the topsoil with one third compost. Add some general fertiliser plus a cup of superphosphate or bone meal and mix well.
Watering and feeding: This plant does not need a lot of attention once established. Water during dry weather and feed during spring.
Pruning: Cut the Virginia creeper back in early spring to shape and to control its growth.
Uses: Ideal for growing on building facades and walls.
Varieties: P. tricuspidata (Boston ivy) also has handsome vine-like leaves but takes longer to cover a wall and does not cling as well as P. quinquefolia. It does, however, have more spectacular colouring in the autumn.

Repotting a plant When a plant like the Australian bower plant has outgrown a pot on the patio, for example, water it well and lay the pot on its side. Use a hosepipe to wash the potting soil out, starting from the sides. By doing this, the roots will be flexible so that the plant can be pulled out of the pot without breaking either the pot or the plant.

Petrea volubilis
Petrea/Purple wreath, Perskransie

Size: 2–3 m

Growth habit: Deserves to be one of the best-known climbers in South Africa. Once it gets going, this showy creeper is easy to grow; it needs strong support and assistance in climbing. A scrambling, woody plant with large, rough leaves, it gets covered in 20-cm sprays of small, star-like, purple flowers from spring to summer. Prefers warmer climates to perform really well. Stays evergreen in subtropical climates but sheds its leaves in colder climates.

Planting: Dig a hole, 60 cm square and deep, and mix two thirds of the topsoil with one third compost and kraal manure. Add some general fertiliser plus a cup of superphosphate or bone meal and mix well.

Watering and feeding: Water this plant regularly, especially during very hot, dry weather. It does not need to be fed once it is established.

Pruning: Not necessary.

Uses: Attractive on its own or trained over an arch or pergola.

Varieties: 'Albiflora', the white form, has beautiful flowering racemes of pure white flowers. Leaves are a slightly paler green than those of the purple petrea.

Podranea brycei
Zimbabwe creeper, Zimbabweranker

Size: 10 m

Growth habit: A strong-growing, twining climber. This bignonia-type creeper bears large bunches of pink, trumpet-shaped flowers at the ends of its branches. The compound leaves are dark green and lance shaped.

Planting: It prefers fertile, well-drained soil in a hot situation. Dig a hole, 60 cm square and deep, and mix two thirds of the topsoil with one third compost and kraal manure in the bottom of the hole. Add some general fertiliser plus a cup of superphosphate or bone meal and mix well.

Watering and feeding: Water during hot, dry weather and feed during spring with a general fertiliser for flowering plants.

Pruning: Cut this creeper back hard in late winter to promote fresh new growth.

Uses: Lovely over a pergola or against a tall wall, but needs strong support. Tolerates heat and drought.

Varieties: *P. ricasoliana*, the Port St John's creeper, is similar to the above but bears lighter pink flowers and prefers subtropical coastal areas.

Gardening for butterflies Provide enough nectar-producing flowers to attract butterflies. Scented and trumpet-shaped flowers with long tubes are especially attractive to butterflies, and they in turn will attract birds that prey on them to the garden. Do not use insecticides if you intend to attract butterflies to the garden.

Pyrostegia venusta
Golden shower, Gouereën

Size: 10 m

Growth habit: Few climbers are as colourful as the golden shower when in full flower, as it cascades like a molten waterfall of orange trumpets. It is a vigorous grower and needs lots of space to grow. It flowers for many months, from soon after Christmas until winter when there isn't a lot of colour in the garden. Its shiny, dark green foliage is just as lovely. It flourishes in warmer gardens but can survive moderate frost.

Planting: Not fussy about soil type, but will benefit if planted well. Dig a hole, 60 cm square and deep, and mix two thirds of the topsoil with one third compost and kraal manure in the bottom of the hole. Add some general fertiliser plus a cup of superphosphate or bone meal and mix well.

Watering and feeding: Does not need a lot of attention. Relatively drought tolerant once established but will benefit from water during dry weather. Feed with a general fertiliser for flowering plants during spring, and water in well.

Pruning: Cut back after flowering to control its size.

Uses: Golden shower may be grown as a screen on very hot surfaces such as corrugated iron roofs. Ideal for covering a pergola or fence quickly.

Senecio tamoides
Canary creeper, Kanarieklimop

Size: 2–4 m

Growth habit: One of the showiest indigenous climbers available. It is vigorous, evergreen to semi-evergreen and needs the support of a wall or other plants. It is covered in large, showy heads of yellow, daisy-like flowers from April until June. Dies back in severe winters, but usually recovers to flower again the following autumn.

Planting: Not very fussy but will benefit from a well-prepared hole. Dig a hole, 60 cm square and deep, and mix two thirds topsoil with one third compost and kraal manure in the bottom of the hole. Add some general fertiliser plus a cup of superphosphate or bone meal and mix well.

Watering and feeding: Not very demanding but will perform better if it receives regular water and feeding at least once during the active growth season.

Pruning: Can be cut back to ground level after flowering and it will recover quickly.

Uses: Excellent for covering a fence or pergola quickly. Makes a lovely container plant for the patio, or to cover a pillar.

Bird-friendly gardening Incorporate indigenous climbers like canary creeper, black-eyed Susan and starry wild jasmine into an existing garden to provide natural food and shelter for birds. This will help to create a variety of habitats to attract as many bird species as possible. Also put up a bird feeder, especially in the winter months.

Stephanotis floribunda
Stephanotis, Madagaskar-jasmyn

Size: 2,5 m

Growth habit: This is a twining climber which is also known as the 'bride's flower'. The charming white blooms of this Madagascan beauty are not only stunning against the dark green of its thick, glossy, oval leaves, but they have a delicate, sweet fragrance. Starry, waxy flowers are carried in clusters and appear from spring to autumn. Prefers hot and humid climates.

Planting: Use good quality potting soil for containers. Otherwise dig a hole, 50 cm square and deep, and mix two thirds of the topsoil with one third compost and kraal manure in the bottom of the hole. Add some general fertiliser plus a cup of superphosphate or bone meal and mix well.

Watering and feeding: Water and feed regularly during the active growth season.

Pruning: Cut back in winter before new growth starts.

Uses: Excellent container plant, or for covering a small trellis.

Strongylodon macrobotrys
Jade vine, Jaspisklimop

Size: 3 m

Growth habit: This Philippine plant is one of the most spectacular of all flowering climbers. It is suited to the subtropical areas of the country and enjoys humidity, thriving along KwaZulu-Natal's Coast. Long trusses with unusual sea-green flowers, 50 cm and longer, cascade down. It flowers from spring up to the middle of summer. This woody climber with shiny, dark green foliage needs strong support and looks its best over a tall pergola.

Planting: Prefers well-drained soil. Dig a hole, 60 cm square and deep, and mix two thirds of the topsoil with one third compost and kraal manure in the bottom of the hole. Add some general fertiliser plus a cup of superphosphate or bone meal and mix well.

Watering and feeding: Not very demanding once established. Water during dry weather and keep the root area well mulched. Feed with a general fertiliser for flowering plants during spring, and water in well.

Pruning: Not necessary.

Uses: Ideal for growing on high pergolas where the flowers can cascade, from spring well into summer.

Pruning When using secateurs, make the cut close to a bud at a slight angle away from the bud so that moisture can run off. To remove thicker branches, use a saw and remove the branch piece by piece to prevent breaking and tearing. Remove these cleanly against the main stem, to prevent a fertile breeding ground for insects and pests.

Thunbergia alata
Black-eyed Susan, Swartoognooi

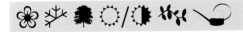

Thunbergia grandiflora
Sky flower/Bengal trumpet vine, Bloutrompetter

Size: 3–7 m

Growth habit: This vigorous but light annual climber is perennial in hot areas and is easy to grow. It has a twining growth habit with deep green leaves. Large, trumpet-shaped, open flowers are bright orange with black throats and appear from early summer to autumn. It self-seeds easily.

Planting: Use good quality potting soil for container planting. Otherwise, dig a hole, 60 cm square and deep, and mix two thirds of the topsoil with one third compost and kraal manure in the bottom of the hole. Add some general fertiliser plus a cup of superphosphate or bone meal and mix well.

Watering and feeding: Water regularly during summer. Feed with a general fertiliser for flowering plants during spring, and water in well.

Pruning: Prune lightly in spring.

Uses: Excellent for hot, dry areas, this creeper has many uses, from covering banks, terraces, trellises and pillars to trailing from hanging baskets. Ideal container plant where a light climber is needed for the hot summer months.

Size: 3–5 m

Growth habit: A fast-growing, vigorous climber with large, heart-shaped leaves. Drooping clusters of large, gloxinia-type, tubular, pale lilac flowers with a yellow throat are borne in summer and autumn. Prefers hot, humid climates and must be protected against hot summer winds. Looks lovely when hanging over a balcony or steep slope.

Planting: Prefers fertile, well-drained soil. Dig a hole, 60 cm square and deep, and mix two thirds of the topsoil with one third compost and kraal manure in the bottom of the hole. Add some general fertiliser plus a cup of superphosphate or bone meal and mix well.

Watering and feeding: Water regularly in hot, dry weather. Not very demanding. Feed with a general fertiliser for flowering plants during spring, and water in well.

Pruning: Not necessary.

Uses: Excellent for covering a trellis, fence or pergola.

Winter July is the ideal time to check garden features for signs of damage and to start repairs on trellises, paving, walls, fences and pergolas. Most climbing plants are dormant during this time and many will have shed their foliage, enabling you to reach more difficult areas which would otherwise be covered in foliage and growth.

Trachelospermum jasminoides
Star jasmine, Sterjasmyn

Size: 5 m

Growth habit: The star jasmine is an extremely useful twining plant for either sun or shade. Healthy looking with dark green leathery leaves, the star jasmine is not only showy with its glossy leaves and masses of shiny, white, star-like flowers, but it also has a delightful fragrance. Initially slow growing, it grows faster once established.

Planting: Dig a hole, 60 cm square and deep, and mix two thirds of the topsoil with one third compost and kraal manure in the bottom of the hole. Add some general fertiliser plus a cup of superphosphate or bone meal and mix well.

Watering and feeding: Quite drought tolerant once established but will benefit from extra water during dry weather. Feed with a general fertiliser for flowering plants during spring, and water in well.

Pruning: Cut back straggly shoots and congested branches in autumn.

Uses: May be trained into a shrub or used as a ground cover. Excellent as a container plant and ideal for covering a pillar, pergola or trellis. Develops into a thick, dark mat when used as a pergola covering.

Varieties: 'Yellow Star' is similar to the above but with lovely yellow flowers.

Wisteria sinensis
Chinese wisteria, Bloureën

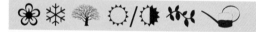

Size: 10 m

Growth habit: This vigorous, woody-stemmed, deciduous, twining climber is popular for pergolas in cold climates. Prized for grape-like bunches of drooping, lavender-blue flowers in spring. Flowers are slightly scented and appear before leaves. Can be trained into a weeping shrub. Tolerates heat, drought and frost but will not do well in subtropical climates.

Planting: Prefers fertile, well-drained soil. Dig a hole, 60 cm square and deep, and mix two thirds of the topsoil with one third compost and kraal manure. Add some general fertiliser plus a cup of superphosphate or bone meal and mix well.

Watering and feeding: Needs little attention once established. Water during dry weather and feed in late summer with a general fertiliser for flowering plants.

Pruning: Prune after flowering in early summer, and not in late winter before flowering. If plants do not flower well, prune roots in a circle about 90 cm from the stem in winter by pushing a spade down into the soil.

Uses: Cover pergolas where shade is needed in summer but not in winter. Needs sturdy support. Excellent bonsai subject.

Varieties: 'Alba' has fragrant, pea-like, white flowers. 'Amethyst' bears light rosy-purple flowers with a sweet fragrance in late winter.

Winter frost Frost kills most insect pests except those that hide in the compost heap, under stones, in climbers and hedges. Watch out in spring when these come to life and start putting out bait for snails and slugs, or take appropriate preventative measures by spraying or dusting with insecticide where necessary.

Perennials and ground covers are indispensable as they provide continuity of colour throughout the seasons. They multiply with ease and many tolerate considerable neglect. In addition some are drought resistant so they save time, money and labour. Perennials are plants that live for more than one season, with herbaceous rather than woody stems. They generally die down in winter, but their root systems remain intact for a number of years. Most ground covers are low-growing perennials or shrubs with a horizontal growth habit.

Prepare the soil well before planting perennials or ground covers as they will grow in the same place for a few years before being lifted and divided to replant. Dig over the soil to a depth of two spades and work in a large quantity of compost and well-rotted manure, together with some general fertiliser and superphosphate or bone meal. Once the plants are established, water in liquid fertilisers to keep them in good condition.

After the flowering period, you should remove old flowers and stems, leaving most of the foliage to conserve the plant's energy and store up enough food for the next season. Some perennials, usually those used for ground covering, have evergreen foliage and remain attractive throughout the year. Once plants have become overcrowded, a general rule is to divide early spring-flowering perennials in autumn, and late summer- and autumn-flowering ones in spring.

Perennials and ground covers are ideal plants for low-maintenance gardening. Remember to plant large patches of the same plants together to make a bold statement instead of mixing them up, which could look very busy.

perennials & ground covers

Acorus gramineus 'Variegata'
Sweet flag

Size: 30 x 30 cm

Growth habit: Sweet flag is a tuft-forming, evergreen, perennial, grass-like plant, with creamy-green, variegated leaves crowded on short rhizomes. It bears inconspicuous flower-spikes in spring and summer and is grown for its foliage. Propagate by division in autumn.

Planting: Plant in boggy areas or in containers in shallow water, or use as a ground cover.

Watering and feeding: Watering not necessary if grown in boggy areas. Cut back occasionally to control its spread. Feed during spring with a general fertiliser.

Uses: Sweet flag is excellent as a bog plant or in shallow water at pond edges. Looks stunning massed together as a ground cover. This plant has been used in folk medicine, perfumes and food flavourings.

Varieties: *A. gramineus* 'Ogon' has bright gold and green variegated foliage, and is good for moist areas.

Agapanthus praecox subsp. orientalis
Blue agapanthus, Blou agapant

Size: 50 x 50 cm

Growth habit: A popular and versatile garden plant, this is a strong, clump-forming, rhizomatous perennial with arching, strap-shaped leaves and dense, fleshy roots. In summer, large umbels of flowers in shades of blue and white, depending on the cultivar, are borne on tall, erect stems. Remove spent flowers regularly. It withstands conditions of neglect very well.

Planting: Not very fussy, but will benefit from enriched, well-drained soil. To prepare the bed, dig over the soil and work in a lot of compost and well-rotted manure, together with some general fertiliser and superphosphate or bone meal.

Watering and feeding: Water regularly in spring and summer. Feed in spring with a general fertiliser for flowering plants.

Uses: This plant is ideal for edging along a fence, wall or driveway. Excellent for mass plantings, on dry slopes and near the coast. Attracts birds and butterflies.

Varieties: *A. praecox* subsp. *orientalis* 'Albidus' is similar, but has white flowers. *A. africanus*, 30 cm tall, is compact, clump-forming and has white or blue flowers on short stems in summer. It is good for border edging and cut flowers. *A. africanus* 'Tinkerbell', 20 cm tall, has cream and green variegated leaves and blue flowers in summer. Not a prolific bloomer but excellent for its variegated foliage in sun and shade.

Dividing agapanthus and watsonias These perennials tend to decline a little when transplanted. To avoid this happening, dig carefully around the main clump and remove some of the outer growth or corms by cutting them off with a spade. The main plant will flower as normal.

Ajuga reptans 'Burgundy Glow'
Carpet bugle, Senegroen

Size: 15 cm

Growth habit: This low-growing, perennial ground cover spreads by surface runners, forming a mat of leafy rosettes of predominantly pink leaves against an ivory background. It does well in moist soil in a sunny but not hot position. In spring spikes of deep blue flowers are common to all *A. reptans* varieties, some of which have slightly different requirements. A trouble-free plant.

Planting: It prefers moist soil conditions. Dig over the soil and work in a lot of compost and well-rotted manure, with some general fertiliser and superphosphate or bone meal.

Watering and feeding: Water regularly to keep soil moist. Feed with a general fertiliser for foliage plants during spring, and water in well.

Uses: Ideal for shady places in corners and courtyards.

Varieties: *A. reptans* 'Atropurpurea' does well in similar conditions but has glossy, dark purple leaves. 'Multicolour' has bronze, pink and yellow variegated leaves, and needs more sun than some other ajugas to retain its colour. 'Variegata' has grey-green leaves splashed with cream, and needs shade and moist soil. 'Catlins Giant Cavalier' has larger, metallic-green/purple foliage, grows much more vigorously than other varieties and flourishes in a semi-shade position.

Alstroemeria aurea
Peruvian lily/Inca lily, Inkalelie

Size: 75 cm

Growth habit: This deciduous perennial, dormant in winter, spreads by means of fibrous roots. Foliage is twisted, narrow and lance-shaped, and concentrated on the upper half of the wiry stems. From spring to summer it bears spires of spotted and streaked orange-red, trumpet-shaped flowers. There are several choice hybrids of brick-red, pink, purple, white and yellow. Easy to grow, it is usually propagated by division.

Planting: It prefers enriched, well-drained soil. To prepare the bed, dig over the soil and work in a large quantity of acid compost and well-rotted manure, together with some general fertiliser and superphosphate or bone meal. In cold inland regions it needs a thick mulch during winter when it is dormant.

Watering and feeding: Water regularly during the active growth season. Feed during spring with a general fertiliser for flowering plants.

Uses: Popular as a cut flower, it is greatly sought after by gardeners and flower arrangers. Shorter hybrids make excellent container plants for the sunny patio. Attracts butterflies.

Varieties: 'Jazze Deep Rose' is a miniature with deep pink flowers all year. 'Red Heat' bears brick-red flowers in spring and autumn and is a good cut flower. 'Sussex Gold' has yellow flowers with dark brown stripes.

Picking Inca lilies When picking Inca lilies for the vase, you should pluck out the entire flower stem at root level with a sharp tug; there is no need to cut the stem off at the base. Be careful, however, not to overwater these plants as soil-borne pathogens could infect the plant in the wound under constant damp conditions.

Anemone x hybrids
Japanese anemone, Japanse anemone

Size: 1 m

Growth habit: A must for every garden, this fibrous-rooted perennial flowers in autumn and is one of the most elegant and lovely of plants. It has mid-green, deeply lobed leaves and saucer-shaped flowers of either white or pink. It is almost evergreen in milder climates.

Planting: Its main requirements are cool roots and moisture. To prepare the bed, dig over the soil and work in a large quantity of acid compost and well-rotted manure, together with some general fertiliser and superphosphate or bone meal. Keep plants well mulched with compost.

Watering and feeding: Water regularly during the active growing season and feed with a general fertiliser for flowering plants during spring. Water less during the dormant period.

Uses: A fine cut flower and lovely planted in groups towards the middle and back of the perennial border.

Varieties: 'Queen Charlotte' has pale purple, semi-double flowers. 'Hadspen Abundance' has dark wine-red, single flowers. 'Honorine Jobert' has dark green foliage with single, white flowers.

Arctotis acaulis
Marigold, Botterblom

Size: 30 cm

Growth habit: This compact, perennial ground cover has silver-grey foliage. Its large pink, red, orange or yellow daisy-like flowers with dark centres flower from spring to summer. Flowers need full sun to open fully. Remove spent flowers regularly to prolong flowering period.

Planting: Prefers well-drained, sandy soil. To prepare the bed, dig over the soil and work in some compost with general fertiliser and superphosphate or bone meal.

Watering and feeding: Do not overwater. Feed with a general fertiliser during spring, and water in well.

Uses: Excellent for covering large dry banks. It can also be grown in containers on the hot patio. Attracts butterflies.

Varieties: *Arctotis* x hybrids: 'Flame' is spreading, with grey-green foliage and bright orange flowers almost all year. 'Orange Fire' is spreading, with grey-green foliage, and large orange flowers in spring and summer. 'White Wonder' is spreading, with grey-green foliage and creamy flowers from spring to summer. 'Wine' has light green foliage and pink flowers all year. 'Yellow Cup' is low growing, with grey-green foliage and yellow flowers all year. *A. purpureus* is a perennial ground cover with grey-green foliage and purple-pink flowers in spring and summer.

Dividing perennials To split overgrown clumps of perennials easily, they must first be dug up. Place two gardening forks, back to back, into the middle of the clump and press the handles towards each other, which will split the clump in half. Replant only the newer outer plants.

Argyranthemum frutescens
Marguerite daisy, Magrietjie

Size: 1 x 1 m

Growth habit: This ever-popular beauty goes on flowering all year round. An upright-growing, bushy perennial with deeply lobed, bright green to blue-green leaves, it starts producing daisies when it is still small. Its colours are white, pink and yellow, in single and double forms. Easy to grow and propagate by slip, it deserves a place in every garden. Cut back in late winter to encourage new growth. Remove spent flowers regularly to prolong the flowering period.

Planting: It prefers light, well-drained soil. Dig a hole about 40 cm square and deep. Mix two thirds of the topsoil with one third compost in the bottom of the hole, add half a cup of bone meal or superphosphate and mix well.

Watering and feeding: Water when dry and feed with a general fertiliser during spring.

Uses: Excellent in the mixed perennial border or in containers. Attracts butterflies.

Varieties: Several cultivars are available: 'Fairy Tale' has pink flowers with yellow centres that fade to cream; 30 cm tall. 'Goldy' has bright green foliage with golden-yellow flowers all year; 50 cm tall. 'Ruby Red' has bright green foliage, single rose-red flowers; 80 cm tall. 'Snow Queen' has bright green foliage, single, white flowers all year; 1 m tall.

Asparagus densiflorus 'Mazeppa'
Foxtail fern, Katstert

Size: 30 x 50 cm

Growth habit: An evergreen perennial, this low-growing cultivar is a compact, bushy ground cover with dark green foliage. It bears small, white flowers in spring, and these are followed by red berries.

Planting: To prepare the bed for planting, dig over the soil and work in a large quantity of compost and well-rotted manure, together with some general fertiliser and superphosphate or bone meal.

Watering and feeding: Water when dry and feed during spring with a fertiliser for foliage plants.

Uses: Excellent as a ground cover when planted in large groups. Pretty plant for containers and hanging baskets.

Varieties: 'Cwebe' is compact and low growing with purple-brown new growth. 'Myersii' has needle-like, mid-green foliage up to 50 cm long, with white flowers in summer, followed by red berries. Very ornamental and a good tub subject for the shady patio. 'Sprengeri' has stems up to a metre long, loosely covered in fine, needle-like leaves. It has small, white, honey-scented flowers that eventually turn to small, red berries. Excellent for flower arranging and hanging baskets.

Broken clay pots Do not discard broken clay pots; rather break them up into smaller pieces and use in pots to help water drain out and to keep soil from being washed away. Place a piece over each drainage hole and cover with a layer of sand before filling with potting soil. Then plant perennials like asparagus or New Guinea impatiens in the pots.

Bergenia cordifolia
Heartleaf saxifrage

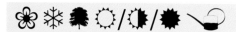

Size 50 x 50 cm

Growth habit: This very popular perennial looks good throughout the year. Flowering late in winter to early spring, the lilac- to rose-coloured panicles stand out above their large, glossy, leathery leaves. In dry areas it prefers more shade. Remove all the spent flowers regularly to prolong the flowering season. Divide the overcrowded clumps in late spring, after flowering.

Planting: Not very fussy about soil. To prepare the bed, dig over the soil and work in a large quantity of acid compost and well-rotted manure, together with some general fertiliser and superphosphate or bone meal.

Watering and feeding: Water regularly during dry weather. It needs little attention once established. Keep well mulched with compost. Feed with a general fertiliser for flowering plants in spring.

Uses: Grows well near streams or pools and makes a charming ground cover when planted in large groups.

Canna indica x hybrids
Canna, Kanna

Size: 1,2 m

Growth habit: This strong-growing, rhizomatous perennial has large leaves and bright flowers in summer in a range of colours from red, pink and orange to yellow and cream. Hybrids are available with purple-bronze foliage as well as variegated leaves. Break out flower stems at ground level to prolong the flowering period. Divide rhizomes in early spring.

Planting: To prepare the bed, dig over the soil and work in a large quantity of compost and well-rotted manure, together with some general fertiliser and superphosphate or bone meal.

Watering and feeding: Water well during hot, dry weather. Feed with a general fertiliser and a mulch of well-rotted manure during spring.

Uses: Excellent in large groups or as clumps in the background perennial border.

Varieties: A few named hybrids are: 'Bridesmaid' which has green foliage with pink flowers; 1 m. 'Marshmallow' has green leaves, apricot-pink flowers; 1 m. 'Pretoria' has variegated yellow and green foliage with orange flowers; 1 m. 'Tropicana' has red and pink striped foliage, orange flowers; 80 cm. 'Richard Wallace' has pale green leaves and bright yellow flowers; 90 cm. 'Tropical Rose' has green foliage and light pink flowers; 60 cm.

Using fertiliser Most fertilisers are highly concentrated and should never come into direct contact with roots or stems as this will cause root and tissue burn. To avoid this, mix fertiliser well with soil so that it will be evenly distributed, and water well after fertiliser application.

Carex morrowii 'Variegata'
Japanese sedge

Size: 30 x 30 cm
Growth habit: An evergreen, clump-forming sedge with drooping, grass-like leaves, it is vertically striped with white and green. Fluffy seed heads are insignificant and appear during summer. Divide overgrown clumps during autumn.
Planting: It prefers moist soil conditions. To prepare the bed, dig over the soil and work in some compost and well-rotted manure, together with some general fertiliser and super-phosphate or bone meal.
Watering and feeding: Water regularly during hot, dry weather and feed during spring with a general fertiliser for foliage plants.
Uses: Excellent ground cover when massed together, or in the rock garden. Works well in containers on the patio.
Varieties: *C. comans* 'Select', a bronze-coloured sedge, is excellent in shady areas and ideal for contrast plantings. *C. hachijoensis* is a tuft-forming, perennial sedge with green foliage that reaches a length of 20 cm. Cut back foliage when it becomes untidy. Ideal near water features and when massed together. *C. hachijoensis* 'Evergold' is a tuft-forming, perennial sedge with drooping leaves that are yellow-white down the centre with a green edge. Excellent patio plant.

Carissa macrocarpa 'Green Carpet'
Dwarf Natal plum, Dwergnatalpruim

Size: 0,3 x 1 m
Growth habit: This low-growing, dense, spreading shrub has glossy foliage. It has large, jasmine-like, scented, white flowers that appear in spring, followed by crimson, oval fruits in summer. Fruits are edible. The plant can be cut back to control its size after summer flowering. Rather slow at first but spreads quite fast once it is established.
Planting: It is not fussy about soil types. To prepare the bed, dig over the soil and work in a large quantity of compost and well-rotted manure, together with some general fertiliser and superphosphate or bone meal.
Watering and feeding: Water during hot, dry weather and feed during spring with a general fertiliser. Does not need a lot of attention once established.
Uses: Excellent thorny ground cover for hot and dry areas, on slopes and in wildlife gardens. Makes a great low hedge or foreground plant. Birds love the fruits.

Waterlogged soil Only aquatic plants – for example Louisiana iris, some crinum species, arum lilies and papyrus or sedges – can grow in waterlogged soil. Water can, however, be drained from these areas by installing underground drainage so that other plants can successfully be cultivated in these areas.

Chlorophytum comosum
Hen-and-chickens/Spider plant, Hen-en-kuikens

Size: 30 cm

Growth habit: This evergreen, rhizomatous perennial has grass-like leaves, striped with white, yellow or cream. It bears insignificant white flowers on long, arching flower-spikes that produce new tufts of leaves where they touch the ground. The tufts take root and make the hen-and-chicken spread.

Planting: Prefers well-drained soil. Dig over the soil and work in a lot of compost and well-rotted manure, with general fertiliser and superphosphate or bone meal.

Watering and feeding: Water regularly and feed with a general fertiliser during spring.

Uses: A quick-spreading ground cover under large trees. Excellent in hanging baskets and containers on the shady patio.

Varieties: *C. comosum* 'Gold Nugget' is compact, 150 mm tall, and has white-and-green striped leaves. It tolerates full sun. 'Picturatum' has soft, arching, grass-like leaves with a central yellow stripe and grows in shade or semi-shade. 'Variegatum' is similar but with white leaf margins. 'Vittatum' is much the same but has a white to cream central stripe, excellent in hanging baskets. 'Bonnie' is a new introduction and is a hybrid of *comosum* with attractive curling leaves in compact clusters. For pots or hanging baskets.

Chondropetalum tectorum
Thatching reed, Dekriet

Size: 1,5 x 2 m

Growth habit: This restio from the fynbos regions of the southwestern Cape is a tussock-forming perennial with dark green, reed-like stems called culms. It has flowering stems with terminal heads of showy, papery brown inflorescences. Separate male and female plants in restios constitute the main difference between restios and grasses. To tidy a restio, old culms can be removed once new shoots are about 5 cm tall, taking care not to damage new growth.

Planting: This plant prefers well-drained, acidic soil. Dig a hole 60 cm square and deep. Mix two thirds of the topsoil with one third acid compost in the bottom of the hole, add half a cup of bone meal or superphosphate and mix well. Keep the plant well mulched to keep the roots cool and also to reduce water evaporation.

Watering and feeding: Does not need a lot of attention once established but will produce more robust growth with regular watering and liquid feeding during the active growth season.

Uses: A lovely feature plant, it makes interesting flower-arranging material.

Traditional clay pots Paint ethnic containers with a stone sealer on the inside or on both sides before using them for planting perennials like hen-and-chickens. This will prevent them from breaking or falling apart. Before planting, make sure to drill adequate drainage holes into these containers if there are no holes.

Chrysanthemum maximum
Shasta daisy, Shastamadeliefie

Size: 50 cm

Growth habit: This clump-forming perennial has smooth, green foliage which may be toothed or lobed. It bears snowy-white, single and double daisy-like flowers with pale golden centres on tall leafy stems, varying from the miniatures at 15 cm high to cultivars reaching 50 cm. It flowers through summer to early autumn. It should be divided regularly every two to three years during spring. Remove spent flowers often to prolong the flowering period.

Planting: It needs fertile, well-drained soil. To prepare the bed, dig over the soil and work in a large quantity of compost, together with some general fertiliser and superphosphate or bone meal.

Watering and feeding: Undemanding, but it will benefit from water during dry weather and feeding in spring with a general fertiliser for flowering plants. Do not overfeed as this will only cause leafy growth with very few flowers.

Uses: Excellent in the perennial border and ideal for cutting, the flowers last well in the vase. Attracts butterflies.

Varieties: *C. maximum* 'Esther Read' has beautiful double, white flowers.

Clivia miniata
Bush lily/Saint John's lily, Boslelie

Size: 75 x 50 cm

Growth habit: This popular, clump-forming perennial is indigenous to the Eastern Cape, KwaZulu-Natal and eastern Mpumalanga. Flowering in spring, with clusters of bright orange flowers rising among its leathery, dark green, strap-like leaves, it is most attractive and easy to grow. Flowers are followed by red berries. Divide overgrown clumps during autumn or after flowering in spring when roots start to appear above the soil level. Watch out for amaryllis caterpillars during spring and summer.

Planting: It prefers organic, rich but well-drained soil. To prepare the bed, dig over the soil and work in a large quantity of compost and well-rotted manure, together with some general fertiliser and superphosphate or bone meal. Keep the plant well mulched with leaf compost.

Watering and feeding: Not very demanding. It will benefit from water during hot, dry weather and a feeding with a general fertiliser for flowering plants during early spring.

Uses: Excellent for shady areas under trees or in containers on the shady patio.

Varieties: *C. miniata* 'Lutea', the yellow form, is becoming more readily available.

Compost container For a regular and cheap supply of compost, make your own by layering organic material – like leaves, twigs and cut-up branches, vegetable skins and manure – in a round container with sturdy mesh wire. Keep it damp but not soggy. It should be ready after about eight weeks when it is decomposed and crumbly.

Convolvulus sabatius
Ground morning glory, Dwergpurperwinde

Size: 20 cm

Growth habit: This trailing perennial, fast spreading by underground rhizomes, is not invasive. With leaves of soft green, its flowers are an attractive lilac-blue in summer to late autumn. These flowers differ from true morning glories in that they open and stay open all day; they also open in succession over a long season. The plant can be cut back to promote bushier growth after flowering.

Planting: To prepare the bed, dig over the soil and work in some compost and well-rotted manure, together with some general fertiliser and superphosphate or bone meal.

Watering and feeding: Not demanding, it will benefit from water during hot, dry weather and a feeding with a general fertiliser for flowering plants during spring.

Uses: Highly recommended ground cover, it is ideal on steeply sloping banks and scrambling over walls and container edges. Attracts butterflies.

Cynara scolymus
Globe artichoke, Artisjok

Size: 1,5 m

Growth habit: This very attractive herbaceous perennial has silver-grey foliage. The heart of the immature flower bud is edible. It has large, thistle-like silver buds which open into mauve-purple flowers in early summer. Clump-forming, it spreads by suckers which can be removed from the overgrown mother plant every three to four years, in early spring, and replanted. It grows quite large for a perennial and needs enough space to develop.

Planting: It is easy to grow in most well-drained soil types. To prepare the bed, dig over the soil and work in a large quantity of compost and well-rotted manure, together with some general fertiliser and superphosphate or bone meal.

Watering and feeding: This is not a demanding plant; give water when dry and feed it during spring with a general fertiliser for foliage plants.

Uses: Excellent for contrast planting in the mixed shrub border or rock garden, and the flowers also make good cut flowers. Attracts butterflies.

Garden shredder Invest in a garden shredder to effectively dispose of garden litter like leaves and branches. Add the shredded litter to the compost heap. Coarser material obtained from the shredder, such as shredded branches, can be used to make an excellent mulch among perennials.

Dianella tasmanica 'Variegata'
Flax lily, Vlaslelie

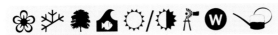

Size: 50 x 30 cm

Growth habit: This clump-forming perennial has sword-shaped leaves that are striped in green and white. It bears small, pale blue flowers on long, slender stems in summer, followed by light blue berries. It is drought tolerant once established but needs ample water to flower and fruit well. The green-leafed form produces dark blue berries. Divide overcrowded clumps in autumn after a few years.

Planting: It prefers rich, well-drained soil. To prepare the bed, dig over the soil and work in a large quantity of compost and well-rotted manure, together with some general fertiliser and superphosphate or bone meal.

Watering and feeding: Water the flax lily regularly during hot, dry weather and feed during spring with a general fertiliser for foliage plants.

Uses: Excellent for colour and texture contrast in the mixed perennial border. It also looks lovely near water or massed together as a ground cover under tall trees.

Varieties: 'Yellow Stripe' is similar to the above but has yellow striped leaves and is slightly shorter.

Diascia integerrima
Twin spur, Pensie

Size: 30 x 40 cm

Growth habit: This colourful indigenous perennial occurs from the southwestern Cape to KwaZulu-Natal. Plants grow into small herbaceous bushes. Masses of pink flowers with twin spurs are borne for several months in summer. Cut back after flowering to encourage bushy new growth and to promote new flowering.

Planting: It will grow in almost any soil but will perform better in fertile, well-drained soil. To prepare the bed, dig over the soil and work in a large quantity of compost and well-rotted manure, together with some general fertiliser and superphosphate or bone meal.

Watering and feeding: It is not a demanding plant. Water when dry and feed during spring with a general fertiliser for flowering plants.

Uses: Excellent when planted massed together as a ground cover. Lovely in the rock garden or as a border in front of larger perennials or shrubs.

Varieties: *D.* x hybrid 'Joyce's Choice' has light green foliage with salmon-pink flowers throughout the year. *D.* x hybrid 'Lilac Queen' has dark green foliage with lilac-pink flowers all year round. *D.* x *stachyoides* 'Salmon Supreme' has light green leaves and salmon-coloured flowers all year.

Holiday hint Mulch flower beds with a thick layer of compost and then water deeply before going away on holiday. This will help to conserve moisture while you are away.

Dichondra repens
Wonder lawn, Wondergras

Size: 5 cm

Growth habit: This low-growing, creeping, lush green perennial is very neat in appearance. It is an excellent lawn substitute in low-traffic and shady areas in which normal grass struggles to grow. It forms a dense mat with rounded leaves; the flowers are insignificant. It is easily grown from seed at any time of the year, but preferably in spring or autumn. Can become invasive if not controlled near other grass-type lawns.

Planting: To prepare the area to be sown, dig over the soil and work in a large quantity of compost and well-rotted manure, together with some general fertiliser and superphosphate or bone meal. Rake over to create a fine, even surface. Sow and water with a fine sprinkler.

Watering and feeding: Water when dry. Feed during spring with a liquid fertiliser for foliage plants.

Uses: Ideal for direct sowing in open ground, bare patches and between stepping stones.

Dietes bicolor
Peacock flower/Yellow wild iris, Reënlelie/Uiltjie

Size: 60 x 40 cm

Growth habit: This large clump-forming, versatile perennial is indigenous to the Eastern Cape. Dark green leaves are stiff and sword-shaped. In late spring wiry, arching stems appear with yellow flowers, which have a brownish blotch at the base of each alternate petal. Single flowers last for one day only but new flowers open continually. It seeds itself freely.

Planting: It will grow in almost any soil, but will benefit from compost-enriched soil. To prepare the bed, dig over the soil and work in a large quantity of compost and well-rotted manure, together with some general fertiliser and superphosphate or bone meal.

Watering and feeding: Water this plant during very dry and hot weather. Feed with a general fertiliser during spring, and water in well.

Uses: It is very good for mass planting, especially in dry, shady or sunny areas.

Varieties: *D. grandiflora* is similar, but it has iris-like white flowers with yellow and mauve markings.

Clean fingernails Scrape your nails over a cake of soap before working with soil. This will help to clean your nails very quickly and easily after you have, for example, finished replanting divided perennials.

Dymondia margaretae
Silver carpet

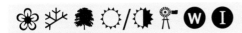

Size: 3 cm

Growth habit: This flat-growing, neat and attractive ground cover is indigenous to the southern Cape. It is a herbaceous perennial with small, silver-grey and blue-green leaves. The silver carpet has small, daisy-like, yellow flowers, borne during the spring and early summer.

Planting: It prefers well-drained soil. To prepare the bed, dig over the soil and work in some compost together with some general fertiliser and superphosphate or bone meal.

Watering and feeding: Water during very hot and dry conditions. It is not a demanding plant. Feed with a general fertiliser during spring, and water in well.

Uses: Makes an excellent ground cover between sleepers and stepping stones. It is also very good for stabilising soil on steep slopes. This plant is drought tolerant.

Echeveria x hybrids
Echeveria

Size: 15 cm

Growth habit: This mostly silver-grey succulent forms fleshy, symmetrical rosettes usually low at soil level. Spikes of red, pink or yellow, bell-shaped to cylindrical flowers are produced at different times of the year. Propagate from offsets or leaf cuttings during spring and summer.

Planting: Soil must be very well drained. To prepare the bed, dig over the soil and work in a large quantity of compost and well-rotted manure, together with some general fertiliser and superphosphate or bone meal.

Watering and feeding: Water during hot, dry weather from spring to summer, reducing the watering to little or none during winter. Feed with a general fertiliser during spring, and water in well.

Uses: Excellent as a ground cover massed together in dry, well-drained areas. It also looks lovely in a container or rock garden in hot, dry areas. Drought tolerant.

Varieties: *E. elegans* has small rosettes of blue-green leaves with red margins, and pinky-red, bell-shaped flowers.

Succulents Use indigenous succulents (many perennials are succulents) and aloes in containers and in areas close to hot paving and walls where a lot of heat is reflected and where other plants have difficulty to flourish.

Echinacea purpurea
Pink rudbeckia/Coneflower

Size: 50 cm

Growth habit: This tough, clump-forming perennial has thick edible roots. It is drought resistant and dormant in winter. Daisy-like, mauve-pink or purple flowers appear in summer on 80-cm stems. It has a raised, golden cone and rough, slightly toothed leaves. Remove spent flowers regularly to prolong flowering. Divide overgrown clumps in winter to early spring.

Planting: It prefers well-drained, fertile soil. Dig over the soil and work in a lot of compost and well-rotted manure, with some general fertiliser and superphosphate or bone meal.

Watering and feeding: Water when dry and mulch clumps during spring with compost. Feed with a general fertiliser for flowering plants during spring, and water in well.

Uses: Beautiful in the mixed perennial border, it provides an excellent cut flower. It has a wide range of uses as a medicinal herb and its dried roots are used to increase the body's resistance to disease. Attracts butterflies.

Varieties: *E. purpurea* 'Magnus' has very large, dark pink flowers and grows up to 1 m tall. 'Kim's Knee High' bears clear pink flowers with a red-tipped orange cone in midsummer, with a second flush in autumn on 40-cm stems. 'White Swan' bears ivory-white flowers with a mahogany-brown centre on tall stems during midsummer.

Elegia capensis
Fountain reed, Fonteinriet

Size: 2 x 1 m

Growth habit: This restio is indigenous to the southwestern Cape. It is strong growing and clump forming. This ornamental plant produces upright stems with whorls of foliage that look like unusual feathery reeds, crowned by brown inflorescences. Propagate it by division of the underground rhizomes in early spring. Cut untidy stems at ground level to promote new growth.

Planting: Needs moist and sandy soil. Dig a hole 50 cm square and deep. Mix two thirds of the topsoil with one third compost in the bottom of the hole, add half a cup of superphosphate or bone meal and mix well.

Watering and feeding: Water regularly to keep the soil moist at all times. Keep plants well mulched with compost to help conserve moisture.

Uses: One of the most beautiful form plant species for the bog garden or next to a water feature. Makes for interesting flower arranging material.

Waterwise planting Group plants with the same water requirement – like aloes, succulents and drought-tolerant ground covers – in the same bed to save water and time by concentrating on watering plants with higher water requirements grouped in another bed.

Erigeron karvinskianus
Mexican daisy/Santa Barbara daisy

Size: 35 cm

Growth habit: It is a fast-spreading and hummock-forming, herbaceous perennial. This dainty little plant has narrow, lobed leaves and is covered in small, white daisies tinged with pink throughout the year. It spreads with lax stems which take root at the nodes and can be invasive in mild climates through self-seeding. Cut back hard during winter to promote new, bushy growth.

Planting: The Mexican daisy prefers well-drained soil. To prepare the bed, dig over the soil and work in a large quantity of compost, together with some general fertiliser and superphosphate or bone meal.

Watering and feeding: Water it regularly during hot, dry weather. Feed once during spring with a general fertiliser for flowering plants.

Uses: Ideal for rock gardens, the mixed perennial border and for edging pathways, it is also excellent in large hanging baskets and containers in full sun.

Felicia amelloides
Kingfisher daisy, Bloumargriet

Size: 60 x 50 cm

Growth habit: This bushy, evergreen, perennial shrub produces sky-blue, daisy-like flowers with bright yellow centres from spring to autumn, but mainly in spring. Fast growing, with bright green, hairy foliage, it is often grown as an annual. Tolerates semi-shade. Also available in a white form. Remove spent flowers after each flush to prolong the flowering season and to keep the bushes in a neat shape. It self-seeds easily.

Planting: It prefers fertile, well-drained soil. Dig over the soil and work in a lot of compost and well-rotted manure, with some general fertiliser and superphosphate or bone meal.

Watering and feeding: Water regularly throughout the year and feed with a general fertiliser for flowering plants in spring.

Uses: Very good for the rock garden or the sunny border.

Varieties: *F. amoena* 'Variegata' is low growing and has green and yellow variegated leaves and small, blue flowers all year. *F. bergiana* (dwarf felicia) is compact, low growing, dark green, with small, blue, daisy-like flowers all year round. *F. erigeroides* is a small, shrub-like plant with pink flowers all year. *F. amelloides* 'Out of the Blue', formerly 'King Fischer', is a new introduction with crisp green leaves that form cushions topped with masses of violet-blue, yellow-centred daisies throughout the year.

Rooting cuttings When making cuttings, dip the lower first centimetre of the plant into a rooting hormone, tipping out a little hormone powder into a small container before using to avoid contaminating the powder. Place the cutting into a damp mixture of sand and peat. Keep the sand damp but not soggy to prevent cuttings from rotting.

Gaura lindheimeri 'So White'
Gaura

Size: 50 cm

Growth habit: This accommodating, tough perennial is clump-forming. A very showy plant, with apple green foliage, it has masses of sprays bearing pure white, butterfly-like flowers on slender stems from spring to autumn. Cut back to ground level after flowering in autumn. Can become invasive if not kept under control.

Planting: It prefers light, well-drained soil. To prepare the bed, dig over the soil and work in a large quantity of compost, together with some general fertiliser and superphosphate or bone meal.

Watering and feeding: Although drought tolerant, it will benefit from occasional watering. Feed with a general fertiliser for flowering plants in spring.

Uses: Excellent in mixed flower borders, it is an interesting cut flower. Attracts butterflies. It is drought tolerant.

Varieties: *G. lindheimeri* 'Siskiyou Pink' grows to a height of about 30 cml, with pink-red flowers from spring to autumn. 'Blushing Butterflies' also grows to about 30 cm, and bears pale pink flowers. Foliage is reddish-green turning a deeper red during winter.

Gelsemium sempervirens 'Lemon Drop'
Carolina jasmine, Valsjasmyn

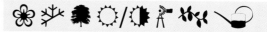

Size: 50 cm

Growth habit: This is a small, rounded ground cover with glossy, dark green foliage and lovely fragrant, yellow, trumpet-shaped flowers during spring. It has a moderate growth rate and all parts of the plant are poisonous. Trim regularly to keep the plant neat and compact.

Planting: To prepare the bed for planting, dig over the soil and work in a large quantity of compost and well-rotted manure, together with some general fertiliser and superphosphate or bone meal.

Watering and feeding: Although quite drought tolerant once established, it will perform better if watered regularly. Feed during spring with a general fertiliser for flowering plants.

Uses: It is an excellent container plant for the patio or for mass planting as a ground cover.

White flowers Plant white-flowering plants and silver-foliaged perennials and shrubs near the patio and pool area to make them stand out in the evening. This will work well for all those gardeners who only have time to appreciate their gardens after work.

Geranium incanum
Carpet geranium, Bergtee

Size: 30 x 30 cm

Growth habit: This low-growing, herbaceous perennial with fine, lace-like, grey-green foliage bears saucer-shaped, pink to mauve flowers throughout the year. It self-seeds easily.

Planting: It will grow in most well-drained soil types. To prepare the bed, dig over the soil and work in a large quantity of compost and well-rotted manure, together with some general fertiliser and superphosphate or bone meal.

Watering and feeding: Water regularly and feed during spring with a general fertiliser for flowering plants.

Uses: Looks lovely in the rock garden or growing among other perennials or small shrubs; it is charming in cottage gardens. Attracts butterflies.

Varieties: *G. maderense* (*G. palmatum*) is a beautiful biennial with fine, feathery leaves. Pink-purple flowers are borne profusely in summer. It grows to 80 cm tall. *G. pratense* (meadow crane's bill) grows 75 cm tall. It has deeply divided, mid-green leaves with crimson-veined, violet-blue flowers. Flowers for most of the summer in attractive mounds. Clumps do best undisturbed. *G. sanguineum* (crane's bill) grows 30 cm high and forms a bushy, flat ground cover with masses of magenta-pink flowers in summer. Also available in a white form.

Hedera helix
Ivy, Klimop

Size: 20 cm

Growth habit: This versatile, woody-stemmed climber is useful as a creeper and ground cover. Prune regularly to retain juvenile leaves and to encourage plants to grow into a dense mat. Virtually any varieties may be used as ground covers in addition to glossy, green-leafed *H. helix* itself.

Planting: It is very adaptable to a wide variety of conditions. For planting ivy as a ground cover, prepare the bed by digging over the soil and working in a large quantity of compost and well-rotted manure, together with some general fertiliser and superphosphate or bone meal.

Watering and feeding: Water ivy regularly and feed during spring with a general fertiliser for foliage plants.

Uses: Excellent ground cover in shade or sun, marsh or rocky outcrop, ivy thrives anywhere and spreads rapidly.

Varieties: *H. helix* 'Baltica' is a small, plain, green-leafed variety. *H. canariensis* 'Gloire de Marengo' (Canary Island) is a large-leafed trailer. *H. helix* 'Glacier' has small, variegated, creamy-white leaves. *H. helix* 'Goldheart' has small, dark green leaves with a golden centre. *H. helix* 'Mosaic' has glossy, dark green leaves with mosaic spots.

Natural pond A pond with gently sloping sides and a variety of marsh plants like arum lilies, sweet flag, papyrus, sedges and water lilies is ideal to attract wildlife to the garden. Provide enough cover for fish and frogs, and flat protruding stones for birds and insects to perch on.

Hemerocallis x hybrids
Day lily, Daglelie

Size: 40 x 40 cm

Growth habit: The day lily is very easy to grow and is an evergreen or deciduous, clump-forming perennial with tuberous, fleshy roots. Lily-like flowers in branched clusters appear from spring to autumn in shades of rust, red, orange and yellow. Flowers open progressively as each flower only lasts for one day. Flowers are also edible. Divide clumps every three to four years in autumn, and cut back the foliage to 10 cm when replanting. Watch out for slugs and snails, aphids and red spider mite attack.

Planting: To prepare the bed, dig over the soil and work in a large quantity of compost and well-rotted manure, with some general fertiliser and superphosphate or bone meal.

Watering and feeding: Water regularly and feed with a general fertiliser for flowering plants in spring.

Uses: Ideal for mass planting or for the herbaceous border.

Varieties: 'Crystal Cupid' with ruffled yellow flowers on short stems is a low-growing miniature that flowers early in the season. 'Fleeta' has dark burgundy flowers. 'Frank Gladney' has coral-pink flowers with golden throats late in the season and is of medium height. 'Lemoine' bears single, salmon-pink flowers. 'Joan Senior' has whitish flowers in mid-season.

Impatiens x 'New Guinea' hybrids
'New Guinea' impatiens

Size: 50 x 40 cm

Growth habit: This fast-growing perennial is popular as much for its attractive foliage as its bright flowers. New Guinea impatiens requires at least four hours' sun a day to retain the colour of its leaves and blooms. The plant provides a great variety of different leaf variegations in greens, yellows, bronzes and pinks, together with many different flower colours from white and pale pink, through mauve, cerise and orange to bright red.

Planting: It prefers moist but well-drained soil. To prepare the bed, dig over the soil and work in a large quantity of compost and well-rotted manure, together with some general fertiliser and superphosphate or bone meal.

Watering and feeding: Water regularly to keep the plant moist and feed with a general fertiliser for flowering plants during spring.

Uses: This is an excellent container plant for colour on the cool to sunny patio. Lovely in the mixed perennial border with afternoon shade.

Varieties: 'Tango' has bright orange flowers and dark green flowers and compact growth. 'Spectra Mixed' features many colours and a variety of decorative foliage.

Hide dying spring foliage Grow spring-flowering bulbs between summer-flowering day lilies to disguise the dying foliage of the bulbs with the fresh new growth from the day lilies in early summer. By the time the bulbs have died down the day lilies will have grown out fully and started to flower beautifully, effectively hiding the dead bulb foliage.

Iris x hybrids
Bearded iris, Baardiris

Size: 40 cm to 1 m
Growth habit:
This hardy, rhizomatous perennial flowers in spring. Divide in December, but only every four to five years. The best way to plant it is to place the rhizome on a hill of soil with the roots separated on either side. The roots should be well covered with soil but the rhizome itself may be exposed for it does well in the hot sun. Planted too deep, it will not flower.
Planting: It prefers well-drained, alkaline soil. Dig over the soil and work in a lot of compost and well-rotted manure, with some general fertiliser and superphosphate or bone meal.
Watering and feeding: Although quite drought tolerant, it will benefit from water during hot, dry summers and feeding during spring with a general fertiliser for flowering plants.
Uses: The iris is easy and rewarding and looks stunning in long, informally shaped clumps. Makes lovely cut flowers.
Varieties: 'Acapulco Gold' has golden yellow flowers, borne in early to mid-spring; 80 cm tall. 'Angel Symphony' has white flowers, borne in early to mid-spring; 85 cm tall. Black Flag' has purple-black flowers, borne in mid-spring; 95 cm tall. 'Glendale' has apricot-pink flowers, borne in mid- to late spring; 90 cm tall. 'Sapphire Hills' has blue flowers, borne in mid-spring; 90 cm tall.

Kniphofia uvaria
Red hot poker, Vuurpyl

Size: 1 x 0,5 m
Growth habit: This strong-growing, rhizomatous perennial grows into a tufted, upright plant with long, bright green grass-like leaves. This species flowers in summer, with dense spikes of tubular red buds that open to yellow flowers on tall, bare stems. Remove spent flowers regularly and divide overgrown clumps in spring. Do not disturb clumps unnecessarily.
Planting: Needs well-drained soil. To prepare the bed, dig over the soil and work in a large quantity of compost, together with some general fertiliser and superphosphate or bone meal.
Watering and feeding: Water regularly, especially during summer. Feed during spring with a general fertiliser for flowering plants. Keep plants well mulched with compost.
Uses: Excellent in large clumps near water, or in the mixed perennial border. Attracts nectar-feeding birds.
Varieties: *K. linearifolia* bears unusual maroon flowers that become yellow in summer and autumn. *K.* x hybrid 'Yellow Cheer' grows up to 40 cm tall and bears bright yellow flowers in summer. *K. praecox* flowers in winter, with orange buds which open to yellow flowers. It is drought tolerant.

Cut flowers Prolong the vase life of fragile blooms like Inca lilies, agapanthus, Japanese anemone, red hot poker, perennial phlox, cornflower and beach speedwell by adding a teaspoon of sugar and a few drops of household bleach to the water. This will help prevent blooms from wilting and dropping their petals prematurely.

Lampranthus species
Mesembryanthemum, Vygie

Size: 30 cm

Growth habit: This perennial succulent is indigenous to the southwestern Cape. Its size varies from round bushes of about 70 cm high to low-creeping ground covers. Foliage is cylindrical, three sided and smooth. Flowers appear in all shades of pink, purple, orange and yellow and have a glistening sheen on the petals. Flowers only open in full sunshine. The spring-flowering vygie is excellent for the dry garden, where bushes become entirely covered with flowers. Propagate by cuttings taken after flowering.

Planting: It must have well-drained soil. Very easy to grow.

Watering and feeding: This is not a demanding plant. It should be watered occasionaly during winter in summer rainfall regions. Do not overfeed.

Uses: This plant is a must for the dry rock garden or any arid garden. It attracts butterflies.

Varieties: 'Desert Sparkler' has bright orange-red flowers. 'Red Surprise' bears bright red flowers. 'Purple Giant' has large purple flowers. 'Salmon Surprise' features salmon-coloured flowers.

Lantana montevidensis 'Sundancer'
Dwarf lantana, Dwerglantana

Size: 30 x 50 cm

Growth habit: The dwarf lantana is a spreading, compact-growing plant and bears yellow flowers throughout the year. Very elegant, dark green, aromatic foliage. Excellent garden subject for covering large areas in hot climatic regions. This lantana is not invasive. Prune when necessary.

Planting: It prefers well-drained soil. To prepare the bed, dig over the soil and work in a large quantity of compost and well-rotted manure, together with some general fertiliser and superphosphate or bone meal.

Watering and feeding: Water the dwarf lantana during hot, dry weather and feed in spring with a general fertiliser for flowering plants.

Uses: Fine rock garden plant and ground cover for large areas. Excellent container plant on the hot patio. Attracts butterflies.

Varieties: *L. montevidensis*, a low-growing shrub, has a creeping habit and mauve flowers. 'Rosie' is similar, but with light pink flowers in summer. 'Malan's Gold' has yellow-green foliage with lilac flowers in summer. 'White Lightning' is a white-flowering form.

Rock gardens When building a rock garden, try to place rocks in such a manner that they look as natural as possible. Soil must drain well but not be too sandy. For a natural look, plant indigenous perennials like wild iris, marigolds, dwarf Natal plum, kingfisher daisies, vygies, *Othonna* and wild garlic.

Limonium perezi
Giant statice, Reusepapierblom

Size: 50 x 40 cm

Growth habit: This shrubby perennial has large leaves, which are almost stalkless and grow in basal rosettes to form dense clumps. Large heads of flat, crinkle-paper-like, violet-blue and white flowers appear in winter, spring and early summer, and are resistant to sea spray. It self-seeds freely under ideal conditions.

Planting: It prefers well-drained, sandy soil. To prepare the bed, dig over the soil and work in a large quantity of compost, together with some general fertiliser and superphosphate or bone meal.

Watering and feeding: Water during hot, dry weather and feed in spring with a general fertiliser for flowering plants.

Uses: Excellent as a cut flower, it should be cut just as it opens and hung upside down to dry in a cool, airy place.

Liriope muscari 'Variegata'
Lily turf, Perklelie

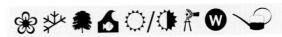

Size: 30 cm

Growth habit: This clump-forming, rhizomatous perennial with cream-striped, grass-like leaves is an excellent ground cover in shaded and semi-shaded positions. Its purple flowers are hyacinth-like, borne on short stems, and appear during summer and autumn. Cut back untidy leaves in early spring, just before new foliage appears. Divide overgrown clumps in spring.

Planting: It prefers well-drained soil. To prepare the bed, dig over the soil and work in a large quantity of compost and well-rotted manure, together with some general fertiliser and superphosphate or bone meal.

Watering and feeding: Water well during the active growing season. Feed with a general fertiliser for foliage plants during early spring.

Uses: Lovely ground cover for edging beds and pathways. It also makes a good container plant.

Varieties: *L. spicata* 'Silver Ribbon,' the creeping lily turf, is a tuft-forming, spreading perennial with silver-green foliage and pink flowers. It is excellent for mass display and colour contrast planting.

Weed roots and bulbils When dividing overgrown perennials where weeds were a problem, be careful to remove all roots and bulbils of weeds that might be left among perennial roots before replanting. Do this by hosing down the root mass of the split perennial to wash out stubborn weed bulbils and roots.

103

Lysimachia nummularia 'Aurea'
Yellow creeping Jenny/Moneywort

Size: 5 cm

Growth habit: This creeping Jenny is a prostrate and vigorous spreader and has a most attractive combination of round-shaped leaves, which are yellow-green in full sun and lime-green in shade. Cup-shaped yellow flowers on short stems are borne during summer and are a bonus. Stems take root wherever they touch damp soil to form a dense mat.

Planting: It prefers soil on the acid side. To prepare the bed, dig over the soil and work in a large quantity of compost and well-rotted manure, together with some general fertiliser and superphosphate or bone meal.

Watering and feeding: Needs to be well watered. Feed with liquid fertiliser during spring.

Uses: Fine for contrast planting. Excellent in damp and boggy areas. Also good between stepping stones in partly shaded areas. Good for hanging baskets.

Varieties: *L. nummularia* is similar but with bright green foliage. *L. congestiflora* 'Outback Sunset' is a low-growing perennial, about 20 cm high, has yellow leaves with green centres and bears clusters of golden-yellow flowers.

Microlepia speluncae
No common name available

Size: 1 m

Growth habit: This strong-growing fern with creeping rhizomes has lovely, soft, papery, pale green fronds covered with sparse, soft hairs, giving it a light, airy appearance. Propagate the plant by division in spring.

Planting: To prepare the bed, dig over the soil and work in a large quantity of compost and well-rotted manure, with some general fertiliser and superphosphate or bone meal.

Watering and feeding: Water regularly to keep the root zone moist. Feed in spring with a nitrogen fertiliser. Keep plants well mulched with compost to help with moisture retention.

Uses: This plant is beautiful in shady areas, and it can take fairly dry conditions. It is an excellent plant to use as a backdrop for clivias and under large tree ferns. Makes an ideal container plant for the shady patio.

Keep root ball intact To keep the root ball of a plant intact without disturbing the root system, cut off the base of the nursery bag, plant with the bag still covering the sides into well-prepared ground, and slip the bag up and over the top once the soil has been firmed down well around the root ball. Water well after planting.

Nepeta mussinii
Catmint, Kattekruid

Size: 25 cm

Growth habit: Catmint is a vigorous perennial with delicate, fine, grey-green, aromatic foliage. It is a low-growing and mat-forming plant, which makes an excellent foil for its lovely lavender-blue flowers. It flowers in summer. Cut back after flowering to keep neat and under control.

Planting: Needs well-drained soil. To prepare the bed, dig over the soil and work in a large quantity of compost and well-rotted manure, together with some general fertiliser and superphosphate or bone meal.

Watering and feeding: Water when dry and feed in spring with a general fertiliser for flowering plants.

Uses: A useful plant for covering low banks and also as an edging in the herbaceous border.

Varieties: *N. cataria*, known as catnip or catmint, is more upright, growing up to 90 cm tall with hairy, aromatic, green foliage. It bears small, white flowers in summer. It is very popular with cats.

Ophiopogon japonicus 'Kyoto Dwarf'
Dwarf mondo grass, Dwerg-mondo-gras

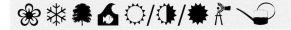

Size: 15 cm

Growth habit: This lovely perennial forms clumps of dark green, leathery, grass-like leaves that reach a length of 15 cm. The leaves of the standard variety are 30 cm. It bears pale mauve flowers, hidden among the foliage, during summer. If an untidy plant is cut short in winter, it will grow beautifully again in spring.

Planting: It prefers moist, well-drained soil. To prepare the bed, dig over the soil and work in a large quantity of compost and well-rotted manure, together with some general fertiliser and superphosphate or bone meal.

Watering and feeding: Water when dry and feed during spring with a general fertiliser for the lawn.

Uses: Highly suited to holding soil along driveways or steep slopes. Excellent, long-lasting ground cover, good between stepping stones or massed together to form a dark green carpet. Can take light traffic occasionally.

Paving Paving can be made very interesting by leaving openings for planting low-growing plants like ground covers or low-growing annuals, or by using natural looking materials such as gravel, small rounded pebbles or rough pine bark chips in between.

Othonna carnosa var. carnosa
No common name available

Size: 10 cm

Growth habit: It is a low-growing, spreading, succulent ground cover with grey, finger-like leaves. It bears small, yellow, daisy-like flowers on thin stalks from spring to autumn.

Planting: It prefers well-drained, fertile soil. To prepare the bed, dig over the soil and work in a large quantity of compost, together with some general fertiliser and superphosphate or bone meal.

Watering and feeding: Water only when very dry, and do not overwater. Feed during spring with a general fertiliser, and water in well.

Uses: This indigenous ground cover is beautiful for colour contrast planting in areas with a temperate climate and also for hot, dry areas. It looks good between stepping stones or next to a paved pathway. It is perfect on slopes and rock gardens, and is ideal for wildlife gardening as the yellow flowers are very attractive to butterflies.

Oxalis depressa 'Pink Star'
Pink clover, Suring

Size: 20 cm

Growth habit: This tuberous, perennial ground cover has green, clover-like leaves and pink flowers from spring to summer. It is fast spreading, and can become weedy.

Planting: It prefers acidic soil. To prepare the bed, dig over the soil and work in a large quantity of compost and well-rotted manure, together with some general fertiliser and superphosphate or bone meal.

Watering and feeding: Water well during winter. Feed with a general fertiliser for flowering plants, and water in well.

Uses: Excellent between stepping stones or as a border next to a pathway.

Varieties: *O. depressa* 'White Star' is similar but with white flowers. 'Bowles White' is compact, growing in winter to 10 cm. It has masses of small, white flowers and is dormant in summer and autumn. *O. purpurea* grows about 7 cm tall and has dark green foliage covered in silky, white hair. Winter growing, it bears pink flowers with a yellow throat.

Utilise water more efficiently Reduce the surface area of the lawn by enlarging flowerbeds and creating gravel pathways through beds planted with tough, drought-tolerant, indigenous plants. Use lots of organic mulch and water-wise ground covers like aptenia, echeveria, *Othonna* and vygies.

Pelargonium x domesticum
Regal pelargonium, Koningspelargonium

Size: 60 x 60 cm

Growth habit: This beautiful perennial shrub has its origins in South Africa. Hybrids are very decorative and form small, sprawling shrubs with woody stems and stiff, pleated, toothed leaves. In spring and summer lovely large clusters of open flowers appear in attractive colours including shades of purple, red, pink and white. Some are bicoloured and others are blotched with more than one colour. Cut back hard after flowering to keep the plant bushy. Remove spent flowers regularly to prolong the flowering period.

Planting: It prefers well-drained, neutral soil. To prepare the bed, dig over the soil and work in a large quantity of compost, together with some general fertiliser and superphosphate or bone meal.

Watering and feeding: Water pelargoniums when dry and feed during the active growth season with a general fertiliser for flowering plants.

Uses: Lovely in pots and as bedding plants.

Varieties: *P. grandiflorum* 'Chocolate' bears dark brown-maroon flowers. 'Pink Cup' has pinkish-orange flowers. 'White Cup' bears white flowers. 'Orange Cup' has orange-coloured flowers.

Pelargonium peltatum
Ivy-leaved pelargonium, Rankpelargonium

Size: 0,3 x 1 m

Growth habit: This trailing perennial is indigenous to the southern and Eastern Cape and has ivy-like, hairless foliage and showy, pink flowers. It is one of the mother plants to many well-known pelargoniums, or geraniums, as they are commonly but incorrectly known.

Planting: It prefers light, well-drained soil. To prepare the bed, dig over the soil and work in a large quantity of compost, together with some general fertiliser and superphosphate or bone meal.

Watering and feeding: Water this plant only when dry. Feed during the active growing season with a general fertiliser for flowering plants.

Uses: Ideal for hanging baskets, to trail over retaining walls, window boxes and pots.

Varieties: *P.* x *zonale*, known as geraniums or zonal pelargoniums, have velvety, round-shaped, undulating leaves and a distinctive darker marking. Flowers are massed on long-stemmed heads and can be either single or double.

Dried manure Use dried manure as a compost activator and sprinkle it over the soil to dig into beds before planting out perennials and vegetables. It can also be used to make liquid manure: place it in a cloth or plastic woven bag and immerse it in a bucket of water, then use this water to feed tired-looking perennials.

Phlox paniculata
Perennial phlox, Meerjarige floksie

Size: 80 cm
Growth habit: It is an upright-growing perennial which bears large spikes of densely packed flowers in summer. Different varieties are available in a range of colours, including white, pink, salmon, lavender, lilac, red and purple, and some have white eyes. It must be cut down after flowering. Divide overgrown clumps in autumn, usually every three to four years. Watch out for powdery mildew and red spider mite. It does not grow well in humid, subtropical climates.
Planting: It prefers fertile, well-drained soil. To prepare the bed, dig over the soil and work in a large quantity of compost and well-rotted manure, together with some general fertiliser and superphosphate or bone meal.
Watering and feeding: Water regularly and feed in spring with a general fertiliser for flowering plants.
Uses: Lovely in the mixed perennial border.
Varieties: *P. maculata* 'Alpha' is an upright perennial with pink flowers. Other varieties have flowers ranging from white to pink, with a distinctive eye in the centre. These are semi-dormant in winter.

Phlox stolonifera
Creeping phlox

Size: 20 cm
Growth habit: An evergreen, spreading, perennial ground cover for cold gardens. During early summer, it bears small cup-shaped flowers in shades of white, blue and pink, depending on the variety. Cut back flowering shoots after they have finished flowering in summer.
Planting: Prefers moist, acid soil. To prepare the bed, dig over the soil and work in a large quantity of acid compost or peat moss, together with some general fertiliser and superphosphate or bone meal.
Watering and feeding: Water regularly and feed with fertiliser for acid-loving plants in spring.
Uses: Lovely ground cover for the rock garden or between and in front of azaleas.
Varieties: *P. subulata* (Alpine phlox) provides a spectacular springtime display, and few ground covers can equal this little beauty, which forms a mat of mid-green leaves and produces purple, pink or blue flowers. Does well in cold gardens.

Larger flowers from perennials If you want to obtain stronger and larger flowers from perennials like phlox and shasta daisies, thin out the new shoots by half during spring. This will channel all the energy into the remaining shoots, resulting in bigger and better flowers.

Phyla nodiflora
Daisy lawn/Lippia

Size: 15 cm

Growth habit: Daisy lawn is a perennial, spreading ground cover and forms a thick mat sturdy enough to serve as a lawn. It has grey-green leaves and small, lilac to rose flowers from spring to autumn. Can be cut with a lawnmower when too high or untidy. Tends to become untidy in winter, and needs to be watered and fed early in spring to bring it back to life. Drought tolerant once established.

Planting: Not very fussy about soil. To prepare the area, dig over the soil and work in a large quantity of compost and well-rotted manure, together with some general fertiliser and superphosphate or bone meal.

Watering and feeding: Water regularly and feed in spring with a general fertiliser for foliage plants.

Uses: Lovely alternative to grass-type lawn in areas where grass would be difficult to maintain. Attracts butterflies.

Plectranthus ciliatus
Speckled spur-flower, Gespikkelde muishondblaar

Size: 25 cm

Growth habit: This herbaceous perennial with a spreading habit grows up to about 25 cm high in light shade. Foliage has maroon-purple reverse to the leaves and stems take root quite easily where they touch the ground. Bears long plumes of lilac to white speckled flowers in autumn. Easily propagated with cuttings.

Planting: It prefers rich, well-drained soil on the acid side. To prepare the area, dig over the soil and work in a large quantity of compost and well-rotted manure, together with some general fertiliser and superphosphate or bone meal.

Watering and feeding: Water well until established, whereafter it only needs to be watered when dry. Feed with a general fertiliser for foliage plants throughout the active growing season.

Uses: Excellent container plant or ground cover for shady areas in subtropical and coastal gardens. Attracts butterflies.

Varieties: *P. ambiguus* (large-flowered plectranthus) is a very showy ground cover for shady areas. Spreading, soft plant with long, narrow purple flowers in autumn. *P. lucidus* is flat-creeping with glossy foliage and bears spikes of white flowers. *P. verticillatus* (gossip) is fast spreading with fleshy, round leaves and spikes of white-mauve flowers in semi-shade.

Spacing ground covers When planting ground covers such as carpet bugle, dwarf Natal plum, ground morning glory, creeping Jenny, *Othonna*, etc., do not plant them too close together. Rather cover spaces in between with organic mulch, allowing plants to establish themselves to their natural height and size and thus reach their full potential.

Polygonum capitatum
Ground polygonum/Knotweed, Knoopkruid

Size: 15 cm

Growth habit: This fast-growing, evergreen ground cover needs to be kept in check. Leaves are attractively coloured and tinged brick red, turning crimson in full sun in autumn. The leaves stay green in the shade. In spring, summer and autumn the plant is festooned with masses of round heads of closely packed, pink flowers. Self-seeds easily and can be invasive if not controlled.

Planting: Not fussy but will benefit from well-prepared soil. Dig over the soil and work in a large quantity of compost and well-rotted manure, together with some general fertiliser and superphosphate or bone meal.

Watering and feeding: Water when dry. Feed during spring with any balanced fertiliser.

Uses: As the ground polygonum is low growing, it is ideal for covering banks and stopping soil erosion in record time.

Potentilla fruticosa
Cinquefoil, Vyfvingerkruie/Ganserik

Size: 1 x 1,5 m

Growth habit: This dense, bushy, perennial shrub has dark green foliage made up out of leaves with 5 smaller leaflets. It flowers in spring to autumn, with large, saucer-shaped, yellow flowers. It thrives in cooler regions, and is not recommended for warm or humid, tropical regions.

Planting: It prefers well-drained, fertile soil. To prepare the area, dig over the soil and work in a large quantity of compost and well-rotted manure, together with some general fertiliser and superphosphate or bone meal.

Watering and feeding: Water when dry and feed during spring with a general fertiliser for flowering plants.

Uses: Excellent for the rock garden or the mixed perennial and shrub border.

Varieties: 'Goldfinger' is a bushy shrub up to 1,5 m tall with large, yellow flowers from spring to autumn. It has dark green foliage. *P. nepalensis* 'Miss Willmott' grows up to 45 cm tall and bears deep pink flowers and strawberry-like foliage. Divide overgrown plants in spring.

Cut flowers When cutting flowers from perennials, the best time is late in the afternoon or early in the morning. Place cut flowers immediately in a container filled with cold water right up to their necks. Store in a cool room away from draughts for about 10 hours before arranging them, thereby allowing them to have a long drink of water.

Primula acaulis
Primrose, Sleutelblom

Size: 25 x 25 cm

Growth habit: This short-lived perennial is usually treated as an annual in South Africa. It is neat and compact with large, flat, scented flowers surrounded by a rosette of green leaves. Flowers come with a great variety of brilliant, clear shades from yellow to bright blue and red. Remove spent flowers and dead leaves regularly to keep the plant neat.

Planting: It prefers fertile, well-drained soil. To prepare the area, dig over the soil and work in a large quantity of compost and well-rotted manure, together with some general fertiliser and superphosphate or bone meal.

Watering and feeding: Water regularly and deeply. Feed during spring with a general fertiliser for flowering plants.

Uses: This is an excellent pot plant for the partly shady patio or for borders.

Varieties: 'Pageant Series' grow up to 15 cm tall and flower very early, excellent for containers. Colours include red with yellow eye, shades of pink with yellow eye, and yellow with scarlet outer edges to name a few. 'Diana Series' grow 15 cm tall, flower early and grow vigorously, with flowers in blue, lemon-yellow, rose, scarlet, white and golden-yellow.

Rumohra adiantiformis
Leather leaf fern, Seweweeksvaring

Size: 90 cm

Growth habit: This fern spreads by means of creeping, branched rhizomes in shady, moist areas of a sheltered garden. Dark green fronds are triangular in shape, leathery and double compound. Divide overgrown ferns in early spring. Watch out for scale and mealy bug.

Planting: It prefers moist, fertile soil. To prepare the area, dig over the soil and work in a large quantity of compost and well-rotted manure, together with some general fertiliser and superphosphate or bone meal.

Watering and feeding: Water and feed regularly throughout the active growth season. Keep on watering the fern in winter to keep roots constantly moist, but not soggy. Feed with a fertiliser for foliage plants once a month, and water in well.

Uses: Excellent for flower arranging. Its leathery, dark green fronds last very well in water when cut.

Mulch for ferns Use dried horse manure to mulch ferns such as leather leaf ferns. This will help the plants to retain moisture and feed them at the same time.

Ruscus aculeatus
Butcher's broom/Box holly, Vuurwerkbos

Size: 1 m

Growth habit: It is a tough, rhizomatous, upright-growing subshrub. It has dark green, stiff, spiny leaves which are actually flattened shoots on which the flowers and fruits are borne. Male and female flowers are small, star-shaped and green and are borne on separate plants, so that the showy, red berries will only appear if both are present. Divide overgrown clumps in spring.

Planting: It is not fussy but will benefit from well-drained soil. To prepare the area, dig over the soil and work in a large quantity of compost and well-rotted manure, together with some general fertiliser and superphosphate or bone meal.

Watering and feeding: Water when dry and feed in spring with a general fertiliser for foliage plants.

Uses: Wonderful cut flower material and excellent as a ground cover under large trees.

Salvia farinacea
Mealy-cup sage, Blou salie

Size: 75 x 50 cm

Growth habit: This fast-growing, upright perennial can be utilised as an annual in cold areas. It grows into a mound with grey-green, lance-shaped foliage, and spikes of intense violet-blue flowers appear during the summer months. Divide overgrown clumps in spring.

Planting: It prefers light, well-drained soil. To prepare the area, dig over the soil and work in a large quantity of compost and well-rotted manure, together with some general fertiliser and superphosphate or bone meal.

Watering and feeding: Water regularly during summer and feed with a general fertiliser for flowering plants.

Uses: Excellent for the mixed perennial border or rock garden. Attracts butterflies.

Varieties: *S. farinacea* 'Victoria' is similar to the above but with deep blue flowers on long, bluish stems.

Healthy soil Think twice before using chemical pesticides for killing pests. There are many organisms which are beneficial to us like earthworms, bees, butterflies, and numerous soil-dwelling micro-organisms that will also disappear when coming into contact with pesticides.

Santolina chamaecyparissus
Lavender cotton, Sipreskruid

Size: 50 cm

Growth habit: This small, aromatic shrub is native to the Mediterranean coastal areas. Its lovely, silvery-grey foliage is divided into tiny segments, with rounded, yellow flowers borne on long stalks in summer. Remove any spent flowers and untidy stems in autumn to encourage new growth.

Planting: It must have well-drained soil. To prepare the bed, dig over the soil and work in a large quantity of compost and well-rotted manure, together with some general fertiliser and superphosphate or bone meal.

Watering and feeding: Water regularly during winter, and feed in spring with a general fertiliser for flowering plants.

Uses: It is excellent for colour contrast planting in the perennial border or as a ground cover on sloping areas.

Scabiosa columbaria 'Butterfly Blue'
Cornflower, Koringblom

Size: 50 x 75 cm

Growth habit: This lovely hybrid perennial produces many flowers of a deep lavender-blue throughout the year. Foliage forms a dense mound and is grey-green to green and finely cut. Flowers resemble pincushions and are borne on slender, erect stems. Dead flower heads should be removed for perpetual flowering. Does best in full sun. Divide overgrown clumps in early spring.

Planting: Prefers well-drained, alkaline soil. To prepare the bed, dig over the soil and work in a large quantity of compost, together with some general fertiliser and superphosphate or bone meal.

Watering and feeding: Water it regularly and feed during spring with a general fertiliser for flowering plants.

Uses: Lovely in the perennial border and as a ground cover. Flowers last well in the vase. Attracts butterflies.

Varieties: 'Blue Terrace' is prolific and bears blue flowers. 'Pink Mist' bears pink, pincushion-shaped flowers.

Supporting new growth New perennial growth can be supported by pushing branched twigs, slightly shorter than the overall height of the plant, into the soil among the perennials so that new shoots can use the twigs as support, which will help prevent new shoots from flopping over.

Scaevola aemula 'Purple Fanfare'
Fairy fan flower

Size: 25 x 30 cm

Growth habit: It is a herbaceous, evergreen perennial native to Australia and has a spreading, ground-hugging habit. Foliage is thick, coarsely toothed and dark green. It bears lavender-purple, fan-shaped flowers with a yellow centre from late winter throughout summer.

Planting: It prefers light, well-drained soil. To prepare the bed, dig over the soil and work in a large quantity of compost and well-rotted manure, together with some general fertiliser and superphosphate or bone meal.

Watering and feeding: Water when dry and feed during spring with a general fertiliser for flowering plants.

Uses: Ideal for hanging baskets and makes a lovely colourful ground cover in areas with a temperate climate.

Varieties: 'Pink Fanfare' bears pink flowers with a yellow eye. It is also available in a white-flowering form. 'Sunfan' is a compact grower bearing lots of mauve flowers from spring to autumn. 'Sunfan' is ideal for outdoor containers and hanging baskets.

Solidago virgaurea
European goldenrod, Goudroede

Size: 50 cm

Growth habit: Solidago is a rhizomatous perennial with showy, dense, yellow plumes that rise well above lance-shaped, mid-green leaves from late summer to autumn. The plant forms a neat, round bush. The goldenrod can become invasive and must be controlled. Divide overgrown clumps in autumn or spring.

Planting: It prefers fertile, well-drained soil. To prepare the bed, dig over the soil and work in a large quantity of compost and well-rotted manure, together with some general fertiliser and superphosphate or bone meal.

Watering and feeding: Water it regularly and feed during spring with a general fertiliser for flowering plants.

Uses: An excellent florist's flower. Wonderful for the mixed perennial border where colour is needed towards autumn.

Varieties: 'Golden Crown' grows 80 cm tall, with plumes of fine, yellow flowers in summer. Ideal cut flower.

Wider pathways, less maintenance Make paths through beds wider than necessary in order to allow ground covers to spread out without growing over the walkway. This will save a lot of time when trimming growth back regularly.

Stachys byzantina
Lamb's ears, Lamsoor

Size: 25 cm

Growth habit: This evergreen perennial has a dense, spreading growth habit. Its small, mauve-pink flowers appear during summer but this ground cover is in fact more sought after for its soft and woolly-looking silvery-white foliage than for its flowers. Foliage tends to become mushy during heavy rain or during cold, humid and wet weather. Severe frost will damage the leaves but the plant will quickly recover in spring. It is drought tolerant. Cut lamb's ears back in spring in order to promote new growth.

Planting: Must have well-drained, moderately fertile soil. To prepare the bed, dig over the soil and work in a large quantity of compost, together with some general fertiliser and superphosphate or bone meal.

Watering and feeding: Water only when dry, and feed during spring with a general fertiliser for foliage plants.

Uses: Lovely ground cover or border plant for colour contrast. Effective edging plant for pathways.

Varieties: Also available in a lime-green form.

Sutera campanulata
White phlox, Witfloksies

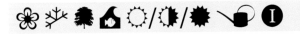

Size: 7,5 cm

Growth habit: This fast-growing, spreading perennial ground cover is indigenous to the Eastern Cape. The foliage is rounded and bright green, forming a lovely background for masses of dainty white flowers throughout the year. It needs ample water if grown in full sun, but prefers a semi-shaded position to look its best.

Planting: Prefers rich, fertile soil. To prepare the bed, dig over the soil and work in a large quantity of compost and well-rotted manure, together with some general fertiliser and superphosphate or bone meal.

Watering and feeding: Water regularly and feed during the active growing season with a balanced general fertiliser.

Uses: A fine container plant, it also does well at the coast, enjoying compost-enriched soil.

Varieties: *S. cordata* is a very neat, fast-growing, trailing ground cover with white or mauve, star-like flowers from autumn to spring. It can be grown in sun or shade. Good in hanging baskets.

Bog plants in ordinary beds Create a bog garden by digging a hole as large as the area needed for planting arum lilies or Louisiana irises. Line the hole with heavy-duty plastic, trim the edges at soil level and fill with enough water to form a dam at the bottom. Fill with a mixture of compost and soil and plant bog plants into this area. Water normally.

Trifolium repens 'Atropurpurea'
Black shamrock, Swart klawer

Size: 10 cm

Growth habit: This herbaceous perennial forms a striking, low-spreading ground cover of shamrock-like, black-purple and green leaves. It bears small, insignificant heads of pea-like, white flowers in summer. Needs a sunny, hot position on the dry side. It is a vigorous grower and can become invasive if not kept under control. Divide overgrown plants in spring. Spreads by means of self-seeding as well.

Planting: Prefers well-drained soil. To prepare the bed, dig over the soil and work in a large quantity of compost and well-rotted manure, together with some general fertiliser and superphosphate or bone meal.

Watering and feeding: Water when dry and feed in spring with a general fertiliser for foliage plants.

Uses: This is an excellent ground cover for colour contrast planting and rock gardens.

Tulbaghia violacea
Wild garlic, Wildeknoffel

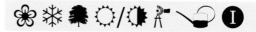

Size: 30 x 20 cm

Growth habit: Wild garlic is indigenous to the eastern summer rainfall regions of South Africa. A bulbous perennial plant, it is clump-forming with strong-smelling, garlic-scented, grey, strap-like leaves. It bears sweetly scented umbels of mauve flowers on long stems almost throughout the year but mostly in summer. Leave undisturbed as long as possible for best flowering. Overgrown clumps can be divided in early spring when necessary.

Planting: It is not fussy. To prepare the bed, dig over the soil and work in a large quantity of compost and well-rotted manure, together with some general fertiliser and superphosphate or bone meal.

Watering and feeding: Water when dry. It will benefit from feeding in spring with a general fertiliser for flowering plants.

Uses: Excellent ground cover for large areas. It is traditionally believed to keep snakes away.

Varieties: *T. violacea* 'Silver Lace' is a beautiful perennial with white-edged, blue-grey leaves that become pink in cold winters. It bears delicate, mauve flowers in summer.

How deep to plant When planting out a perennial bought from the nursery into the garden, make sure the existing soil level in the container or plant bag is at the same level as the garden soil when planted. This ensures successful growth without any problems.

Verbena peruviana
Verbena, Ysterkruid

Size: 5 cm
Growth habit: This perennial ground cover spreads rapidly. It has dark green, irregularly shaped and toothed leaves. It is free flowering with masses of rounded heads composed of small flowers in shades of white, red, pink and purple that appear from spring to autumn. Remove spent flowers to encourage a longer flowering period.
Planting: Does well in virtually any soil. To prepare the bed, dig over the soil and work in a large quantity of compost and well-rotted manure, together with some general fertiliser and superphosphate or bone meal.
Watering and feeding: Water it when dry and feed during spring with a general fertiliser for flowering plants.
Uses: Excellent, colourful ground cover for sunny beds. Attracts butterflies.
Varieties: 'Dragon Eye' grows about 15 cm high. It has a spreading growth habit and dark blue flowers. 'Forest Fire' is similar but with bright red flowers.

Veronica longifolia
Beach speedwell

Size: 1 m
Growth habit: This clump-forming, herbaceous perennial has deep green, narrow, tapering and toothed leaves. During summer it produces upright racemes of closely packed purple-blue flowers on 10-cm stems. They should be cut down after flowering. Divide the overgrown clumps in spring. Easy to grow.
Planting: Not fussy about soil. To prepare the bed, dig over the soil and work in a large quantity of compost and well-rotted manure, together with some general fertiliser and superphosphate or bone meal.
Watering and feeding: Water regularly and feed in spring with a general fertiliser for flowering plants.
Uses: Beautiful perennial for the middle or background mixed perennial border. Flowers last well in the vase.
Varieties: *V. spicata* 'Rosea' is suitable for both sun and semi-shade, and has mid-green, oblong, toothed leaves and spikes with pink flowers.

Dishwashing liquid Use a few drops of household dishwashing liquid as a wetting agent when spraying insecticides or fungicides. This will prevent the chemical from being washed off by irrigation water or a sudden shower of rain after spraying. It serves the same purpose as commercial wetting agents specially formulated for this purpose.

Vinca major 'Variegata'
Periwinkle, Maagdeblom

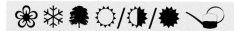

Size: 25 cm

Growth habit: Periwinkles are slender-stemmed, trailing perennials which make ideal ground covers. Foliage is round-shaped and variegated with yellow and green. Attractive purple blue flowers appear during spring. Plants flower better when they get more sun. They may become invasive and must be controlled by cutting back the trailing stems in winter.

Planting: Not fussy about soil, but will benefit from enriched soil. To prepare the bed, dig over the soil and work in a large quantity of compost and well-rotted manure, together with some general fertiliser and superphosphate or bone meal.

Watering and feeding: Water regularly during hot, dry weather and feed in spring with a general fertiliser for foliage plants.

Uses: Lovely as a ground cover in semi-shaded areas or in hanging baskets and containers, with its showy, long, trailing stems hanging down.

Other species: *V. minor* 'Illumination' grows only about 15 cm tall and has very pretty, small, golden-yellow foliage with a green margin. Bears blue flowers from spring to summer.

Viola hederacea
Australian violet, Australiese viooltjie

Size: 10 cm

Growth habit: This is an evergreen, creeping perennial with a vigorous, spreading habit. It has attractive, pale green leaves and bears lovely, short-stemmed, mauve and white flowers with a violet-like appearance during summer. Can become invasive if not controlled. Prefers semi-shaded positions. Propagate by division in early spring.

Planting: To prepare the bed before planting, dig over the soil and work in a large quantity of compost and well-rotted manure, with some general fertiliser and superphosphate or bone meal.

Watering and feeding: Water regularly and feed with a general fertiliser for flowering plants in spring.

Uses: This is one of the most charming ground covers for shade or semi-shade, and it does very well even with a full morning of sun.

Varieties: *V. hederacea* 'Baby Blue', a mini-violet, is similar but has much smaller, deeper blue flowers. Extremely fetching, it is not a vigorous grower.

Buy perennials economically When buying perennials look out for those pots or bags that are really full and well established, so that you can divide and split the root ball to obtain as many new plants as possible and thus cover a larger area when planting them out into the garden.

Viola odorata
English violet/Sweet violet, Viooltjie

Size: 15 cm

Growth habit: This spreading, rhizomatous perennial prefers cool, moist soil conditions and is an old favourite. It bears fragrant, deep purple, pink or white flowers and dark, heart-shaped leaves. It performs at its best in light shade. It flowers in late winter and early spring. Divide overgrown clumps in spring; it is also self-seeding.

Planting: It needs moist, well-drained soil that is not too rich. To prepare the bed, dig over the soil and work in a large quantity of compost, together with some general fertiliser and superphosphate or bone meal.

Watering and feeding: Water regularly. It is not demanding. Feed with a fertiliser for flowering plants during spring, and water in well.

Uses: Much-loved florist's flower. Excellent ground cover for edging in semi-shaded positions.

Varieties: *V. odorata* 'The Czar' bears fragrant, blue flowers in spring.

Zantedeschia aethiopica
Arum lily, Aronskelk/Varkoor

Size: 1 x 0,5 m

Growth habit: This tuberous perennial is indigenous to the Western Cape, KwaZulu-Natal and Mpumalanga. It is a moisture-loving plant with attractive, white spathes with large, glossy, somewhat arrow-shaped, broad leaves. Flowers during winter and spring in winter rainfall areas and during spring and summer in summer rainfall areas. Divide overgrown clumps in spring.

Planting: It prefers moist, rich soil. To prepare the bed, dig over the soil and work in a large quantity of compost and well-rotted manure, together with some general fertiliser and superphosphate or bone meal.

Watering and feeding: Water regularly and feed with a balanced fertiliser during the active growing season.

Uses: It has excellent, long-lasting cut flowers. Lovely for damp, shaded areas or bog gardens.

Varieties: *Z. aethiopica* 'Green Goddess' (green arum lily) is a popular variety and provides wonderful cut flowers. 'Speck Leaf' has lovely, white-spotted green leaves and white flowers. *Z. pentlandii* (yellow arum lily) is deciduous, and has deep yellow blooms. It does well in positions in sun to semi-sun. *Z. rehmannii* (pink arum lily), also deciduous, is another sun-lover.

Arum lilies Leave them in the ground as long as possible, without disturbing them, until they start to become too overcrowded. Keep them mulched with lots of compost and well-rotted manure, and water deeply at least twice a week during summer.

Bulbs are not only colourful, they are among the easiest of plants to grow. Many of the bulbs in our gardens are indigenous to South Africa and have been hybridised overseas. They make wonderful cut flowers and many are fragrant as well.

Bulbs are perennial storage organs and their foliage remains green after flowering for some time to be able to manufacture food for the next season's growth and flowers. Let the foliage die down naturally after flowering before cutting it off.

When buying bulbs, follow the planting instructions on the package, which will include planting depth, spacing and the position for sun or shade. Prepare the soil in advance and plant bold groups of the same species to show them to their best advantage. Bulbs are also excellent container plants for spring and for general use on the patio.

Treated bulbs are those that receive a special cold treatment to force them into flower earlier, as opposed to untreated bulbs which will flower much later in the season. Tulips and hyacinths are examples of bulbs commonly sold as treated bulbs

There are two major planting seasons for bulbs: late autumn (late March to early June) for winter/spring-flowering varieties, and spring (early August through to late October) for dahlias, gladioli and a number of other summer-flowering varieties, with liliums being planted from May through to September.

Summer-flowering bulbs include allium, amaryllis, begonia, chlidanthus, dahlia, eucomis, galtonia, gladiolus, hippeastrum, lilium, nerine, sprekelia and tuberosa. Some winter-flowering bulbs are anemone, babiana, dutch iris, freesia, hyacinth, ixia, lachenalia, leucojum, muscari, narcissus, ornithogalum, ranunculus, sparaxis, tritonia and tulip.

bulbs

Allium neapolitanum
Florist allium, Ster van Persië

Size: 0,3 m
Growth habit: This close relative of the onion is a deciduous, bulbous plant, dormant during summer. It bears umbels of white flowers on 25-cm stems in late winter and early spring. It does very well in semi-shaded positions and looks stunning when planted close together in a large group. It can be left in the soil for many years without lifting every season. Not prone to diseases or attack by insects.
Planting: It prefers well-drained soil. Plant in autumn when the soil has cooled down. Prepare the bed by loosening the soil to a depth of 20 cm, mixing in a 5-cm layer of compost and kraal manure at the same time. Plant bulbs twice as deep as the diameter of the bulb, mulch and water deeply.
Watering and feeding: Water regularly throughout the growing season. Does not need any extra feeding.
Uses: Alliums make excellent cut flowers or container plants for early spring. Very good for the rock garden or when grouped together in the mixed border.

Amaryllis belladonna
Belladonna lily/March lily, Belladonnalelie

Size: 0,5 m
Growth habit: Endemic to the winter rainfall region of the southwestern Cape, this large, deciduous, winter-growing bulb is dormant during summer. A large umbel of fragrant, pink to white, trumpet-shaped flowers on tall stems appears during autumn, before the strap-shaped leaves emerge. Plants can, however, remain evergreen in the summer rainfall regions if watered regularly. Do not move bulbs for many years as they don't take well to being transplanted, and so may not flower for a few seasons. They are susceptible to the amaryllis caterpillar or lily borer.
Planting: It prefers well-drained, fertile soil. Prepare the soil by digging a thick layer of compost into the soil to a depth of 30 cm. Plant bulbs during early summer with the neck of the bulb at soil level.
Watering and feeding: Water them only after leaves have appeared and bulbs show active growth. Do not need a lot of attention. Feed once with a bulb food in late summer.
Uses: Very good in the rock garden or in containers.

Amaryllis caterpillars Plant large clumps of indigenous *Albuca* bulbs, the natural host plant for these caterpillars, to entice moths away from clivia and amaryllis plants. Plants can also be sprayed with garlic spray to act as a repellent.

Anemone coronaria x hybrids
Wind flower, Anemoon

Size: 0,2 m

Growth habit: One of the most popular winter-growing bulbs in South Africa. It is a deciduous, tuberous rhizome, which is dormant during summer. Flowers are single ('De Caen') or double ('St Brigid') and colours range from white to blue, red and purple, usually with a contrasting centre colour. This compact little plant has masses of blooms, which multiply with picking and make delightful cut flowers. Avoid planting in a position that has hot afternoon sun. It is susceptible to mildew if watered late in the afternoon, or during long periods of damp weather.

Planting: Plant during autumn in batches to prolong the flowering period. Prepare the bed by loosening the soil to a depth of 20 cm, mixing in a 5-cm layer of compost and kraal manure at the same time. Plant tubers in well-drained soil with the pointed end facing downwards or to the side and cover with about 2 cm of soil.

Watering and feeding: Keep plant constantly moist at root level. Once planted it needs little attention except for regular, deep watering and cutting to keep it flowering for longer. Water once with liquid fertiliser when flowers start to appear.

Uses: Gives beautiful cut flowers for spring. It is also an excellent subject in the colour border.

Babiana striata x hybrids
Babiana/Baboon flower, Bobbejaantjie

Size: 0,2 m

Growth habit: The babiana is endemic to the southwestern Cape. A winter-growing corm, it is dormant during summer. Foliage is linearly ribbed and hairy. During spring, spikes with star-shaped flowers appear, with flower colours ranging from white and cream to blue, mauve and red, some with contrasting centres. It is not necessary to lift corms in the winter rainfall regions. Lift corms in early summer in the summer rainfall regions for replanting in autumn. Foliage is susceptible to red spider mite during warm, dry weather.

Planting: Plant corms during autumn when the soil temperature has cooled down. The babiana prefers sandy, well-drained soil. Prepare the bed by loosening the soil to a depth of 20 cm, mixing in a 5-cm layer of compost and kraal manure at the same time. Plant corms at least 8 cm deep.

Watering and feeding: Water regularly in winter to keep the root zone moist. Feed with bulb food once a month when plants have started to flower until foliage starts to die down.

Uses: Lovely in the rock garden or in pots on the sunny patio.

Planting bulbs A general rule is to plant bulbs with the pointed side facing up at a depth of about twice the diameter of the bulb. Anemone corms, however, need to be planted with the point facing downwards, and ranunculus must be planted with the claws facing downwards.

Begonia x hybrids
Tuberous begonia, Begonia

Size: 0,3 m
Growth habit: The tuberous begonia is dormant in winter. It prefers humid, cool, summer conditions and has lovely, decorative foliage with large camellia-like flowers in vivid shades of red, orange, yellow and white. It flowers in summer and autumn. It can be grown in the open ground in dappled shade. When using the begonia outdoors, avoid draughts and windy situations. The begonia is susceptible to mildew under damp growing conditions. Snails and slugs are also very partial to the foliage.
Planting: It prefers a light and well-drained medium, enriched with lots of compost. Plant the tubers with the indented side facing upwards, covered with about 30 mm of compost-enriched soil.
Watering and feeding: Water and feed regularly. Stake the heavy stalks to prevent them from breaking.
Uses: Excellent in hanging baskets, pots and window boxes on the lightly shaded patio.

Chlidanthus fragrance
Peruvian daffodil, Peru-affodil

Size: 0,1 m
Growth habit: The Peruvian daffodil grows in summer and is dormant during winter. Three to four bright yellow, scented, trumpet-shaped flowers are borne in spring before the narrow, semi-upright, strap-shaped leaves appear. Foliage is susceptible to amaryllis caterpillars; watch out for this pest during midsummer. Bulbs can be left undisturbed in the ground in winter, or you can lift and store them until the next spring. Propagate by offsets in early spring.
Planting: Plant in early spring in compost-rich soil. Prepare the bed by loosening the soil to a depth of 20 cm, mixing in a 5-cm layer of compost and kraal manure at the same time. Plant bulbs about 5 cm deep and group them together.
Watering and feeding: Water regularly during the active growing season. Feed with special bulb food once in early summer when foliage is starting to grow actively.
Uses: Good container plant for the patio, or for a sunny spot in the perennial border.

Daffodils that don't flower They may have been planted too late, that is after May. They may also have suffered a dry spell, which causes the bulbs to abort their flower buds, or they may not have been fed well after flowering the previous season.

Dahlia x hybrids
Dahlia

Size: 0,2–2 m

Growth habit: This upright-growing, herbaceous plant has hollow, woody stems. It grows in summer and is dormant during winter. New hybrids give flowers in many shapes, sizes and colours from midsummer until early winter. The tall variety needs staking. Lift tubers during early winter in areas with severe frost and store in a cool, dry place. Powdery mildew can be a problem during wet weather. Aphids and thrips may also attack plants and need to be dealt with when noticed.

Planting: Needs well-drained soil. Plant tubers in compost-enriched beds in late spring. Do not use fresh manure, as this will cause tubers to rot. Keep plants well mulched.

Watering and feeding: Water regularly and do not let the soil dry out between waterings as this will cause the plants to wilt, making them more susceptible to disease and attack by insects. Reduce watering when foliage turns yellow in late autumn. Feed with a general fertiliser for flowering plants once a month during the active growing season.

Uses: Tall varieties are ideal for the background border, with shorter varieties in the front to create a colourful display in the perennial border. Excellent cut flowers. Pick only those flowers with the centre still in bud, having only the outer petals open. When picked fully open, flowers will not last.

Eucomis autumnalis
Pineapple lily, Wildepynappel

Size: 0,75 m x 0,5 m

Growth habit: This upright-growing bulb plant is indigenous to the Eastern Cape, Free State and KwaZulu-Natal. It grows in summer and is dormant in winter. Cylindrical flower-spikes are packed with star-shaped flowers of green, white, cream or purple and crowned with a tuft of small leaves or bracts, resembling a pineapple. Flowers are followed by triangular fruits. Foliage is broad and strap-shaped with wavy edges. Dormant bulbs left undisturbed in the ground will show signs of regrowth early in the following spring.

Planting: The pineapple lily will grow in almost any soil enriched with compost. Prepare the bed by loosening the soil to a depth of 20 cm, mixing in a 5-cm layer of compost and kraal manure at the same time. Plant bulbs with the neck of the bulb level with the soil surface.

Watering and feeding: Water regularly and mulch with compost to help with moisture retention. They will also benefit from a general fertiliser for flowering plants applied at monthly intervals throughout summer.

Uses: Flower-spikes make popular flower-arranging material. Excellent indigenous bulb for the perennial border in full sun.

Varieties: *E. comosa* bears a spike of pink flowers and has a pinkish cast to the foliage.

Perennial bulbs Use perennial bulbs like belladonna lily, crocosmia, spider lily, pineapple lily, galtonia, tuberose, Maltese cross, watsonia and blue squill instead of annual bulbs that need to be replaced every season. Perennial bulbs multiply in the garden and can be lifted and divided when dormant to plant up other areas, thus being much more economical.

Freesia x hybrids
Freesia, Kammetjie

Size: 0,25 m

Growth habit: An indigenous bulb producing flowers with a beautiful scent during spring. Modern hybrids all have trumpet-shaped flowers, borne like a cockscomb on thin 30-cm stems. Colours include blues and purples, pinks, reds and oranges, and the yellows and whites which are the most fragrant. Foliage is lance-shaped and arranged in a fan pattern. Leave corms in the soil for the next season, or lift (only once the foliage has died down) in early summer and store in a dry place at room temperature. Freesias are usually disease- and trouble-free, but foliage may be attacked by slugs and snails.

Planting: Prefers light, well-drained soil. Prepare the bed by loosening soil to a depth of 20 cm, mixing in a 5-cm layer of compost and kraal manure at the same time. Plant corms in autumn, with a covering of 5 cm of soil.

Watering and feeding: Water regularly to keep soil moist at root level. If planted for an annual display no special feeding is necessary. Feed with a general fertiliser for flowering plants if the corms are to be used for the next season. Keep corms mulched with compost.

Uses: Wonderful cut flowers. Can also be planted in groups in the rock garden or perennial border.

Galtonia candicans
Berg lily, Berglelie

Size: 1 m

Growth habit: This summer-growing bulb is indigenous to the Drakensberg range and is dormant during winter. Its foliage forms an erect tuft of fleshy, grey-green leaves. Waxy, white, pendant, bell-shaped flowers on stout flower-spikes can be expected during summer for about six weeks. You can leave it in the same spot for up to four years before lifting and dividing it during winter to replant just under soil level in spring. It flowers better if left undisturbed for a few years. Foliage attracts slugs and snails during wet weather, but it is otherwise disease free.

Planting: It prefers fertile, well-drained soil. Prepare the soil by digging a thick layer of compost and well-rotted manure into the soil to a depth of 30 cm. Plant bulbs during spring with the neck of the bulb at soil level.

Watering and feeding: Water regularly until the foliage dies down. Feed with a general fertiliser for flowering plants during the active growing season. Keep plants well mulched with compost.

Uses: Plant in clumps for a spectacular effect in the mixed perennial border.

Spring- and winter-flowering bulbs
Make a note or mark the place where you plant your winter- and spring-flowering bulbs in autumn so that you do not disturb them when they have died down.

Gladiolus x hybrids
Gladiolus/Sword lily, Swaardlelie

Size: 0,5 m

Growth habit: This is a genus of cormous perennials which grows in summer or winter, depending on the species. It varies from the small, indigenous species to the magnificent, colourful hybrids used mainly for cut flowers. The smaller, indigenous species from the winter rainfall regions grows in winter, and the tall-stemmed hybrids used for cut flowers grow in summer. The gladiolus corm should be treated as an annual, as growing it for a second season is not feasible, due to diseases. Thrips is the most common pest, with attack by red spider mite not so common. Both pests should be treated.

Planting: Prefers well-drained, sandy soil. Prepare the bed by loosening the soil to a depth of 20 cm, mixing in a 5-cm layer of compost and kraal manure at the same time. Plant corms in batches to prolong the flowering period from early summer until early winter. Plant about 100 mm deep.

Watering and feeding: Water regularly to keep the root level moist at all times. Feed every two weeks with liquid fertiliser for flowering plants.

Uses: Well-known cut flowers. To cut them for the vase, simply uproot the corm and cut the stem at the desired length. They also look magnificent grouped together in the background perennial border.

Hippeastrum x hybrids
Amaryllis/Christmas flower, Maartlelie

Size: 0,3 m

Growth habit: This summer-growing bulb is dormant in winter. Flowers are either single and large or double and trumpet-shaped, in colours ranging from white to rose, pink, salmon, orange, red, and red with white stripes. Miniature hybrids are also available. Three to four flowers are borne on a tall, sturdy stem and grow together with strap-shaped foliage. Leave bulbs in the soil without lifting them in areas where winters are mild.

Planting: Prefers well-drained soil. Prepare the bed by loosening the soil to a depth of 20 cm, mixing in a 5-cm layer of compost and kraal manure at the same time. Make sure to leave the neck and shoulder of the bulb above soil level.

Watering and feeding: Water regularly but take care not to overwater. Soil should be kept just moist to prevent root rot. Feed with a general fertiliser for bulbs during the active growth season, to ensure good flowering for the next season.

Uses: Stunning grouped together in a bed. Also excellent pot plants and cut flowers.

Varieties: *H.* 'Pink Flamingo' is an evergreen lily that flowers in autumn. Flowers are bell-shaped, pale pink with dark pink veins. Dark green foliage has a prominent white stripe in the centre. Excellent garden or container plant in full shade for subtropical areas.

Potting soil mix Make your own potting soil by mixing 3 parts compost with 2 parts good quality topsoil and 1 part clean river sand. Add a fistful of superphosphate and a fistful of 5:1:5 general fertiliser to each wheelbarrow load of the above mixture, and mix well. You can use this mix in containers to plant your winter- and spring-flowering bulbs.

Hyacinthus orientalis x hybrids
Hyacinth, Hiasint

Size: 0,2 m

Growth habit: Popular winter-flowering bulb for indoors, with highly scented inflorescences in either purple, white, blue or pink. Bulbs are dormant during summer. In late winter a cylindrical inflorescence with bell-shaped flowers appears among the upright, strap-shaped leaves. The inflorescence can become top-heavy and should be staked to prevent breaking. Not prone to many pests and diseases.

Planting: Do not plant before April. It prefers cool, well-drained, sandy soil. Prepare bed by loosening soil to a depth of 20 cm, mixing in a 5-cm layer of compost and kraal manure at the same time. Make sure bulbs are just covered with soil.

Watering and feeding: Ensure that soil is always moist but not soggy at root level. It does not need special feeding as it is treated like an annual in South African gardens, but needs special treatment to make it flower again the next season.

Uses: Excellent pot plant for indoors. Also popular for growing in a special vase with the base of the bulb just above the water level. Outdoors, they complement daffodils and tulips when planted together. However, they should not be planted in mixed colour beds, for different coloured hyacinths flower at different times, producing a patchy effect. Rather plant in drifts of one colour.

Iris x hybrids
Dutch iris, Hollandse iris

Size: 0,5 m

Growth habit: The Dutch iris originated from crossbreeding the iris species from southwestern Europe with an iris species found in northwestern Africa. Untreated bulbs have a long dormancy period during summer and flower late in the season. The foliage of the Dutch iris is upright and grass-like. Flowers are borne on tall stems and come in shades of white, yellow, blue or purple. Leave bulbs in the ground during summer if the soil is well drained. You can also lift them in summer, store them at room temperature in a cool, dry place and plant them again in autumn. The plant is susceptible to attack by thrips and aphids.

Planting: Plant in late autumn when the soil temperature has cooled down. Prepare the bed by loosening the soil to a depth of 20 cm, mixing in a 5-cm layer of compost and kraal manure at the same time. Plant bulbs about 5 cm deep.

Watering and feeding: Water regularly to keep moist at root level. Keep plants well mulched to help retain moisture and to feed them.

Uses: Well-known cut flower, much beloved by florists. It should be cut in the bud stage with only a little colour showing. Also beautiful when planted close together in groups in the perennial border.

Bulbs in glass vases
Grow a hyacinth or daffodil bulb in a tall glass vase by filling it with pebbles or glass beads and water. Wedge the bulb in the neck of the vase. Keep in a dark place until leaves have sprouted, then place on a cool windowsill indoors.

Ixia x hybrids
Corn lily/Wand flower, Kalossie

Size: 0,5 m
Growth habit: Ixia grows in winter and is dormant during summer. It is a cormous plant with grassy leaves and dainty, star-like flowers, carried at the tips of long, wiry stems. The garden hybrids have a wide range of colours including purple, red, mauve, pink, green, yellow and white, usually with a dark contrasting centre. Lift corms in early summer and store in a dry place at room temperature until next autumn. Aphids may be a problem but generally, corn lilies are trouble free.
Planting: It prefers sandy, well-drained soil in full sun. Prepare the bed by loosening the soil to a depth of 20 cm, mixing in a 5-cm layer of compost and kraal manure at the same time. Plant corms about 3 cm deep.
Watering and feeding: Water regularly to keep moist at root level. Mulch the plant well to help retain moisture. Water until foliage starts to die down in summer. Fertilise bulbs with a general fertiliser after flowering if they are to be kept for the next season.
Uses: Striking when planted in large groups in the perennial border. Can also be used for cut flowers.
Varieties: *I. viridiflora* is a beautiful Ixia species bearing turquoise-blue flowers.

Lachenalia species
Cape cowslip, Viooltjie

Size: 0,2 m
Growth habit: This small, bulbous plant is indigenous to the Western Cape and Eastern Cape. It grows in winter and is dormant during the summer months. Colourful tubular flowers include purple, red, orange and yellow, often variegated with others in pastel shades of pink, mauve and blue. Foliage forms a rosette of either flat, open leaves or upright leaves which may be speckled with purple spots, depending on the species or hybrid. Lift bulbs in summer and store in a dry place at room temperature until late autumn. Store potted bulbs which have died down in their pots by keeping them dry and under cover during the summer months. Aphids can be a problem and should be dealt with when noticed.
Planting: It prefers light, sandy soil. Prepare the bed by loosening the soil to a depth of 20 cm, mixing in a layer of compost. Plant bulbs about 4 cm deep.
Watering and feeding: Do not overwater, but keep the root level moist throughout the active growing season. Fertilise with a general fertiliser for flowering plants after flowering, to ensure the next season's flowers. Stop watering them once the foliage has died down.
Uses: Very good container plant and also ideal for a sunny rock garden or front border.

Lachenalia bulbs Propagate your own Cape cowslips by making leaf cuttings early in the growing season, using only fully grown leaves. Place the cut-off side of the leaf cutting about 2 cm deep into washed river sand. Small bulbs will form on the edge and can be removed once their own roots have developed.

Leucojum aestivum
Snowflakes, Sneeuvlokkies

Size: 0,3 m

Growth habit: This winter-growing bulb is dormant during summer. Snowflakes have lovely, bell-shaped, white flowers with a distinct green dot at the apex. Flowers hang in clusters from a 35-cm stem. Leave the bulbs in the soil until they become overcrowded after three to four years. Snowflakes are trouble free and not susceptible to diseases or pests.

Planting: It prefers rich fertile soil. Transplant bulbs during autumn in compost-enriched soil.

Watering and feeding: Water regularly to ensure that the soil never dries out completely, especially at root level. Keep plants well mulched to help preserve moisture. Feed once with special bulb food in early winter when foliage is starting to grow actively.

Uses: Ideal for woodland gardens or as a border under large shrubs. Also lovely as cut flowers in early spring.

Lilium longiflorum
Saint Joseph's lily, Sintjosefslelie

Size: 1–2,5 m

Growth habit: In Pretoria they start flowering in October and continue, cultivar by cultivar, until February. As all lilies prefer a cold winter, they do particularly well on the Highveld and in the Free State. Plant them on the south or east side of the house, and never on the west, for they enjoy a cool root-run. Tall varieties need to be staked if planted in windy spots.

Planting: Dig in lots of compost to a depth of at least 35 cm before planting lily rootstocks. Plant about 15 cm deep.

Watering and feeding: Water regularly until foliage starts to die down. After flowering, feed with a general fertiliser for flowering plants, to build up the bulbous rootstock for the next season. Use a mulch to keep the roots cool and to help with moisture retention and feeding.

Uses: Excellent cut flowers; also provide colour in the background of the mixed border.

Varieties: A few good cultivars (according to flowering time): from September to early November try 'Avignon' (orange-red), 'Montreux' (pink), 'Connecticut King' (yellow) or 'Mont Blanc' (white); from November to December, *L. longiflorum* (Saint Joseph's lily) gives a white trumpet; from November to January, try 'Casablanca' (white), 'Stargazer' (pink) or 'Citronella' (yellow tiger lily).

Pot character To make a concrete pot look old, scratch the surface with a pot scourer, steel brush or coarse river sand and paint it with liquid manure or natural yoghurt. Keep it in the shade and moisten it regularly; it will soon turn green from moss growing on the surface. It will look great planted with spring-flowering bulbs.

Muscari armeniacum x hybrids
Grape hyacinth, Druifhiasint

Size: 0,2 m

Growth habit: This small, winter-growing bulb is dormant during summer. It has fleshy, grass-like foliage and small, bell-shaped flowers on a central stem. Colours range from deep blue and mauve to white. Leave bulbs in the ground for up to three years before lifting and dividing overcrowded plants in early summer. The grape hyacinth is not prone to attack by pests and diseases.

Planting: It prefers fertile, well-drained soil. Replant stored bulbs in autumn. Prepare the bed by loosening the soil to a depth of 20 cm, mixing in a 5-cm layer of compost and kraal manure at the same time. Plant bulbs about 5 cm deep.

Watering and feeding: Water regularly to keep the soil at root level moist at all times, but not waterlogged. Keep bulbs well mulched with compost. Fertilise with a general fertiliser for flowering plants or bulb food after flowering to build up reserves for the next flowering season.

Uses: Very good container plant for spring; pots can be brought indoors when in flower. They are also excellent planted in drifts to contrast with other spring-flowering bulbs.

Narcissus x hybrids
Daffodil/Narcissus, Affodil

Size: 0,3 m

Growth habit: A winter-growing bulb, dormant in summer. It has blue-green, strap-shaped, upright-growing foliage. The flowers are usually yellow but combinations of yellow, white, cream, orange and pink exist. Bulbs not planted before 21 June must be discarded as it will be too late for them to grow and flower. Leave bulbs in the ground for four to five years before lifting and dividing overcrowded plants.

Planting: Prepare the bed by loosening the soil to a depth of 20 cm, mixing in a 5-cm layer of compost and kraal manure at the same time. Plant bulbs about 10 cm deep and cover with a mulch of compost. Keep bulbs in the vegetable compartment of a refrigerator and plant a batch every two weeks for prolonged flowering.

Watering and feeding: Water deeply to keep soil moist at root level. Stop watering when foliage dies down. Fertilise once at the start of flowering with bulb food or a general fertiliser for flowering plants.

Uses: Popular cut flower in spring. Ideal in the lawn, in containers or in the mixed perennial border.

Varieties: 'Flower Carpet' (yellow) is the first cultivar to flower. 'Mount Hood' (white) is lovely in the winter garden.

Moles If moles are a problem in your garden, use wire baskets in which to plant your bulbs. Cover the whole basket with soil and lift it at the end of the season. You could also try burying mothballs in beds where moles are a problem.

Nerine bowdenii
Nerine, Nerina

Size: 0,3 m

Growth habit: A summer-growing bulb, dormant during winter. It has narrow, strap-like leaves and tall stems with about 10 large, pink or white flowers in an umbel during late summer. Bulbs may not all flower every year and should be planted in groups. Leave in the ground for at least four to five years before lifting overcrowded plants in winter. Guard against amaryllis caterpillars and mealy bug.

Planting: It prefers fertile, well-drained soil. Prepare the bed by loosening the soil to a depth of 20 cm, mixing in a 5-cm layer of compost and kraal manure at the same time. Plant bulbs with the neck of the bulb at soil level.

Watering and feeding: Water regularly and feed periodically with bulb food or general fertiliser for flowering plants during the active growing season. Keep well mulched with compost.

Uses: Excellent, long-lasting cut flowers. Lovely in large groups for shady areas under big trees.

Ornithogalum thyrsoides x hybrids
Chincherinchee, Tjienkerientjee

Size: 0,5 m

Growth habit: This bulb is indigenous to the southwestern Cape and grows in winter. It is dormant during summer. Many star-shaped, creamy-white flowers with a buff eye appear in late spring on a tall inflorescence. Broad leaves are fleshy and usually lie flat on the ground but can also be upright. Leave bulbs in the ground for several years before lifting and dividing overcrowded plants. Throw away any plants showing signs of virus disease. They are otherwise not prone to attack by pests and other diseases.

Planting: It prefers sandy, well-drained soil. Prepare the bed by loosening the soil to a depth of 20 cm, mixing in a 5 cm layer of compost at the same time. Plant the bulbs in autumn about 5 cm deep.

Watering and feeding: Water regularly to keep the soil moist at root level at all times. Reduce watering when the foliage starts to die down. When in flower, feed with bulb food or a general fertiliser for flowering plants.

Uses: Wonderful, long-lasting cut flower. Easy to grow in groups in the mixed perennial border.

Varieties: *O. dubium*, the yellow chincherinchee, bears orange-yellow, star-shaped flowers in spring.

Healthy compost To avoid infecting future compost, never add diseased plant material – like cut-off diseased dahlia foliage or weeds that have gone to seed – to the compost heap. Rather destroy this plant material by burning or discarding it.

Polianthes tuberosa x hybrids
Tuberose, Soetamaling

Size: 0,5 m

Growth habit: This is a summer-growing, tuberous per-ennial, dormant during winter. Tuberoses flower during mid-summer, when stems of up to 1 m tall appear, packed with highly scented, waxy, white flowers, which may be single or double. Leave tubers in the ground over winter, until the next season. Lift in early winter when plants have become over-crowded and plant during early spring. Watch out for aphids and thrips on fresh shoots.

Planting: It prefers well-drained soil. Prepare the bed by loosening the soil to a depth of 35 cm, mixing in a 5-cm layer of compost and kraal manure at the same time. Plant tubers about 20 cm deep with the pointed ends facing up.

Watering and feeding: Water regularly throughout spring and summer and mulch plants in spring with a thick layer of well rotted manure. Feed with liquid fertiliser in early summer when flowers start to appear.

Uses: Excellent, highly fragrant cut flower. It is also lovely in the mixed perennial border, planted in a group towards the middle of the bed.

Ranunculus asiaticus x hybrids
Ranunculus/Persian buttercup, Ranonkel

Size: 0,3 m

Growth habit: One of the most popular spring-flowering plants, the ranunculus offers masses of thickly doubled flowers, on compact little plants. It grows in winter and is dormant in summer. The flowers multiply with picking and range in colours from purple and red to orange, yellow, cream, white and pink. Leave in the ground for the following season. However, it is not really worthwhile keeping them, as they grow easily from seed or new tubers. Watch out for mildew during humid, warm weather. Slugs and snails are also very partial to the foliage.

Planting: The soil must be well drained. Prepare the bed by loosening the soil to a depth of 20 cm, mixing in a 5-cm layer of compost at the same time. Plant claw-like, tuberous roots with the claws facing downwards in autumn and keep moist at root level.

Watering and feeding: Except for regular, deep watering and cutting to keep the plants flowering, no extra care is needed once the initial planting is over. Keep the soil cool with a mulch. Feed once with liquid fertiliser when flowers start to appear.

Uses: Excellent cut flowers. Beautiful for a colourful display in beds and borders.

Bulbs for next season Feed bulbs well before and after flowering, to help the foliage manufacture and supply food for the bulbs. Let the foliage die down naturally before cutting it off, to ensure a successful display for the following season. The bulb develops the new flower bud during its dormancy period.

Sparaxis x hybrids
Harlequin flower/Sparaxis, Fluweeltjie

Size: 0,3 m
Growth habit: Indigenous to the southwestern Cape, this easy-to-grow, cormous perennial grows in winter and is dormant in summer. During late winter and early spring brilliantly coloured, star-shaped, marked flowers appear on slender stems. Colours include shades of red, pink, orange, yellow and purple. Flowers open from the bottom of the stem progressively towards the top of the flowering stem. Leave corms in the soil, if it is well drained.
Planting: Prepare the bed by loosening the soil to a depth of 20 cm, mixing in a 5-cm layer of compost and kraal manure at the same time. Plant corms about 5 cm deep, in autumn.
Watering and feeding: Water regularly to keep the soil moist at root level. Mulch plants with compost to help with moisture retention. Keep watering until the foliage dies down. If you are going to keep the corms for the next season, fertilise them after flowering with a general fertiliser for flowering plants, or a bulb food.
Uses: Wonderful for spring colour in the border or rock garden.

Sprekelia formosissima
Maltese cross, Malterserkruis

Size: 0,2 m
Growth habit: This is a summer-growing bulb, dormant during winter. An unusually formed, dark red flower, about 10 cm across, appears during spring and early summer on a 20-cm stem. Foliage is strap-shaped and upright. Leave bulbs in the ground over winter or lift them in autumn and store in a cool, dry place. Watch out for amaryllis caterpillar on the foliage.
Planting: It prefers fertile, rich, well-drained soil. Prepare the bed by loosening the soil to a depth of 20 cm, mixing in a 5-cm layer of compost and kraal manure at the same time. Plant in spring with the neck just above ground level.
Watering and feeding: Water regularly throughout spring and summer. Keep plants well mulched with compost to help with moisture retention. Feed once with liquid fertiliser when flowers start to appear.
Uses: Great as pot plants or in groups under large trees with dappled shade.

Garlic spray Make garlic tea by blending two whole bulbs of garlic with two red chillies and one cup of water. Strain and make up a concentrate by adding enough water to make up 2 litres. Dilute one cup of this concentrate in 2 litres of water and use as spray to repel aphids, spider mites, white fly, mealy bug and amaryllis caterpillars.

Tritonia x hybrids
Blazing star, Kalkoentjie

Size: 0,3 m

Growth habit: This cormous plant is indigenous to the winter rainfall regions of South Africa. It bears cup-shaped flowers on a slender stem in a range of colours from orange, salmon, to cream and white. Flowers appear from late spring to early summer, later than most spring-flowering bulbs. Easy to grow. Leave corms in the ground over winter in well-drained soil. They are not prone to attack by pests and diseases.

Planting: It prefers sandy, well-drained soil. Prepare the bed by loosening the soil to a depth of 20 cm, mixing in a 5-cm layer of compost at the same time. Plant corms about 4 cm deep during autumn.

Watering and feeding: Water regularly during winter and spring. Feed with special bulb food once a month until leaves start to die down. Continue to water and feed after flowering, if the corms are to be kept for the next season, until the foliage dies down.

Uses: The blazing star is lovely in the perennial border. It also extends the border's flowering period.

Tulipa x hybrids
Tulip, Tulp

Size: 0,3 m

Growth habit: Spectacular flowers are goblet-shaped and borne upright on a sturdy stem; foliage consists of about four broad, lance-shaped leaves. The tulip grows in winter and is dormant in summer. Often an early bloomer, though always late when it is for sale in garden centres and nurseries. In fact, you should not plant it before late April through May, either in pots or in cool soil outside. It is not worth your while to keep the bulbs, as they require special treatment to ensure flowers for the next season.

Planting: It prefers fertile, well-drained soil. Prepare the bed by loosening the soil to a depth of 20 cm, mixing in a 5-cm layer of compost and kraal manure at the same time. Plant bulbs so that they are covered by about 5 cm of soil.

Watering and feeding: Keep soil moist at root level at all times. Because tulips are treated as annuals in South Africa, no special feeding is needed.

Uses: Tulips are very popular cut flowers. If planting them out in the open, it is advisable to plant at least 10 to 30 bulbs of one colour to get a massed effect. Beautiful in containers for spring colour on the patio.

Treated or forced tulips These are bulbs that have been specially treated by subjecting them to a cold temperature to force them into flower earlier. Treated bulbs will all flower uniformly earlier than normal, last longer and grow taller. Plant them as soon as possible, within 10 days at most after treatment, to ensure success.

Modern roses are very adaptable and can be grown throughout the country, except in very hot areas with high humidity and on the beachfront. Once planted, roses give years of endless joy. They need an open, airy position where they get at least six hours of sun a day. If full sun is not available, remember morning sun is more beneficial than afternoon sun. To obtain beautiful flowers you should remember to prune, spray, water and feed them regularly.

Roses will grow in any well-drained soil that is slightly on the acid side. Prepare holes well in advance by digging a hole 65 cm square and deep, removing all weeds. Add well-rotted compost and peat and at the same time dig in half a cup of superphosphate or bone meal and half a cup of general fertiliser per hole.

These beauties need a lot of water, particularly during the hot summer months. Keep them well mulched with organic material like compost. They have a fine hair root system and do not like to have their roots disturbed. Roses are gross feeders and should receive a general fertiliser for roses or flowering plants at the rates recommended on the bag for use on different-sized plants, at monthly intervals after pruning.

Generally, hybrid tea roses are pruned back to one third of their growth to allow sturdy shoots to develop. Prune out the oldest stems and so ensure a robust plant from the outset. The occurrence of scale and other pests is reduced when infested branches are removed. Spray the pruned bushes with lime sulphur (8:1 strength) followed 10–14 days later by another spray at half strength (16:1). If, however, a high percentage of new growth is present, it is better to spray with Oleum.

roses

1. Blossom Magic
3. Iceberg

2. Clair Matin
4. Rose Celeste

1. Graham Thomas
3. Molineaux

2. Margaret Roberts
4. Sharifa Asma

Climber roses

Size: 2,5–4 m

Growth habit: Nothing can beat the choice in these roses for colour, size and fragrance of the flowers. There are climbers with hybrid tea, floribunda or miniature flowers, all giving a spectacular show either during spring or throughout summer.

Pruning: Remove all old, diseased and thin canes in winter. Cut back healthy canes to about one third of their length to promote new shoots and flowers.

Uses: Good for training up walls, along a fence, over a pergola or arch. Can climb up a tree or cover a lamppost.

Varieties: 'Blossom Magic' has floribunda-type, semi-double prolific, large, fragrant, bright rose-pink blooms. Easy to grow and train over walls, pillars or pergolas. 'Clair Matin' bears floribunda-type, semi-double, fragrant, shell-pink blooms with golden stamens. Vigorous growth produces many long, willowy branches, excellent for training over pergolas or on posts. 'Iceberg' bears floribunda-type, double white blooms with a pink flush. Fine vigorous rose to form a loose hedge or to train over a pergola, with repeated continuous flowering. 'Rose Celeste' bears fragrant, delicate, porcelain-pink, hybrid-tea-shaped, fragrant blooms. Vigorous and prolific bloomer. Great as a quick cover for a wall, pergola or hedge.

English roses

Size: 1–2 m

Growth habit: Some varieties grow much taller than others. They have a shrubby growth habit, ideal for the mixed shrub border. Many varieties make excellent cut flowers. They are the most fragrant roses, not excluding the old roses. 'David Austin', a hybrid breed of English rose, retains all the attributes of the antique varieties, such as fragrance and a very frilly double form, with the many advantages of modern roses. These include stronger bushes, which are more compact and have the ability to flower more profusely over a longer period.

Varieties: 'Graham Thomas' has glistening, yellow flowers with a powerful tea rose fragrance. Blooms prolifically and has healthy foliage. Excellent, tall-growing garden rose. 'Margaret Roberts' has large, soft pink blooms and strong, old rose fragrance. Vigorous, branching growth habit. Excellent hedging rose. Flower petals are used in potpourri. 'Molineaux' has light yellow blooms deepening to copper, with a tea rose fragrance. Tall-growing shrub with flowers distributed all over from the base to the top of the bush. 'Sharifa Asma' bears delicate, blush-pink blooms fading to white on the outer petals, with a strong, fruity fragrance. Short, upright growth habit. Blooms can be scorched by very hot sun.

Suckers on roses Always remove suckers, usually fresh green in colour, on rose bushes to prevent the rootstock onto which the rose has been grafted from robbing the grafted part of essential nutrients and moisture. Suckers arise from below the graft union and have different foliage from that of the grafted rose.

1. Duet   *2. Johannesburg Garden Club*
3. Iceberg   *4. Pearl of Bedfordview*

Varieties of Flower Carpet ground covers:
1. Coral   2. Pink   3. Red   4. Yellow

Floribunda roses

Size: 0,75–1 m
Growth habit: Floribunda roses are shrubby plants and bear clusters of flowers at the ends of their stalks, so offering a colourful garden display. They are also useful for cut flowers. They usually have very little fragrance but are on the whole more robust and disease resistant than hybrid teas.
Uses: They are very good for mass colour effect and can also be grown in large containers.
Varieties: 'Duet' has medium, salmon-pink blooms. Vigorous, healthy grower, very floriferous. Can be grown at the coast. Free-flowering 'Johannesburg Garden Club' has coral pink single flowers. It has medium-high growth and can be pruned or cut back with a hedge-trimmer. Ideal for landscaping and containers. 'Iceberg' is our most popular floribunda. Clusters of pure white blooms appear continuously. It also produces fragrant cut flowers. An excellent medium-sized garden rose with healthy growth, it can also be grown at the coast. Should be pruned less severely, cut back just below the old flowers. 'Pearl of Bedfordview' has clusters of pearl-white, semi-double blooms with a touch of pink, which are produced profusely. Excellent medium-sized bedding rose with healthy foliage and vigorous growth habit. It can be grown at the coast.

Ground cover roses

Size: 0,5 x 1 m
Growth habit: Ground cover roses are rampant, shrubby plants that spread over the ground, usually up to 50 cm tall. Blooms are borne in clusters. Modern hybrids have good disease resistance and make excellent plants for covering banks or as mass plantings in large gardens. Remove spent flowers regularly to encourage new blooms.
Uses: They are also very good as container plants or even in hanging baskets on the sunny patio.
Varieties: 'Flower Carpet Coral' has slightly ruffled, single, coral-coloured blooms. Compact growth and shiny, dark green, disease-resistant foliage. Excellent for mass planting or tub culture. 'Flower Carpet Pink' has prolific, bright pink flowers. Compact growth and shiny, dark green, disease-resistant foliage. Ideal for mass planting and containers. 'Flower Carpet Red' has prolific, glowing red, single blooms. Compact growth and shiny, dark green, disease-resistant foliage. Perfect for mass planting and containers. 'Flower Carpet Yellow' has rich yellow flowers with a red blush. Compact growth and shiny, dark green, disease-resistant foliage. Dense, low-growing habit. Suitable for mass planting and containers.

Roses in containers To successfully grow a rose bush in a container, the container should not be smaller than 45 cm in diameter. Use good quality potting soil and feed once a month with rose fertiliser during the active growth season. Water regularly.

1. *Burning Sky*   2. *Esther Geldenhuys*
3. *Pascali*   4. *Peace*

1. *Amoretta*   2. *Ocarina*
3. *Rise 'n Shine*   4. *Starina*

Hybrid tea roses

Size: 1–1,5 m

Growth habit: Hybrid teas are bush roses with a strong, upright growth and produce exquisite, long-stemmed flowers and pointed buds. Flowers are usually borne singly; side shoots may appear on the stem. Many are fragrant; modern varieties are stronger and healthier than earlier varieties.

Uses: Do not blend well with other plants in the shrub border, but are excellent for beds, rose borders and formal gardens.

Varieties: 'Burning Sky' has glossy, dark green foliage and long, pointed buds on tall stems. Unusual shades of lavender, purple, bright pink and ruby-red appear at different stages as the blooms open. Moderately fragrant. Bushy plants are free flowering. 'Esther Geldenhuys' is strong growing and one of the best for long-lasting cut flowers. Buds are coral pink and open to pink blooms. Strong basal shoots form huge candelabra. 'Pascali', one of the best white roses for cutting, produces profuse and perfectly shaped blooms. An upright, vigorous grower with healthy foliage. Do not prune too hard in winter. 'Peace' bears pointed, slightly rounded buds which open to creamy, golden-yellow blooms, edged with rose-pink. Blooms have a slight fragrance. A moderately high grower with glossy, dark green foliage. Do not prune too hard in winter.

Miniature roses

Size: 0,4 x 0,4 m

Growth habit: Miniature roses grow up to about 40 cm tall and sometimes more, according to growing conditions. They bear dainty little flowers and make excellent cut flowers for small posies.

Uses: Miniatures are ideal for small gardens, tubs, window boxes and pots, to finish off a bed or as single specimens.

Varieties: 'Amoretta' has pointed buds that open to white blooms with deep cream centres. Bushy growth with very few thorns and healthy, light green foliage. Can be grown at the coast and cut back at any time of the year. 'Ocarina' is one of the best miniature roses with light vermilion, double blooms blending to yellow at the base and reverse of petals. Foliage is glossy and healthy; new shoots have a bronzy tinge. Excellent miniature rose for all purposes, also at the coast. 'Rise 'n Shine' is the best miniature yellow rose. Bears large, perfect buds which open to double, clear yellow blooms. They are excellent cut flowers. Vigorous growth habit with healthy foliage and can be cut back throughout the year. 'Starina' has perfectly shaped buds that open to scarlet-vermilion blooms with a creamy white reverse. Has a productive, healthy and vigorous growth habit. Fine container rose.

Replanting a rose When replacing a rose, be sure to remove at least 10 large, heaped spades full of the old soil and replace with fresh topsoil before planting another rose in the same hole. Roses do not grow well in the same soil in which other roses or peach trees were previously planted.

Annuals are essential for providing year-round colour in the garden.

These lovely plants offer the most immediate and spectacular rewards as they grow from seed to flower in one season.

Many hybrid varieties that cater for almost any situation are available from most garden centres either as seedlings or in seed packets. You can easily transform an empty bed into a kaleidoscope of colour with a few trays of seedlings or, with a little more effort, a few packets of seeds.

Annuals are very versatile because of the great variety in colour and shape of plants and flowers. They are either tall or small, bold or feathery, trailing or upright growing, shade or sun loving, and there is always one of them suitable for some position. Many annuals make excellent cut flowers for the vase; they are ideal for small gardens; lovely for forming a border for larger plants or for bold splashes of colour in containers. It is essential to remove spent flowers regularly to prolong the flowering period of these plants.

It is very easy to plant annuals. Prepare the soil before planting out seedlings by digging the bed over to a depth of a fork and at the same time incorporating a 5-cm layer of compost. It is not essential to add any fertiliser at this stage, but a light sprinkling of superphosphate or bone phosphate at a rate of a closed handful per square meter will benefit all plants, as phosphate encourages root development and lots of flowers.

Seedling trays must be watered before planting out the plants, to help the soil stick to the roots. Late afternoon is the best time to plant out seedlings. Remember to water well after transplanting. When you're planning your annual beds, try to group related colours together for a pleasing picture rather than having many groups of contrasting colours, which may look busy when in flower.

annuals

Acroclinium roseum
Everlasting/Paper daisy

Size: 40 x 15 cm

Growth habit: A moderately fast-growing, upright annual with grey-green, lance-shaped leaves. Pink, daisy-like, semi-double flowers with papery petals appear in summer. Keep a lookout for aphids.

Planting: Sow the seed directly into well-drained loam or sandy soil during autumn or spring. Thin out the seedlings to space them about 25 cm apart, discarding the thinned seedlings as they do not transplant well. Flowers should appear approximately 10–12 weeks after sowing.

Watering and feeding: Water when dry. Feed every 14 days with liquid fertiliser.

Uses: The flowers dry very well, making them ideal for dried flower arrangements.

Varieties: *A. roseum* 'Reselected Giants Mixed' grow up to 60 cm tall and the flowers are red, pink or white.

Althaea rosea
Hollyhock, Stokroos

Size: 1,4–2,5 m

Growth habit: A popular plant with tall spikes of flowers appearing from summer to autumn. When sown in autumn, it acts like a biennial, but sown in spring it is an annual. Flowers are either single or double with ruffled petals. Foliage is rounded and lobed, with a rough texture. Many varieties are available in a range of colours including pink, purple, cream and yellow. Spray for rust during wet weather.

Planting: Prefers rich, well-drained soil. Sow directly in soil or in trays, and space seedlings 30 cm apart. Germination takes place about 10–14 days after sowing. Plants start to flower approximately 28 weeks after sowing.

Watering and feeding: Water regularly in dry weather. Feed once a month with a general fertiliser for flowering plants.

Uses: Makes a lovely tall border plant for backgrounds in cottage gardens.

Varieties: 'Chaters Double Rosette' has peony-shaped double flowers and is about 1,5 m tall. 'Spring Carnival' has double flowers in a large range of colours, about 1,25 m tall.

Sowing seed When sowing seed remember never to cover the seed with a thicker layer of soil than twice its diameter. Very fine seed can be mixed with clean, dry river sand to obtain a more even distribution; these seeds do not need to be covered. Water only with a fine mist.

Amaranthus tricolor
Joseph's coat, Driekleuramarant

Size: 1 m
Growth habit: A bushy, quick-growing annual with many uses. Some cultivars are used as leaf vegetables and others as brightly coloured bedding plants. Foliage is large and brilliantly coloured. Small, red flowers appear during summer. Keep an eye on the seedlings, as they attract snails, slugs and aphids.
Planting: It prefers well-drained soil. Sow the seed directly in soil or in trays during spring and space the seedlings about 25 cm apart. Germination takes about 10 days. Pinch out the growth point while young to encourage bushy growth.
Watering and feeding: Water regularly. In order to bring out brighter leaf colours, do not feed.
Uses: It is an excellent coloured foliage plant for background and mass plantings in summer.
Varieties: 'Early Splendour' has scarlet-coloured foliage.

Anchusa capensis
Cape forget-me-not, Ostong

Size: 0,3 m
Growth habit: A quick-growing biennial, this plant is usually grown as an annual. It is a bushy, coarse-looking plant with bristly, lance-shaped leaves. It bears clusters of bright blue flowers in spring and these generally last until well into summer. Remove the spent flowers regularly as this will promote the growth of more flowers.
Planting: This plant prefers well-drained soil. Sow the seed in trays or directly into the soil during autumn or spring. Germination takes 10–14 days. Space the seedlings about 20 cm apart.
Watering and feeding: Water regularly. Feed once a month with liquid fertiliser.
Uses: This is a lovely, blue-flowering annual which looks particularly good in the front border.
Varieties: 'Blue Bird' bears clear blue flowers with a white eye from spring to summer.

Sowing flower seed The following can be sown directly or in situ: Cape forget-me-not, Bokbaai vygies, pot marigold, cornflower, satin flower, cosmos, Namaqualand daisies, larkspur, Californian poppy, baby's breath, sunflower, straw flower, sweet peas, mallow, Virginian stocks, love-in-a-mist, marigold, nasturtium and meadow mixes.

Antirrhinum majus
Snapdragon, Leeubekkie

Size: 25–90 cm

Growth habit: The snapdragon is really a perennial, but is generally grown as a winter annual in subtropical areas, and as a spring- to autumn-flowering annual in regions with cooler climates. It is bushy with upright growth and lance-shaped leaves. It bears spikes of tubular flowers with a colour range from red through to yellow, white and pink. Deadhead plants regularly to prolong the flowering period.

Planting: It prefers fertile, well-drained soil. Sow seed in trays during autumn or spring and do not cover after sowing, as light is needed for germination. Space *A. majus* 'Tom Thumb' dwarfs 20 cm apart, and tall 'Animation' series 30 cm apart. Pinch out growing points when plants are 7 cm high to encourage bushy growth.

Watering and feeding: Water regularly and feed with liquid fertiliser once a month.

Uses: Dwarf variety excellent for bedding, and the tall variety for cut flowers and as a very colourful background plant.

Varieties: Many named varieties, also in single colours, are available. 'Dwarf Bells' grows up to 25 cm tall and has open butterfly-type flowers on compact, well-branched plants. 'Animation Series' is a tall, cut-flower variety, growing up to 1 m high, and has a large range of flower colours.

Aquilegia caerulea 'McKana' hybrids
Columbine, Akelei

Size: 60 cm

Growth habit: Although this plant is a perennial, it is regarded as an annual because it is so short-lived. It is bushy and compact, with attractive grey-green, maidenhair fern-like foliage. This graceful plant offers a rainbow of pastel colours in long, spurred, bell-shaped flowers during early summer. Remove spent flowers regularly to prolong the flowering season. Not very long-lived but easily propagated by seed during spring.

Planting: It prefers a light, enriched soil. Sow in early summer and plant out seedlings during March, spacing them 25 cm apart. Seeds take about 10 days to germinate. The plant starts to flower about 28 weeks from sowing.

Watering and feeding: Water regularly and feed once a month with liquid fertiliser.

Uses: Excellent for cutting. Looks lovely in bold clumps behind shorter annuals.

Varieties: 'Heterosis Music Harmony Mixed' grows up to 45 cm tall and bears larger flowers on strong flowering stems.

Seedling soil Prepare seedling soil by mixing sifted garden soil, compost and sand together. Add a handful of bone meal to each bucketful of the mixed soil. To kill pathogens and weed seeds, dampen the soil and bake for 5 to 10 minutes in the oven at 180 °C, or microwave on high for one minute.

Begonia semperflorens
Bedding begonia, Begonia

Size: 20 cm

Growth habit: This shrubby perennial is mostly grown as a bedding annual. It has fleshy foliage and stems, the leaves are rounded and shiny and can be either green or bronze in colour. It is a prolific flowering plant with flowers opening at the branch tips throughout summer. Flower colours range from red and deep rose, to coral, pink and white. Bicolours are available. It can also be propagated by cuttings and transplants well.

Planting: It needs humus-enriched soil. Sow seeds in trays during autumn, winter and spring and do not cover; plants should flower about 18 weeks after sowing. Space seedlings about 20 cm apart.

Watering and feeding: It needs regular watering and liquid fertiliser once a month.

Uses: The begonia is excellent for semi-shaded areas and for containers on the patio.

Varieties: *B. semperflorens* 'Senator', 'Cocktail' and 'Rio' series are bronze-leafed varieties, while the 'Varsity' and 'Ambassador' series are green-leafed. The 'Inferno' and 'Glamour' series are taller, growing up to approximately 40 cm, and they bear larger flowers.

Bellis perennis
English daisy, Engelse madeliefie

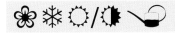

Size: 15 cm

Growth habit: A lovely, biennial bedding plant, considered a weed in England. The plant forms rosettes with small, oval-shaped leaves and produces daisy-like flowers on individual stalks. Either single or double, flowers come in a wide range of pinks, reds, bicolours and white during winter and spring. Widely used as an annual in colder regions.

Planting: Any good garden soil will be adequate. Sow seed directly in the soil in autumn and thin seedlings to space them 15 cm apart. Seeds will germinate in 10–15 days. Plants should reach flowering stage after about 12 weeks.

Watering and feeding: Water and feed regularly.

Uses: Lovely for edging flowerbeds in spring, especially in front of bulbs like daffodils and hyacinths.

Varieties: 'Medicis Series' bears double, ball-shaped flowers in shades of red, rose and white.

Where to plant annuals Some annuals for light shade and semi-shaded positions are alyssum, begonia, columbine, cineraria, flame nettle, Canterbury bells, forget-me-not, impatiens, toadflax, lobelia, nasturtium, fairy primrose and Virginian stocks.

143

Calendula officinalis
Pot marigold, Skotse gousblom

Size: 20–40 cm

Growth habit: This is a popular winter- and spring-flowering annual with round, flat single or double flowers. Colours range from cream to yellow and orange. It has pale green, lance-shaped, aromatic leaves. The plant self-sows easily.

Planting: Sow directly into beds during autumn, and cover seed. Germination occurs within 7 days. Thin out to space 25 cm apart, and pinch out tips to encourage bushy growth. They should flower 10 weeks after sowing.

Watering and feeding: Water when dry. Do not overfeed as this will cause lush growth with very few flowers.

Uses: This annual was once widely used as a medicinal and culinary herb because of its antiseptic properties. It is very easy to grow as a bedding or border plant. Good cut flower.

Varieties: 'Bonbon Mixture' is a bushy dwarf variety up to 25 cm tall, with large, double flowers. 'Pacific Beauty' has a mixture of yellow, orange and salmon-coloured flowers with darker petal tips and grows up to 40 cm tall.

Callistephus chinensis
Aster/China aster, Chinese aster

Size: 30–70 cm

Growth habit: This fast-growing, bushy annual has an upright habit and is usually grown as a cut flower but asters also make lovely bedding plants. Foliage is mid-green, oval-shaped and toothed. Flowers resemble large daisies and are borne on long flower stalks during late spring and summer. It is available in a wide range of single and double flower shapes and colours, including purple, blue, red, rose, pink and white. To avoid wilt disease, do not grow in the same bed in successive years.

Planting: Sow during spring and autumn in trays or directly into beds. Space 25 cm apart. Plants should flower 15 weeks after sowing. It is a good idea to make successive sowings to prolong the flowering season.

Watering and feeding: Water regularly and feed once a month with liquid fertiliser.

Uses: Excellent cut flower, also good in the back of the mixed annual border.

Varieties: 'Matsumoto Mixture' is a disease-resistant, cut-flower variety, growing up to about 50 cm tall, and bearing double flowers which have a clear yellow centre. 'Rainbow Upright Mixture' has brightly coloured, single and double flowers on 70 cm stems.

Bushy seedlings To encourage bushiness in young plants, pinch out the lead shoot. This will cause the side shoots to develop, helping the plant to grow into a healthy and bushy specimen.

Campanula medium
Canterbury bell, Kantelberg-klokkie

Size: 40–60 cm

Growth habit: A slow-growing biennial, this plant is usually grown as an annual. It is has an upright growth habit with narrow leaves. Bell-shaped flowers are borne on numerous tall spikes and may be single, semi-double or double, and appear during late spring and summer. Colours range from white and rose, to mauve and purple. Stake stems and deadhead regularly. Watch out for slugs.

Planting: It prefers moist, fertile and well-drained soil. Sow in trays during summer and autumn and barely cover seeds. Space seedlings 25 cm apart. The plant needs about 12 weeks to reach flowering stage.

Watering and feeding: Water regularly and feed with liquid fertiliser once a month.

Uses: Excellent border plant in semi-shaded positions.

Varieties: Compact dwarf varieties like 'Deep Blue Clips' and 'White Clips' make excellent bedding plants.

Capsicum annuum
Ornamental pepper, Sierrissie

Size: 20–30 cm

Growth habit: A fairly fast-growing perennial, used as an annual. It is a very close relative to the edible sweet pepper and chilli. The bushy plant has oval, mid- to dark green leaves with white flowers, followed by colourful fruits either round or elongated in shape. Fruits turn from green or yellow to red or orange in winter.

Planting: Sow during summer in seed trays and space seedlings 10 cm apart. Germination takes 10–14 days.

Watering and feeding: Water and feed regularly.

Uses: Excellent container plant or colourful bedding plant in hot climates.

Varieties: 'Masquerade' bears long fruits which turn from purple to yellow, orange and then red. 'Medusa' bears non-pungent, twisted, cone-shaped fruits which reach a length of 5 cm. When held upright, they have a snaky appearance. Fruits start out as cream, turn to yellow then orange and finally to bright red. The plant is compact, up to 20 cm tall. 'Red Missile' bears tapered fruits changing from cream to orange and finishing a bright red.

Potager Make a potager garden by planting vegetables, herbs and flowering plants like annuals and perennials around a sundial or birdbath in a geometric pattern.

145

Celosia argentea
Celosia/Cockscomb, Hanekam

Size: 30–60 cm

Growth habit: A fast-growing, brilliantly coloured bedding plant for summer. It is upright, with flower heads which are plumed or crested. Colours range from red, bronze, orange to yellow. Some varieties even have bright red or golden yellow foliage. It is better adapted for hot climates.

Planting: Sow in trays during spring, and space seedlings 20 cm apart. Germination takes around 7–10 days. They should start to flower after about 12 weeks.

Watering and feeding: Water regularly and feed once a month with liquid fertiliser.

Uses: Celosia is a good option for providing bright colour in the summer annual bed or border. Some of the plumose types are excellent for cut flowers.

Varieties: 'Kimono Series', a dwarf variety that grows only 20 cm tall, has plume-shaped flowers in many bright colours, including red, rose, salmon, orange, yellow and cream. 'Coral Garden' bears large crested flowers up to 30 cm tall.

Centaurea cyanus
Cornflower, Koringblom

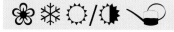

Size: 0,5–1 m

Growth habit: This is an erect annual with weak stems and a well-known weed in cereal crops in Europe. Flowers appear in summer and are borne in sprays in a colour range of whites, pinks, reds, purples and blues. Deadhead regularly in order to prolong the flowering period.

Planting: Sow the seeds in autumn or spring, directly into the soil or in trays, and cover seeds lightly. Space seedlings 25 cm apart. Germination takes about 7–10 days. Flowering takes place approximately 14 weeks after sowing.

Watering and feeding: Water regularly and feed once a month with liquid fertiliser.

Uses: Excellent cut flowers and when grouped as a bedding plant, but with a rather short flower display.

Varieties: 'Montana' bears cornflower-blue flowers and grows up to 60 cm tall.

Short of space Where space for a separate vegetable garden is a problem, vegetables and herbs can very effectively be grown in beds among annual flowers and perennials. Containers are also great space-savers for growing veggies and herbs.

Chrysanthemum species
Annual chrysanthemum, Eenjarige krisant

Size: 15–50 cm

Growth habit: These brilliant bedding plants deserve to be planted more widely as they are very easy to grow and flower for a long period.

Planting: Sow directly in soil throughout the year except in areas with very cold winters. Cover seeds thinly; they should germinate within 7–14 days. Thin seedlings out and space them 25 cm apart.

Watering and feeding: Water regularly and feed once a month with liquid fertiliser.

Uses: Good bedding and edging plants.

Varieties: *C. carinatum* (painted daisy) has brightly coloured, daisy-like flowers with concentric rings of contrasting colours ranging from red, pink, orange, yellow to white and fleshy foliage. They make lovely cut flowers. *C. multicaule* is a dwarf spreading plant bearing bright yellow ,daisy flowers, excellent for borders. *C. paludosum* bears small, single, white daisies, and makes a useful border plant. It should flower around 14 weeks after sowing.

Clarkia amoena
Satin flower/Godetia, Satynblom

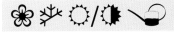

Size: 30–40 cm

Growth habit: A fast-growing, very free-flowering annual with lance-shaped leaves and upright stems. Spikes of open funnel-shaped flowers are single or double in single colours or bicolours, blotched or striped, and appear in summer. Colours are in shades of pink, mauve and white. Watch out for fungus disease during damp conditions.

Planting: It prefers a well-drained, slightly acid soil. Sow seed during spring directly in soil or in trays, and cover seed slightly after sowing; space seedlings 25 cm apart. Flowers appear about 15 weeks after sowing.

Watering and feeding: Do not fertilise with nitrogen and do not overwater; allow plants to dry out between waterings.

Uses: A colourful and easy-to-grow annual useful for bedding and cut flowers.

Varieties: 'Bouquet Mixed' bears flowers in shades of red, pink, salmon and lilac.

Hanging baskets When preparing to plant up a wire hanging basket with annuals, use a lining of plastic between the coir or moss and the potting soil to help prevent the soil from drying out too quickly. Remember to provide some draining holes in the plastic lining for excess water to drain away.

Cleome spinosa
Spider flower, Spinnekopplant

Size: 1,2 m

Growth habit: A fast-growing, bushy annual with an upright growth habit. Foliage is large and palmate in shape, with hairy prickly stems bearing flowers with long, purple stamens. This gives flowers a spidery appearance. It flowers in summer. The scented flowers are pink, white, lilac or purple. Remove spent flowers regularly and watch out for aphids.

Planting: Sow directly in soil in spring and thin out to space 50 cm apart. Seed should germinate after about 14–20 days. It should flower after about 12 weeks.

Watering and feeding: Water regularly and feed once a month with liquid fertiliser.

Uses: This large annual makes an excellent background plant in beds or against walls.

Varieties: 'Colour Fountain' has a mixture of pink, purple, lilac and white flowers. 'Rose Queen' bears clear pink flowers.

Coleus x hybrids
Flame nettle, Josefskleed

Size: 35 cm

Growth habit: Fast-growing, bushy perennial grown as an annual. Foliage has many colour varieties ranging from green to purple, pink, yellow and white. Flowers are insignificant compared to the colourful foliage. Pinch back to encourage bushy growth and remove flowers to prolong the plant's life. Easily propagated by softwood cuttings.

Planting: Sow in trays during spring and space the seedlings 25 cm apart.

Watering and feeding: Water regularly and feed once a month with liquid fertiliser.

Uses: Colourful foliage plant for containers and a good bedding plant for semi-shaded areas.

Varieties: 'Rainbow Series' is compact, grows up to 30 cm tall and has colourful foliage streaked with red, salmon, yellow and green. An excellent container plant. 'Fiji Superfine' is a mixture of dwarf plants with large, brightly coloured, fringed and serrated leaves.

Flowing lines An open, uncluttered lawn surrounded by beds shaped with flowing lines and edged with colourful annuals always looks lovely. Informal planting in the surrounding beds gives a more natural look to the garden.

Consolida ambigua
Larkspur, Ridderspoor

Size: 60 cm

Growth habit: Fast-growing, upright annual with a branching habit and finely divided, feather-like leaves. The seeds are poisonous. Long, upright spikes of tightly packed flowers in white, pink, red or blue are borne during summer. Stake the tall varieties. Watch out for snails and slugs and also for powdery mildew.

Planting: It prefers rich, well-drained soil. Sow the seed directly into the soil or in trays during autumn or spring. Space seedlings 30 cm apart; they should start to flower 20 weeks from germination, which takes about 3 weeks.

Watering and feeding: Water regularly and feed once a month with liquid fertiliser.

Uses: This is a very popular plant for cut flowers and also for dried arrangements.

Varieties: 'Giant Imperial Series' is a cut-flower variety, with flower colours including lavender-blue, rose, pink, salmon and white.

Cosmos bipinnatus
Cosmos, Kosmos

Size: 30–90 cm

Growth habit: This is an easy-to-grow annual, with feathery foliage. It is popular mainly for its white, pink or maroon cut flowers, which look like single dahlias in late summer. Deadhead the plant regularly to prolong the duration of flowering. Watch out for mildew in humid weather.

Planting: Sow the seed directly into the soil during spring, cover the seed lightly and space the seedlings about 25 cm apart. Do not overwater. It should produce flowers approximately 10–12 weeks after germination.

Watering and feeding: Water regularly during hot, dry weather. Feed once a month with liquid fertiliser.

Uses: Cosmos make excellent cut flowers.

Varieties: *C. sulphurous* has coarser foliage, and it produces flowers in shades of yellow and orange.

Collected seeds Store seeds in envelopes, label and date them. Spray the envelopes with a general pesticide before storing in a box to prevent seeds from being eaten or damaged by insects, and keep them in a cool, dry place.

Delphinium x elatum
Delphinium, Pronk-ridderspoor

Size: 0,3–1,5 m

Growth habit: This tall perennial has an upright, loosely branching growth habit, and is usually grown as an annual. It bears tall, central spikes of semi-double flowers in all shades of blue, purple, pink and white, which appear in early and late summer. Stake tall cultivars. Plant where it is sheltered from strong winds.

Planting: Sow in spring or autumn in trays. The germination temperature is below 18 °C, as high temperatures will inhibit germination. Space seedlings 35 cm apart. The plant takes 14–21 weeks to flower.

Watering and feeding: This is a gross feeder and needs compost and manure-enriched soil with regular feeding.

Uses: Good for bedding and cut flowers.

Varieties: 'Belladonna Improved' has sky blue flowers, excellent for cut flowers. *D. grandiflorum* (butterfly delphinium) grows up to 40 cm tall, and is bushy and branching, with deep blue flowers in spring. It should flower approximately 20 weeks after germination.

Dianthus barbatus
Sweet William, Baardangelier

Size: 15–40 cm

Growth habit: A slow-growing, bushy biennial with dark green foliage and flat clusters of fragrant flowers in red, pink, rose, white and purple, or bicolour with zoned and eyed flowers. Flowering time is late spring and early summer. It self-seeds readily. Keep a lookout for aphids, caterpillars and rust disease.

Planting: It prefers well-drained, slightly alkaline soil. Sow seed in trays in spring or autumn, and space seedlings 15 cm apart. Plant in alkaline soil for best results. It should flower after about 16 weeks from germination.

Watering and feeding: Water regularly and feed once a month with liquid fertiliser.

Uses: Ideal for mass planting in beds.

Varieties: *D. chinensis* (Indian pink) grows up to 20 cm tall and has scented flowers in shades of pink, red and white, with a contrasting eye.

Sandy soils Improve sandy soil by working in lots of organic material like well-rotted manure and compost, which will help to bind the soil and to retain moisture.

Digitalis purpurea
Common foxglove, Vingerhoedjie

Size: 0,5–1 m
Growth habit: The foxglove is really a biennial, but can be regarded as an annual because it is short lived. It is an erect plant with light green, woolly leaves and long spikes of pendulous, spotted flowers. The colour of the flowers may vary from purple and pink to white or pale yellow. All parts of the plant, especially the leaves, are poisonous. Cut spent flower-spikes down to ground level after spring flowering to encourage secondary spikes. It self-seeds freely.
Planting: It prefers fertile, well-drained soil. To prepare the bed before planting out seedlings, dig the soil over and work in a large quantity of compost and well-rotted manure, together with some general fertiliser and superphosphate or bone meal.
Watering and feeding: Water regularly and feed during early spring with a general fertiliser for flowering plants.
Uses: It is beautiful in the background perennial border. Medicinal properties for the treatment of heart ailments have been known since ancient times. Attracts butterflies.
Varieties: 'Excelsior Hybrids' have very large flowers and lovely clear colours.

Dimorphotheca species
African daisy, Namakwalandse madeliefie

Size: 30 cm
Growth habit: Indigenous to the winter rainfall areas of the Cape and Namaqualand, this annual has a sprawling growth habit. Daisy-like flowers with a dark centre, and glistening petals which may be white, yellow, orange or salmon-pink, appear in late winter and spring. Flowers only open in sunshine. Very easy to grow. Watch out for fungal disease during hot, humid weather.
Planting: Sow directly into well-drained soil from March to May and thin out to space 15 cm apart. The plant should flower 9 weeks from sowing.
Watering and feeding: Water when dry. Water once with liquid fertiliser when plants start to form buds.
Uses: A wonderful choice for hot, sunny and dry areas.
Varieties: *D. pluvialis*, also known as the rain daisy, is low growing with large, white flowers that have a purple tinge on the underside of the petals. *D. sinuata* is the orange-flowering Namaqualand daisy. 'Pastel Shades Mix' is a mixture of flower colours including cream, salmon, pale orange and yellow.

Foxgloves The drug digitalis is obtained from the second year's young foliage of the foxglove plant. All parts of the plant are poisonous when eaten, with most of the poison concentrated in the leaves. If taken in overdoses, digitalis can be lethal.

Dorotheanthus bellidiformis

Mesembryanthemum/Livingstone daisy, Bokbaaivygie

Size: 10 cm

Growth habit: This is a low-growing, spreading, annual succulent with light green leaves that contain shining surface cells. Daisy-like flowers appear in early summer, and they come in brilliant, glistening shades of many colours including red, pink, purple, orange, yellow and white, but not in blue.

Planting: Sow from March to May directly in beds or in trays, and do not cover the seed. Space the seedlings about 15 cm apart. It should start to flower approximately 12 weeks after germination.

Watering and feeding: Do not overwater. Feed once with liquid fertiliser when buds start to develop. Do not overfeed as too much fertiliser will cause the plants to develop foliage instead of flowers.

Uses: This plant is excellent for poor soil conditions and for coastal gardens. It is lovely in rock gardens and for massed displays or borders.

Eschscholzia californica

Californian poppy, Kaliforniese papawer

Size: 25 cm

Growth habit: This short-lived perennial, regarded as an annual, is the official floral emblem of California. The plant has grey-green, feathery foliage. Flowers are cup-shaped and come in a colour range including cream, yellow, rose, red, orange and mauve with a silky sheen. Flowers mainly in spring but can flower on and off in summer and autumn. Flowers need sunshine to open. Remove spent flowers regularly to prolong the flowering season. It self-seeds easily.

Planting: Easy to grow in poor, well-drained soil. Sow during autumn or spring directly into beds. Space seedlings 20 cm apart by thinning out. Discard thinned seedlings as they do not transplant well. It should take 12–14 weeks to flower.

Watering and feeding: Water regularly. Feed once a month with liquid fertiliser.

Uses: Excellent for mass displays or as an edging for the mixed perennial border.

Varieties: 'Mission Bells' is a dwarf variety with double flowers in orange and yellow shades.

Garden friends Poisonous insecticides used to kill aphids or other insects may also kill the ladybirds that eat the aphids. Both adult ladybirds and their larvae will clean up aphids, mealy bug, white fly and scale. Centipedes also are friends, as they feed on grubs and slugs. Think twice before using insecticides, or try organic alternatives.

Gaillardia x grandiflora
Blanket flower/Indian blanket, Kombersblom

Size: 25–60 cm
Growth habit: A mound-forming perennial with slightly lobed, hairy leaves, usually grown as an annual. Flowers are daisy-like, in single or double forms, ranging in colour from red to yellow. It has a long flowering season, from early summer until the first frosts appear. Deadhead regularly to prolong the flowering period.
Planting: Sow during autumn in trays, and space seedlings 200 mm apart. Should take about 16 weeks to flower.
Watering and feeding: Water when dry and feed once a month with liquid fertiliser.
Uses: Easy to grow and very useful in poor to dry soils. Also suitable for cut flowers.
Varieties: 'Plume Series' is a dwarf type annual only 30 cm tall, with large, double, ball-shaped flowers in summer. 'Picta Series' is a tall-growing annual, up to 60 cm, and excellent as a cut flower. Flowers are double.

Gazania x hybrids
Gazania/Treasure flower, Botterblom

Size: 20–30 cm
Growth habit: Indigenous to the winter rainfall regions of the Cape. This clump-forming perennial, grown as an annual, has green leaves that are grey underneath. Daisy-like flowers in shades of orange, red, and yellow are borne year round, but mainly in spring and early summer. It self-seeds freely.
Planting: It prefers sandy, fairly dry, well-drained soil. Sow seed directly in soil or in trays throughout the year and thin to space seedlings 20 cm apart. Germination takes 7–14 days.
Watering and feeding: Do not overwater. Water once a month with liquid fertiliser.
Uses: Ideal for brilliant colour in sunny places and containers like window boxes. Excellent as ground covers and rock garden plants in well-drained soil.
Varieties: Some named varieties are: 'Day Break Bronze', dark brown flowers; 'Day Break Orange', large orange flowers; 'Day Break Pink', large pink flowers; 'Day Break Red Stripe', large yellow- and red-striped flowers; 'Day Break Yellow', large yellow flowers; 'Moonglow', double, bright yellow flowers; 'New Moon', creamy-white flowers with a dark yellow centre; 'Pink', grey foliage with pink flowers; 'Raspberry', green leaves and small, light red flowers; and 'Tangerine Tango', green foliage with double, orange-yellow flowers.

Sweet basil Grow this annual herb in all the areas where flies are a problem as it is a very effective fly repellent. Different basil varieties with green and maroon leaves can look very attractive planted in groups near the patio or pool.

Gypsophila elegans
Baby's breath, Bruidsluier

Size: 70 cm

Growth habit: A well-branched, quick-growing annual. Small, starry flowers in white or pink are borne in large sprays. It has a short life of about 10 weeks. Make sure to sow consecutive weeks to ensure a longer display for the garden.

Planting: Add a handful of lime to the soil before sowing directly into beds. Sow in spring or summer and space seedlings 20 cm apart. The plant should flower about 8 weeks from germination.

Watering and feeding: Water regularly to keep moist at all times. Feed with liquid fertiliser every 2 weeks.

Uses: A fast-growing annual grown for flower arranging and for its misty effect in flower beds.

Varieties: 'Covent Garden Market Strain' has large, pure white flowers. *G. muralis* 'Gypsy' is a dwarf variety with delicate pink flowers, ideal for containers and hanging baskets. It flowers about 10–12 weeks after germination. *G. paniculata* is a perennial variety and popular for cut flowers, also easy to grow from seed. This plant should flower about 20 weeks after germination.

Helianthus annuus
Sunflower, Gewone sonneblom

Size: 1–3 m

Growth habit: A fast-growing, upright annual. It is not only a giant plant with huge, daisy-like flowers, but multi-stemmed, smaller varieties are also available that are excellent for cut flowers. The plant has hairy, often sticky leaves and stems. Flowers form wide yellow flower heads in summer. It is very easy to grow. Stake tall varieties. Different varieties with shades of yellow to rust-brown flowers make popular cut flowers.

Planting: Sow in spring to summer in trays or directly into beds. Space seedlings 50 cm apart.

Watering and feeding: Water and feed regularly.

Uses: Showy cut flowers.

Varieties: 'Orit' grows to 1,6 m tall and bears large, bright yellow flowers in 10 weeks from sowing. 'Sonja' grows up to 1 m tall with dark yellow flowers which have a dark centre, and produces many side branches. Flowers within 8 weeks from sowing. 'Valentine' grows 1,5 m tall and produces lemon-yellow flowers with black centres and flowers 9 weeks from sowing.

Hot water Avoid scalding plants with hot water from a hosepipe that has been lying in the hot sun. Let all the hot water run out first, before watering your plants.

Helichrysum bracteatum
Straw flower/Paper daisy, Sewejaartjie

Size: 0,4–1 m
Growth habit: A short-lived perennial which is usually grown as an annual. It is upright growing with hollow stems and thin green leaves. The everlasting flowers look like double daisies with straw-like petals in bright colours ranging from scarlet, purple, orange, pink, yellow to white. Flowering time is spring and summer.
Planting: It needs well-drained soil. Sow directly in soil or in trays during autumn or spring. Space the seedlings 35 cm apart in well-drained soil; the plant should flower about 16 weeks from sowing.
Watering and feeding: Water and feed regularly.
Uses: Very popular cut flower for drying. Cut flowers when half open, tie stems in bunches and hang them upside down in a cool, dry place away from sunlight.
Varieties: 'Bright Bikinis' are short plants, growing up to 40 cm tall, with many brightly coloured flowers.

Impatiens walleriana
Busy Lizzie, Vlytige Liesbet

Size: 20–50 cm
Growth habit: This succulent-stemmed plant is one of the most popular summer annuals, and comes in every colour except yellow and brown. It flowers and grows throughout the year in subtropical climates. Cut back leggy plants.
Planting: Sow in trays during spring and do not cover seeds as they require light for germination. Space seedlings 20 cm apart in compost-enriched soil. You can propagate them from cuttings. The plant flowers 12 weeks after germination.
Watering and feeding: Water regularly and feed once a month with liquid fertiliser to prolong the plant's life and also the flowering period.
Uses: Splendid bedding plant for semi-shade to shaded areas. Very good container plant for the shady patio.
Varieties: 'Accent Series' are short plants, growing up to 20 cm tall, strong and very free flowering. 'Super Elfin Series' grow slightly taller to approximately 30 cm, with very uniform growth and plenty of large flowers. *I. balsamina* (balsam) cultivars are unbranched plants of up to 70 cm tall with single and double flowers.

Avoiding hoar frost damage In dry continental areas, water the garden after two o'clock in the afternoon to allow plant foliage to be wet by nightfall. Cold winds and frost are more devastating in a dry garden than in a wet one.

Lathyrus odoratus
Sweet pea, Pronk-ertjie

Size: 0,3–2 m

Growth habit: This vigorous climbing annual is one of the joys of the winter garden. Flower colours available range from dark purple, maroon, pink, rose, salmon, blue and white. Although few diseases trouble sweet peas, use nets against birds, for they consider the young shoots a great delicacy.

Planting: Choose a sunny, north- or east-facing position for your bed and prepare the soil well in advance. Put up the trellis before sowing. The best time to sow sweet peas is from February to April, at a depth of 1,2 cm. Keep soil cool and damp, but not saturated. The plant should flower 14 weeks after germination. Pinch back when 8 cm tall, retaining a few strong shoots, then start training with plastic budding tapes.

Watering and feeding: Water copiously several times a week, and, once in bud, feed fortnightly with a liquid fertiliser.

Uses: Sweet peas make lovely scented cut flowers. The more they are cut, the more they flower.

Varieties: 'Mammoth Series' is a climbing variety with large flowers on long stems. 'Bijou Choice Mixed' is a dwarf bush variety about 50 cm tall, with good quality cut flowers. 'Little Sweetheart Mixed' is a low-growing, bushy variety, 30 cm high, with fragrant flowers.

Lavatera trimestris
Mallow, Eenjarige malva

Size: 60 cm

Growth habit: This lovely, easy-to-grow annual is moderately fast growing and has a bushy, branching growth habit. Leaves are feathery lobed and downy. Flowers are trumpet-shaped in silky pink or white and appear during summer to autumn. This is a short-lived annual. Deadhead regularly to prolong the flowering period.

Planting: It prefers well-drained soil. Sow seed directly into the soil during spring or autumn. The plant should flower the following summer. Seedlings do not transplant well. Space seedlings 30 cm apart.

Watering and feeding: Water regularly and feed once a month with liquid fertiliser.

Uses: This plant is good for edging the perennial border or in front of shrubs.

Varieties: 'Silver Cup' has small, compact bushes covered with large, rose-pink flowers. 'Mont Blanc' is a dwarf variety with pure white flowers. 'Pink Beauty' bears large, pale-pink flowers with darker pink veins.

Useful pruned branches Use cut-off branches that are sturdy enough to form a wigwam to act as support in flowerbeds. This will allow plants like sweet peas to grow onto the branches instead of growing them onto a trellis or staking them.

Linaria maroccana
Toadflax, Weeskindertjies

Size: 20–40 cm

Growth habit: This fast-growing annual bears flowers resembling miniature snapdragons. It has an upright, bushy growth habit with lance-shaped, pale-green leaves. Masses of small flowers are borne in winter and spring and come in shades of red, pink, purple, yellow or white. It self-seeds easily.

Planting: It prefers well-drained, sandy soil. Sow during autumn directly into the soil in a sunny position. Mix the fine seed with sand to get a more even distribution. Space the seedlings 20 cm apart.

Watering and feeding: Do not overwater. Feed once a month with liquid fertiliser.

Uses: This plant is suitable for the rock garden, borders and in cottage-style gardens.

Varieties: 'Fairy Bouquet' grows 20 cm tall and is bushy in growth habit with a mixture of flower colours. 'Northern Lights' is taller, growing up to about 35 cm, and bears flowers on tall spikes in many shades.

Lobelia erinus
Lobelia, Bloulobelia

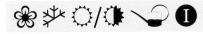

Size: 15 cm

Growth habit: Indigenous to the southwestern Cape, this low-growing annual is well known for its blue flowers. It has a tufted, semi-trailing growth habit with dense, oval to lance-shaped leaves, either green or with a bronze tinge. The lobelia is available with flowers in shades of blue, lilac, rose and white and it flowers from spring to autumn. It self-seeds readily.

Planting: It prefers light, enriched soil. Sow during autumn or spring in trays and transplant seedlings in small clumps rather than as individual plants. Space clumps 15 cm apart. The plant should flower 14–16 weeks after germination.

Watering and feeding: Water regularly and feed every two weeks with liquid fertiliser.

Uses: One of the most popular dwarf edging plants for borders, containers and hanging baskets.

Varieties: 'Crystal Palace' is compact with bronze foliage and deep violet-blue flowers. 'Moon Series' produces compact, ball-shaped plants with mostly bright green foliage and flowers in shades of blue and white. 'Riviera Series' is a vigorous, compact grower, early flowering with flowers in shades from dark blue to white. 'Fountain Series' has a vigorous, trailing growth habit, ideal for containers, with flowers in shades of blue, rose and white.

Companion plants This simply means the growing of different plants together to avoid problems with pests and diseases. Nasturtiums, for example, will deter harmful insects, while indigenous wild garlic makes a good companion for cabbage, tomatoes, lettuce and squash.

157

Lobularia maritima
Alyssum/Sweet Alison, Heuningblommetjie

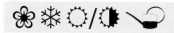

Size: 15 cm

Growth habit: A fast-growing, spreading annual with a bushy growth habit. In flower, the plant looks like a cushion covered in tiny, honey-scented flowers. The flowering period is from spring to autumn. Trim off spent flowers regularly to prolong the flowering period. It self-seeds readily. Flowers in shades of lilac, pink and violet are also available.

Planting: Sow seed directly into soil or in trays throughout the year. Do not cover seed after sowing, as it requires light for germination. Space seedlings 15 cm apart. Flowers should appear 8–9 weeks after sowing.

Watering and feeding: Water regularly and feed once a month with liquid fertiliser.

Uses: One of the most popular annuals for bedding and edge plantings. It is ideal for filling spaces between paving stones.

Varieties: 'Snow Crystals' has pure white, larger than normal flowers on compact, ball-shaped plants. 'Rosie O' Day' bears pink flowers, ideal for semi-shaded positions. 'Royal Carpet' bears violet-purple flowers.

Lupinus hartwegii
Hairy Lupin, Lupiene

Size: 20–80 cm

Growth habit: The annual lupin is a quick winter grower and flowers in spring to early summer. It has a compact, erect growth habit with hairy, dark green leaves. Pea-like flowers are borne on upright spires in shades of blue, yellow, rose and white. Always cut out spent flowers to prolong plant life and to prevent self-seeding.

Planting: Before sowing annual lupins, prepare the soil well in advance, by adding one cup lime to every 1 m², as well as compost. Sow directly into soil during autumn and space seedlings 25 cm apart.

Watering and feeding: Water regularly. Feed once a month with liquid fertiliser.

Uses: Splendid in the perennial mixed border or massed in the background annual bed.

Varieties: 'Giant King Mixed' grows up to about 80 cm tall and bears flowers mainly in shades of blue, white or pink. 'Pixie Delight' is an extra dwarf mixture with brightly coloured flowers. The 'Russel' hybrid is perennial and grows more vigorously. It bears long spikes of strongly coloured flowers in spring and summer.

Annual lupins Sow a crop of annual lupins, and when they have died down, dig them into the garden to enrich the soil with nitrogen before planting another crop of annuals or perennials on the same spot.

Malcolmia maritima
Virginian stock, Strandviooltjie

Size: 20 cm
Growth habit: This is a quick-growing, bushy annual with an upright to sprawling growth habit. From spring to autumn, small, fragrant, four-petalled flowers appear, which range in colour from white, mauve and pink to red. The foliage is oval and grey-green in colour. This plant is easy to grow.
Planting: Sow the seed directly into the soil in a sunny position during spring and space about 10 cm apart. It is one of the fastest annuals from seed to flower, taking only 4 weeks. Sow seed in succession to prolong the flowering period.
Watering and feeding: Water regularly and feed once a month with liquid fertiliser.
Uses: Wonderful for instant colour in containers and beds.
Varieties: 'Compact Large Flowered Mixed' bears larger flowers in shades of pink, mauve and white.

Matthiola incana
Stocks, Vilet

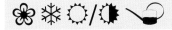

Size: 30–70 cm
Growth habit: Stocks are short-lived perennials or biennials, but are mostly grown as annuals. The plant has soft, velvety, grey-green foliage. Its densely packed flower-spikes come in colours ranging from purple, rose, cream to white during spring. This fragrant annual is not very easy to grow. Do not grow it in a bed where it has previously been grown.
Planting: Prepare the soil with lots of well-rotted manure, general fertiliser and lime. Sow seed in late summer or autumn, directly into soil or in trays. Space seedlings 35 cm apart. Do not handle seedlings by touching their stems – always handle them by the leaves. Generally, dark green seedlings will produce single flowers, and can be discarded when thinning. The plant should flower 10–16 weeks after germination.
Watering and feeding: Water and feed regularly.
Uses: Ten-week stocks are the most popular kind for bedding as they produce branched plants. Non-branching, column varieties are lovely as cut flowers.
Varieties: 'Giant Imperial Austral Mixed' is a branching variety, growing up to 50 cm tall, with mostly double flowers. 'Mammoth Excelsior ' is a non-branching variety, up to 70 cm high, producing tall spikes of scented flowers in mixed or separate colours.

Crop rotation Do not plant the same type of annual in the same bed year after year, as this can cause pests and diseases that thrive on a particular type of plant to multiply greatly. Different plant types attract different pests, so by rotating the plant types pests will not have enough time to multiply and become a problem.

Molucella laevis
Bells of Ireland/Shell flower, Ierse klokkies

Size: 60–90 cm

Growth habit: This is a moderately fast-growing, upright annual. The foliage is rounded in shape and pale green in colour. Generally grown for flower arranging, this curious plant flowers during summer. Small white flowers on a tall stem are enclosed by a green calyx which is bell-shaped, hence the name. It is easy to grow.

Planting: It needs well-drained soil. Sow the seed directly into the soil during spring. Do not cover the seed, and space the seedlings about 30 cm apart. It should flower 12 weeks from germination.

Watering and feeding: Do not overwater, and feed once a month with liquid fertiliser.

Uses: Provides marvellous flower-arranging material, either fresh or dry. Cut stems for drying when the bells change from green to white, and use in dry arrangements.

Myosotis sylvatica
Forget-me-not, Vergeet-my-nie

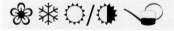

Size: 20–30 cm

Growth habit: This short-lived perennial or biennial is usually grown as an annual for its lovely blue, yellow-eyed spring flowers, which have long been associated with love and remembrance. It is mound forming with fuzzy leaves. It self-seeds easily for the following year.

Planting: Sow the seed directly into beds during autumn. It prefers a damp, semi-shaded position. Space the seedlings about 20 cm apart. The plant should flower 12–14 weeks from germination.

Watering and feeding: Water regularly and feed once a month with liquid fertiliser.

Uses: Ideal for edging or in containers on the sheltered patio. Also makes a good ground cover in mottled shade.

Varieties: 'Alpestris' grows to a height of about 30 cm and bears sky-blue flowers. 'Blue Ball' is more compact and bears indigo-blue flowers.

Soil conditioner Use dried earthworm casings, obtainable from most reputable nurseries, to add to the soil when preparing a new bed for planting out annuals. Earthworm casings are rich in nutrients and natural components to condition the soil, resulting in better growth and healthier plants.

Nemesia strumosa x hybrids
Nemesia/Cape jewels, Wilde leeubekkie

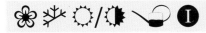

Nicotiana affinis
Tobacco flower, Tabakblom

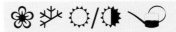

Size: 25 cm

Growth habit: Fast and easy to grow, this bushy annual is indigenous to the winter rainfall regions of the southwestern Cape. It has lance-shaped, prominently toothed, pale-green leaves. Large, open, snapdragon-like flowers appear some 12–14 weeks after sowing in a range of colours including white, yellow, orange, red, lavender, pink and blue. Cut back after the first flush to encourage a second flush. It does not tolerate very hot, humid climates.

Planting: Sow directly in soil or in trays during autumn. Space seedlings 15 cm apart. Pinch out tips of seedlings to encourage bushy growth.

Watering and feeding: Water when dry and feed once a month with liquid fertiliser.

Uses: Fine for bedding and containers.

Varieties: 'Carnival Mixed' are compact dwarf plants with large flowers in a wide range of colours.

Size: 30–40 cm

Growth habit: The tobacco plant was previously grown for its lovely evening fragrance. It was not very decorative, but more compact and colourful varieties are available these days, although with a weaker fragrance. It is a slow-growing, bushy annual flowering towards late summer to autumn. It bears clusters of trumpet-like flowers, the colours of which include red, pink, lime and white. Watch out for snails and caterpillars.

Planting: Sow seed during spring in trays or directly in the soil, and do not cover seed. Space seedlings 25 cm apart. The plant should flower 12–14 weeks after germination.

Watering and feeding: Water regularly and feed with a fertiliser high in potash once a month.

Uses: Lovely bedding plants.

Varieties: 'Havana Series' are bushy dwarf plants up to 40 cm tall with flower colours including pale pink, rose, red, purple and white.

Planting by the moon The best time for sowing is three days before and seven days after full moon. Do not cultivate the soil and do not prune plants during the full moon phase. The best time to plant flowers and crops which produce above ground is during the waxing moon phase. Prune and trim plants during the new moon phase.

Nierembergia hippomanica
Blue cup flower, Nierembergia

Size: 20 cm

Growth habit: This perennial is generally grown as an annual. It is moderately fast growing with a rounded, branching habit and narrow, lance-shaped leaves. Cup-shaped, violet or white flowers appear during summer to autumn. It is easy to grow and can be propagated by cuttings.

Planting: Sow the seed in trays during spring or autumn and space the seedlings about 15 cm apart. The plant should flower approximately 14–16 weeks after germination.

Watering and feeding: Water regularly and feed once every six weeks with a general fertiliser for flowering plants.

Uses: Good for containers, rock gardens and borders.

Varieties: 'Dwarf White Robe' bears pure white flowers. 'Dwarf Purple Robe' has deep violet-purple flowers.

Nigella damascena
Love-in-a-mist, Duiwel-in-die-bos

Size: 50 cm

Growth habit: An upright and fast-growing annual with bright green, feathery foliage. Spurred flowers with many petals appear half hidden within the foliage during spring and early summer, followed by rounded, green seed pods maturing to brown. Love-in-a-mist is available in white, rose and blue. Remove spent flowers regularly to prolong the flowering season. It self-seeds readily.

Planting: Sow in spring to summer directly in soil or in trays, and space seedlings 25 cm apart. Seedlings don't transplant well. Should flower 13 weeks from seed.

Watering and feeding: Water regularly and feed once a month with liquid fertiliser.

Uses: It is grown as a bedding plant and for cut flowers. The plant produces seed-heads which, when dried, are popular for dried arrangements.

Varieties: 'Persian Jewel Mixed' is a lovely mixture with blue, rose and white flowers.

Container snail barrier If ants, snails and slugs attack annuals such as petunias grown in containers, use petroleum jelly or Vaseline smeared in a thick layer around the rim of the container. It won't wash off, and pests will not be able to cross over this barrier.

Papaver nudicaule
Iceland poppy, Yslandse papawer

Size: 30–50 cm

Growth habit: A tuft-forming perennial grown as an annual. Pale green, oval-shaped leaves are toothed with hairy flower stems. Flowers come in shades of red, orange, yellow, pink and white. Varieties with short and tall blooms are available.

Planting: Prepare beds well by digging in lots of compost, well-rotted manure and general fertiliser. Sow during late summer and autumn in trays, and keep germination temperatures below 18 °C. Seedlings don't transplant very well, so handle with care and space 20–30 cm apart. Should flower 24 weeks after germination.

Watering and feeding: Water regularly. Feed every 14 days and nip out the first buds to promote better flower production.

Uses: A popular bedding plant for late winter and spring colour. Iceland poppies also make excellent cut flowers. Pick flowers just as buds start to open and dip stem ends in boiling water before arranging.

Varieties: 'Champagne Bubbles' grows to 45 cm high and bears extra-large flowers in brilliant colours on tall stems. 'Wonderland Series' grows up to 35 cm high and produces large flowers on strong, sturdy stems. *P. rhoes* (Shirley poppy, Flanders poppy) can grow up to 1 m tall and bears flowers in shades of red, pink and white without dark centre markings.

Petunia x hybrids
Petunia

Size: 15–30 cm

Growth habit: There is a variety of size and colour. Flowers are large, funnel-shaped, single or double, some with frilly petals. Watch out for snails. Cut back when straggly.

Planting: Sow uncovered in trays during autumn or spring. Space seedlings 20 cm apart. Should flower after 13 weeks.

Watering and feeding: Water when dry and feed once a month with liquid fertiliser to ensure a second flush.

Uses: An excellent bedding and container plant, and the hotter the sun the better the display.

Varieties: Can be grouped into four categories: Multifloras produce lots of medium-sized flowers and tolerate strong wind and rain. Varieties are the 'Carpet' and 'Primetime' series with the double-flowering range. Grandifloras produce many large flowers, and are less tolerant to adverse weather conditions. Varieties include the 'Supermagic', 'Dream', 'Ultra', 'Daddy' and 'Storm' series, with the 'Supercascades' for hanging baskets and containers. 'Storm' petunias have been specially bred to withstand bad weather. Floribundas bear lots of large flowers with good weather resistance. 'Mirage' is a popular floribunda variety. The Millifloras form compact plants with masses of small flowers, excellent for pots, containers and bedding. Varieties include the 'Fantasy Series'.

Focal point with colour Plant annuals like petunias, lobelias, alyssum or pansies to cover the soil in containers with standards. Plant a patch of brightly coloured annuals like impatiens, begonias or marigolds to draw attention to a statue, water feature or bench in the garden. You don't need to cover large beds with annuals to create a colourful garden.

Phlox drummondii 'Twinkle Star'
Annual phlox, Floks

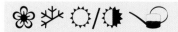

Size: 25 cm

Growth habit: This is a quick-growing, bushy annual. The plant has lanceolate, light green leaves. White-fringed, starry flowers appear in clusters in bright and pastel shades including red, pink, purple, blue, apricot and yellow during summer and autumn. Watch out for snails, red spider mite and powdery mildew. Remove spent flowers regularly.

Planting: Sow seed throughout the year, but it prefers the cooler seasons. Sow in trays and cover seed. They germinate at low temperatures (13 °C is optimum). Space seedlings 20 cm apart in well-drained, compost-enriched beds. Flowers in a wide variety of colours should appear 12 weeks after sowing.

Watering and feeding: Water regularly and feed once a month with liquid fertiliser.

Uses: A very useful annual for bedding and containers.

Varieties: 'African Sunset' is a dwarf variety with lovely colours and very prolific. 'Palona Series' is a dwarf variety with low-branching, compact plants; flowers have a contrasting eye colour.

Portulaca grandiflora
Moss rose/Sun plant, Portulak

Size: 15–20 cm

Growth habit: Low-growing, annual succulent with a spreading growth habit and fleshy, lance-shaped leaves on reddish stems. Large, open, saucer-shaped flowers in bright clashing colours, including scarlet, yellow, orange, pink, purple and white, appear in summer. Flowers close at night and on cloudy days. Easy to grow. Watch out for aphids.

Planting: Sow in spring or summer directly in soil or in trays and cover seed lightly. Space seedlings 15 cm apart. Should start to flower six weeks from seed.

Watering and feeding: Do not overwater. It is not necessary to feed these annuals as this will only cause lots of leafy growth with very few flowers.

Uses: They are effective for edging and as a ground cover, especially in poor soil.

Varieties: 'Sundial Series', a hybrid variety, bears larger flowers with brighter colours; the flowers stay open longer.

Bright annual colour Grow brightly coloured annuals in small groups to attract attention to or to highlight a certain part of the garden. Grow them at the front of the house, in containers on the patio, or at the pool area instead of growing them in large beds, which will need too many annuals to fill. It is more economical to use colour this way.

Primula malacoides
Fairy primrose, Sleutelblom

Size: 20–25 cm

Growth habit: A clump-forming perennial grown as an annual. Oval-shaped leaves are soft, hairy and pale green. Flowers are single or double, in shades of white, rose, pink, lavender and purple. The fairy primrose flowers from winter to spring. Remove spent flowers regularly to prolong the flowering period. It self-seeds readily.

Planting: Sow seed directly in soil or in trays under cool conditions during late summer or autumn. Space seedlings 20 cm apart. Flowers should appear 16 weeks from seed.

Watering and feeding: Water regularly and feed every two weeks with liquid fertiliser.

Uses: A very popular winter and spring bedding annual. Also good in containers on the cool patio.

Varieties: *P. obconica* (poison primrose) is a very popular pot plant and bedding annual with large flowers in shades of blue, orange, pink, white, carmine and rose. Sow in trays during autumn and do not cover seed. Flowers should appear 18 weeks from seed.

Salvia splendens
Sage/Scarlet salvia, Salie

Size: 20–50 cm

Growth habit: A slow-growing, bushy perennial grown as an annual. Foliage is elliptical, fresh green and toothed. Flowers appear on dense, erect spikes during summer until autumn. Colours available are red, burgundy, salmon, white and lavender. Watch out for snails, slugs and caterpillars.

Planting: In spring sow seed in trays and space seedlings 20 cm apart in beds. Pinch out the growing tips to encourage bushier plants. Flowers should appear within 10–12 weeks from seed.

Watering and feeding: Water when dry and feed once a month with liquid fertiliser.

Uses: Ideal annuals for sunny borders.

Varieties: 'Salsa Series' grows 35 cm tall and flowers early in colours including burgundy, salmon, white, scarlet and bicolours. 'Scarlet Bonfire' grows 50 cm tall, has dark green foliage and produces scarlet red flowers. 'Scarlet Dwarf Pygmy' reaches a height of only 20 cm, with compact growth and red flowers.

Removing seedlings from trays Make sure that annual seedlings are well watered before gently pushing them up from the bottom and out of the tray. This will ensure that the whole root ball comes out of the tray. Never pull them out by the stem, as this will cause roots to break off or the stem to snap at soil level.

Schizanthus wisetonensis
Poor man's orchid/Butterfly flower, Skoenlapperblom

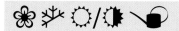

Size: 20–30 cm

Growth habit: A moderately fast-growing, upright annual with a bushy growth habit. It has lance-shaped, light green foliage. During spring to summer it bears orchid-like flowers in bright combinations of violet, purple, pink, crimson, white and scarlet, often flushed with yellow.

Planting: Sow in trays in autumn and space seedlings 20 cm apart. Should flower 14 weeks from germination.

Watering and feeding: Keep moist at all times and pinch back seedlings to encourage bushier growth with more flowers. Feed once a month with liquid fertiliser.

Uses: This plant makes a beautiful addition to any spring border. Also good in containers.

Varieties: 'Angel Wings Mixed' is a dwarf variety, growing up to 30 cm tall. 'Star Parade' is a very compact, ball-shaped plant with bright colours. 'Royal Pierrot Formula Mixed' is low branching with large flowers in shades of pink, purple, violet and white. Excellent pot plant.

Senecio x hybrids
Florist's cineraria, Bloemistecineraria

Size: 30 cm

Growth habit: A slow-growing perennial grown as an annual for potplant culture. Foliage is large, oval-shaped, serrated and dark green. Flowers are daisy-like, in red, pink, blue, purple and white in spring. It cannot survive in climates with high humidity. Watch out for insects and fungal disease.

Planting: Sow seed in trays from January to March. Space the seedlings about 30 cm apart. Should flower 20 weeks from germination.

Watering and feeding: Water regularly and feed once a month with liquid fertiliser.

Uses: Colourful plants for semi-shaded borders in winter and spring. Also delightful pot plants.

Varieties: 'Dwarf Large Flowered Mixed' grows up to 40 cm high and is ideal for outside planting. 'Erfurt Dwarf Palette Mixed' grows 35 cm tall and has medium-sized flowers on compact plants.

Enough space for roots When planting out annual seedlings into beds, make sure that the holes are large enough to accommodate the whole root ball comfortably, fill in the space with soil and firm down gently. If the hole is too small and the root ball is forced into the hole, young roots will become bruised and broken, resulting in poor growth.

Tagetes erecta
Marigold, Afrikaner

Size: 10–60 cm

Growth habit: There is nothing to beat the brassy colour of the marigold for summer colour. It is a fast-growing annual and flower colours include shades of bronze, orange and pale yellow. Tall and short varieties are available and very easy to grow. Flowers are single or double and ball-shaped with small to large varieties. Pinch back to encourage bushy growth and deadhead regularly. Dig marigolds into the soil where eelworms are a problem to get rid of the pest.

Planting: Sow directly in soil or in trays during spring or summer and space seedlings about 25 cm apart. Flowers should appear 8–12 weeks after seed.

Watering and feeding: Water regularly and feed once a month with liquid fertiliser.

Uses: Ideal bedding or border plant for the summer.

Varieties: 'Perfection Series' grows up to 40 cm tall, and has very good weather tolerance and rounded flower heads in yellow or orange. 'Antigua Series' grows up to 25 cm and is excellent for mass displays; flower colours are in shades of yellow and orange. 'Safari Series' dwarf are compact plants, 25 cm tall with large, full, double flowers.

Tropaeolum majus
Nasturtium, Kappertjie

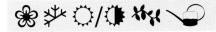

Size: 35 cm

Growth habit: This fast-growing annual is very easy to grow. It has rounded, mid-green leaves. Open, spurred, trumpet-shaped flowers come in a variety of colours ranging from red and orange to pale yellow. The flowers are borne from early summer to autumn.

Planting: Sow seed directly into the soil during spring and summer. Space the seedlings approximately 25 cm apart. Should flower about 10–12 weeks from germination.

Watering and feeding: Do not overwater and do not use nitrogenous fertiliser as the foliage will then cover the flowers.

Uses: These fragrant annuals make lovely cut flowers and are edible too. New hybrids are bushy and suitable for both containers and bedding.

Varieties: 'Jewel Choice Mixed' is a bushy type of nasturtium with lovely, bright flowers.

Eelworms Eelworms or nematodes are small, worm-like insects that attack the roots of many plants, causing stunted growth and eventually the death of the plant. To rid the soil of this pest, grow marigolds (*Tagetes*) during summer in areas where eelworms are a problem.

Verbena x hybrids
Garden verbena/Rose vervain, Ysterkruid

Size: 15–30 cm

Growth habit: A short-lived perennial, grown as an annual, with a trailing and sprawling growth habit. Foliage is dark green and irregularly shaped and toothed. Verbena flowers in summer. A wide range of colours is available including white, pink, scarlet, ruby, mauve and purple, often with a white or red eye.

Planting: Sow during autumn or spring in trays and cover, as darkness aids germination. Space seedlings 30 cm apart and pinch back to encourage bushiness. Flowers appear 10 weeks from germination.

Watering and feeding: Do not overwater or overfeed.

Uses: Popular for rock gardens and sunny borders.

Varieties: 'Romance Series' is only 15 cm high with a dense, spreading growth habit and is free flowering in shades of pink, coral, scarlet, violet, white. 'Quartz Series' grows up to 30 cm high. It has a vigorous growth habit, and flowers in red, blue, salmon, white. Many of the flowers have a white eye.

Viola cornuta
Viola, Viooltjie

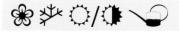

Size: 20 cm

Growth habit: These lovely flowers are really short-lived perennials, grown as annuals, and have little faces in many colours, including crimson-ruby, blue, yellow, white, violet and mixtures. Deadhead regularly.

Planting: Sow violas during autumn; germination takes place between 16 °C and 20 °C. Space the seedlings about 15 cm apart. They should flower 16 weeks from germination.

Watering and feeding: Water regularly and feed with liquid fertiliser once a month.

Uses: They are wonderful as container and bedding plants.

Varieties: 'Bambini Choice Mixed' are bushy plants with many pastel-coloured flowers resembling little faces. 'Prince Henry' is 20 cm tall with small, violet-coloured flowers, excellent for shady areas. 'Viola Princess Series' are compact plants 15 cm tall with yellow or blue flowers, ideal for containers, bedding and rock gardens.

Natural insecticide Nasturtium spray can be made by pouring two cups of boiling water over two handfuls of nasturtium leaves, then leaving it to steep for 15 minutes. Dilute ten drops of this tea in one litre of water to control aphids and red spider mite, or make a stronger dilution for controlling scale insects.

Viola x wittrockiana
Pansy, Gesiggie

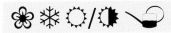

Size: 15–20 cm

Growth habit: A hybrid of compactly branched perennials always grown as annuals. Pansies are larger than violas and usually more patterned. Many varieties are available and long flowering periods make them one of the most popular garden annuals for winter and spring.

Planting: Sow in trays during autumn. Germination takes place between 16 °C and 20 °C. Space seedlings 15 cm apart. Flowers should appear 16 weeks after germination.

Watering and feeding: Water regularly and feed with liquid fertiliser once a month.

Uses: Excellent for winter and spring colour as bedding plants and in borders or for containers.

Varieties: 'Majestic Giants' bears huge flowers in separate colours including crimson, scarlet, purple, blue, yellow and white. 'Roc Series' is an early-flowering variety with good heat tolerance and bushy, compact growth. It comes in a wide variety of colours. 'Velour Series' is very prolific and early flowering in a mixture of colours. Excellent for pot culture and mass bedding display.

Zinnia elegans 'Starbright'
Zinnia, Jakobregop

Size: 30–70 cm

Growth habit: Zinnias prefer warm, dry climates and are erect annuals with terminal flowerheads which are daisy-like and may be single, semi-double or double in colours ranging from scarlet, rose, lilac, orange, yellow and white. Deadhead regularly to prolong the flowering period. They self-seed easily. Watch out for powdery mildew in warm and humid climates.

Planting: Sow seed during summer directly in soil or in trays. The best germination temperature is 25 °C. Space seedlings 20 cm apart. Pinch back seedlings to encourage bushiness. They should flower 10 weeks from germination.

Watering and feeding: To avoid mildew, do not wet the foliage of plants when watering. Feed once a month with liquid fertiliser.

Uses: Zinnias are excellent cut flowers, as well as bedding and border plants for the background.

Varieties: Dahlia-like varieties grow up to 60 cm tall and produce large, double flower heads. Cactus-like varieties also produce large, double flowerheads with petal edges rolled under to create a cactus-type flower form. *Z. angustifolia* 'Starbright Mixed' are bushy annuals with narrow leaves and masses of single, daisy-like flowers in white, yellow or orange. Excellent for hot, dry situations.

Hanging baskets for summer Plant up hanging baskets during October with colourful annuals and perennials like ivy-leaved pelargonium and ground morning glory. Compact annuals with a trailing habit – like lobelia, nasturtiums, petunias, alyssum and *Zinnia elegans* 'Starbright' – are ideal.

INDEX

Page numbers in roman refer to illustrated main entries. Page numbers in *italics* refer to plant varieties or other species discussed under main entries, and entries in **bold** refer to gardening topics or plants discussed in the hints. Those plants with plant breeder's rights (PBR) or trademarks (TM) are marked accordingly.

kappertjie 167
kardinaalsmus 52
karee 31
kareeboom 31
katjiepiering 53
katstert 87
kattekruid 105
Kiggelaria africana 23
kingfisher daisies **102**
kingfisher daisy 97
klimop 99
kliproos 45
Kniphofia linearifolia 101
Kniphofia praecox 101
Kniphofia uvaria 101
Kniphofia x hybrid 'Yellow Cheer' *101*
knoopkruid 110
knotwood 110
kombersblom 153
koorsboom 9
koperblaar 37
koraalklimop 71
koringblom 113, 146
kosmos 149
kraanvoëlblom 68
kransaalwyn 38
krantz aloe 38
krismisroos 54
    eikeblaar- 55
kroton 46
kruipvy 74
Kruschens pink 66

L
Lachenalia species 128, **128**
ladybirds **152**
Lagerstroemia indica 23
lamb's ears 115
Lampranthus species 102
    'Desert Sparkler' *102*
    'Purple Giant' *102*
    'Red Surprise' *102*
    'Salmon Surprise' *102*
lamsoor 115
Lantana montevidensis 102
    'Malan's Gold' *102*
    'Rosie' *102*
    'Sundancer' 102 (TM)
    'White Lightning' *102*
large-flowered plectranthus 109
larkspur **141**, 149
Lathyrus odoratus 156
    'Bijou Choice Mixed' *156*
    'Little Sweetheart Mixed' *156*
    'Mammoth Series' *156*
Laurus nobilis 56
laurustinus 69
Lavandula stoechas 57
Lavatera trimestris 156
    'Mont Blanc' *156*
    'Pink Beauty' *156*
    'Silver Cup' *156*
lavender **57**
lavender cotton 113
lavender tree 21
Lavendula stoechas 'Helmsdale' *57*
Lavendula stoechas subsp. *lusitania*
    'Marshwood' *57*
    'Papillon' *57*
laventel 57
laventelboom 21
lawn in shade **29**
leather leaf fern 111
leaves
    autumn **69**
    fallen **21**, 67
leeubekkie 142
lemoenjasmyn 60
Leonotis leonurus
    var. *albiflora* 57
    var. *leonurus* 57
leopard tree 9, 14, **33**
Leucojum aestivum 129
Leucospermum species 58
    'Ballerina' *58*
    'Highgold' *58*
    'Tango' *58*
Lilium longiflorum 129
    'Avignon' *129*
    'Casablanca' *129*
    'Citronella' *129*
    'Connecticut King' *129*
    'Mont Blanc' *129*
    'Montreux' *129*
    'Stargazer' *129*
lily turf 103
    creeping *103*
lime sulphur **68**
Limonium perezi 103
Linaria maroccana 157
    'Fairy Bouquet' *157*
    'Northern Lights' *157*

lion's ear 57
lippia 109
Lippia repens see *Phyla nodiflora*
liquidambar 24, **24**
Liquidambar styraciflua 24
Liriope muscari 'Variegata' 103
Liriope spicata 'Silver Ribbon' *103*
Livingstone daisy 152
lobelia **143**, 157, **169**
Lobelia erinus 157
    'Crystal Palace' *157*
    'Fountain Series' *157*
    'Moon Series' *157*
    'Riviera Series' *157*
lobelias **163**
Lobularia maritima 158
    'Rosie O'Day' *158*
    'Royal Carpet' *158*
    'Snow Crystals' *158*
locust tree 16
London plane 27
Louisiana iris **89**, **115**
lourier 56
love-in-a-mist **141**, 162
low-maintenance gardening **65**
Loxostylis alata 24
luiperdboom 14
lupiene 158
lupins, annual **158**
Lupinus hartwegii 158
    'Giant King Mixed' *158*
    'Pixie Delight' *158*
    x 'Russel' *158*
Lysimachia congestiflora 'Outback Sunset' *104*
Lysimachia nummularia 104
    'Aurea' 104

M
maagdeblom 118
maartlelie 126
Mackaya bella 58
Madagaskar-jasmyn 80
magnolia 25
Magnolia grandiflora 25
magrietjie 87
maidenhair tree 20
Malcolmia maritima 159
    'Compact Large Flowered Mixed' *159*
mallow **141**, 156
Maltese cross **124**, 133
Malteserkruis 133
Malus floribunda 25
Malus 'Oekonomierat Echtermeyer' 25
Mandevilla amoena 'Alice du Pont' 76
Mandevilla laxa 76
Mandevillea sanderi 'Rosea' 59
Mandevilla splendens see *Mandevilla amoena*
    'Alice du Pont'
Mandevillea x hybrid 'My Fair Lady' 59
manure
    dried **107**
    liquid **107**
maples **10**
March lily 121
marguerite daisy 87
marigold 86, **141**, 167
marigolds **102**, **163**, 167
marmaladebos 68
marmalade bush 68
    yellow 68
Matthiola incana 159
    'Giant Imperial Austral Mixed' *159*
    'Mammoth Excelsior' *159*
meadow mixes **141**
mealy bug **133**, **152**
mealy-cup sage 112
Melaleuca bracteata
    'Golden Gem' *59*
    'Johannesburg Gold' 59
mesembryanthemum 102, 152
Mexican blood trumpet 73
Mexican daisy 87
Mexican flame bush *43*
Mexican orange 45
Mexikaanse trompetblom 73
Microlepia speluncae 104
Milettia grandis 26
miniature date palm 62
miniatuur-dadelpalm 62
mirror bush 47
mitserie 13
mitzeeri 13
moeraseik 29
moles **130**
Molucella laevis 160
moneywort 104
monkey thorn 8
moon, planting by the **161**
moss rose 164
mulch **21**, **67**, **109**
    for ferns **111**
Murraya exotica 60

Muscari armeniacum x hybrids 130
Myosotis sylvatica 160
    'Alpestris' *160*
    'Blue Ball' *160*
Myrtus communis 60
    'Compacta' *60*
    'Variegata' *60*

N
Namakwalandse madeliefie 151
Namaqualand daisies **141**
Nandina domestica 61
    'Pygmaea' *61*
narcissus 130
Narcissus x hybrids 130
nasturtium **141**, **143**, 167
    spray **168**
nasturtiums **157**, **169**
Natal bauhinia *40*
Natal flame bush 10
Natal mahogany 34
natural pond **99**
nematodes **167**
nemesia 161
Nemesia strumosa x hybrids 161
    'Carnival Mixed' *161*
Nepeta cataria 105
Nepeta mussinii 105
nerina 131
nerine 131
Nerine bowdenii 131
'New Guinea' impatiens **87**, 100
Nicotiana affinis 161
    'Havana Series' *161*
nierembergia 162
Nierembergia caerulea see *Nierembergia hippomanica*
Nierembergia hippomanica 162
    'Dwarf Purple Robe' *162*
    'Dwarf White Robe' *162*
nieshout 29
Nigella damascena 162
    'Persian Jewel Mixed' *162*

O
Olea europaea subsp. *africana* 26
olienhout 26
omsambeet 26
Ophiopogon japonicus 'Kyoto Dwarf' 105
orange jasmin 60
organic alternatives **152**
ornamental pepper 145
Ornithogalum dubium 131
Ornithogalum thyrsoides x hybrids 131
ostong 141
Othonna **102**, **106**, 109
Othonna carnosa var. *carnosa* 106
Oxalis depressa
    'Bowles White' *106*
    'Pink Star' 106
    'White Star' *106*
Oxalis purpurea 106

P
painted daisy *147*
palmlelie 48
palms **15**, 30
Pandorea jasminoides
    'Lady Di' *77*
    'Rosea' *77*
    'Southern Belle' *77*
pansies **163**
pansy 169
Papaver nudicaule 163
    'Champagne Bubbles' *163*
    'Wonderland Series' *163*
Papaver rhoes 163
paper daisy 140, 155
paperbark thorn 9
papierbasdoring 9
papyrus **89**, **99**
Parthenocissus quinquefolia 77
Parthenocissus tricuspidata 77
pathways **114**
paving **105**
peacock flower 94
pebbles **61**
Pelargonium grandiflorum
    'Chocolate' *107*
    'Orange Cup' *107*
    'Pink Cup' *107*
    'White Cup' *107*
Pelargonium peltatum 107
Pelargonium x *domesticum* 107
Pelargonium x *zonale* 107
pelargonium
    ivy-leaved 107, **169**
    konings- 107
    rank- 107
    regal 107
pelargoniums, zonal *107*
Peltophorum africanum 27

173

PICTURE CREDITS

AJ = Anthony Johnson, AK = Anneke Kearney, AT = Anthony Tesselaar, AW = Alex White,
DAR = David Austin Roses, DJ = David Johnson, FE = Froman's Eden, GD = Gerhard Dreyer,
HD = Hadeco, JH = Jerry Harpur, JS = Jenny Simpson, KK = Keith Kirsten, KP = Kristo Pienaar,
NG = Nancy Gardiner, SA = Shaen Adey.

Front cover: NG, **Back cover**: left: SA/SIL, centre: AJ/SIL, right: HD, **Half title page**: HD, **4/5**: AJ/SIL,
7: KP/SIL, **8** left: DJ, **9** right: DJ, **12** left: NG, right: KP/SIL, **13** left: DJ, **14** left: JH, right: JS, **15** left: NG,
right: KP/SIL, **16** right: KP/SIL, **17** left: KP/SIL, **18** right: NG, **19** left: KP/SIL, **20** left: KP/SIL, **23** right: AW,
24 left: KP/SIL, right: DJ, **25** right: AW, **27** left: KP/SIL, **28** left: JH, **30** left: AW, right: DJ, **31** left: KP/SIL,
33 left: NG, right: AW, **34** left: KP/SIL, **35** right: FM, **36**: GD/SIL, **39** left: NG, right: KP/SIL, **41** left: AK,
42 left: NG, right: KP/SIL, **43** left: KP/SIL, right: KK, **44** right: NG, **45** left: NG, **46** left and right: NG,
48 left: JS, **49** right: AW, **50** right: NG, **51** right: NG, **54** right: JH, **55** left: JH, **56** left and right: KK,
57 right: KP/SIL, **59** right: NG, **60** left: JH, right: AW, **61** left: JH, right: KK, **62** left: KK, **63** left and right:
NG, **64** right: KK, **65** left: KP/SIL, right: JH, **67** left: KP/SIL, **68** right: KP/SIL, **69** right: JH, **70**: KP/SIL,
71 left: KP/SIL, **72** left: JH, right: NG, **73** left: NG, right: KK, **74** left: KP/SIL, **75** left: KP/SIL, **76** left: NG,
78 left: KP/SIL, **79** right: KK, **80** right: NG, **81** left: KP/SIL, right: NG, **82** right: KP/SIL, **83**: GD/SIL,
85 right: JH, **86** right: KP/SIL, **87** right: NG, **88** right: KP/SIL, **90** right: KP/SIL, **91** right: KK, **92** right: KK,
94 left: AK, right: JH, **96** left: NG, **97** right: KK, **98** left: AW, right: KK, **99** left: KP/SIL, **100** left and right: AW,
101 right: AK, **102** left: KK, right: NG, **103** left: JS, **104** left: KK, **105** left: NG, **107** left: KK, **110** left and right:
AW, **111** left: NG, **112** right: AW, **115** left: NG, right: KK, **117** left: KP/SIL, **118** left: AW, **119** left: KP/SIL,
120: HD, **122** left: HD, right: AW, **123** left: AW, right: KP/SIL, **124** left: HD, right: AW, **125** left and right:
KP/SIL, **126** left: KK, right: KP/SIL, **127** right: HD, **128** right: AW, **129** right: KK, **130** left: HD, right: KK,
131 left: NG, right: HD, **132** left: HD, **133** left: KP/SIL, right: HD, **134** right: KP/SIL, **135**: AJ/SIL, **136** left:
(1, 3 & 4) AJ/SIL, (2) KK, right: (1) KK, (3 & 4) AJ/SIL, **137** left: (1, 3 & 4) AT, (2) KK, right: (1) AJ/SIL, (2)
NG, (3 & 4) DAR, **138** left: (2) NG, right: (2 & 4) AJ/SIL, (3) JS, **139**: SA/SIL, **140** left and right: NG, **141** left:
AW, **142** left: NG, **143** left and right: KP/SIL, **144** left: AW, right: NG, **145** left and right: KP/SIL, **146** left:
KP/SIL, right: NG, **148** left and right: AW, **149** left: SA/SIL, right: AW, **150** left: AW, right: NG, **151** left: AW,
right: KK, **152** left: JH, right: NG, **153** left: KP/SIL, right: JH, **155** left: KP/SIL, right: KK, **156** left and right:
KP/SIL, **157** right: NG, **158** left: KP/SIL, right: NG, **159** left and right: NG, **160** left: KP/SIL, right: NG,
161 left: AW, **162** left: NG, **163** left: KK, right: NG, **164** left: NG, right: KP/SIL, **165** right: NG, **166** left: KK,
167 left: KK, right: KP/SIL, **168** left: KP/SIL, right: AW, **169** left: KP/SIL, right: KK